MISSION-MINDED
FAMILIES

Saying "YES!" to Jesus and God's Great Commission

Jon & Ann Dunagan

HarvestMinistry.org
MissionMindedFamilies.org
MissionMindedWomen.org

Mission-Minded Families:
Saying "YES!" to Jesus and God's Great Commission

This resource is a updated and revised compilation of two-books-in-one: *The Mission-Minded Child* and *The Mission-Minded Family,* by Ann Dunagan

"And I will establish My covenant
Between Me and you
and your descendants after you
In their generations."

Genesis 17:7

"God's mission is for your family to expand His family."

JON & ANN DUNAGAN
MISSION-MINDED FAMILIES

FOREWARD — by David & Leslie Nunnery
Co-Founders of Teach Them Diligently

What you hold in your hand is an incredibly inspirational resource for all families who are mission-minded and want to pass their passion for serving God on to their children.

It was about 10 years ago that we first came across the original editions of *The Mission-Minded Child* and *The Mission-Minded Family*, and we are so thankful that God brought these books into our lives at the very moment we were sensing His call to serve Him in new ways.

I first found *The Mission-Minded Family* and devoured it-- talking David's ear off most evenings sharing anecdotes and stories I was reading. As we moved ahead into our own missions adventure, the Dunagan's have had a profound impact on our lives. We were inspired by the stories we read and the incredible boldness with which this couple we were reading about walked. We wanted to read more and quickly found *The Mission-Minded Child*, which we ordered right away and dove in as soon as it was delivered.

When God called us to start Teach Them Diligently, the very first people we discussed inviting was Jon and Ann Dunagan who wrote these books, for it was our heart to inspire families to engage in the mission God had given them-- to disciple their children, teaching them diligently to love God and others and to order their lives with the Great Commission in mind. We had no idea how to reach them, though, for we were just a young couple in South Carolina with a God-given dream. I found Ann on Facebook and sent a message that I never expected to receive a reply to. I am so thankful my expectation was wrong, for not only did I receive a gracious response from Ann, but they agreed to join us for our very first Teach Them Diligently event.

A friendship grew and the Dunagan's have joined us every year since then, casting a missional vision for families all across the country.

There have been more times than we could count that we have referred to things mentioned in the Mission-Minded books. Our favorite story is about the blue lamp. We have referenced that story often as we question if something is holding us back from taking the next step God has for us. It is not uncommon for one of us to ask ourselves or our children, "Are you holding onto a Blue Lamp?"

By putting *The Mission-Minded Child* and *The Mission-Minded Family* together in one updated volume, Jon and Ann Dunagan are giving us a wonderful missions resource filled with Gospel principles, practical ideas, and exciting stories. We cannot wait for you to check it out and start your own missions adventure with your family. We imagine that just like us, you'll get a few years down the road and stand in awe of what God has allowed you to do.

David and Leslie Nunnery
Teach Them Diligently
and Worldwide Tentmakers

Mission-Minded Families has been featured on hundreds of radio programs and news articles, including FamilyLife Today, Revive Our Hearts, CBN, PrimeTime America, and The Christian Post. Podcast features include: Moms in Prayer International, The BusyMom, Missions Pulse, The Missions Suitcase, Vibrant Christian Living, 1040 Podcast, and Mission-Minded Families on iTunes.

Wow, what a resource. I couldn't put it down! This compilation of books offers incredible insights to help you redirect your family's focus from temporal accomplishments to eternal rewards through the spreading of the gospel and harvest of souls. What is a mission minded family and how can you become one? *Mission-Minded Families* is a wonderful resource to show you how!

—**RHONDA STOPPE**, evangelist, pastor's wife, speaker, and
    author of 6 books, including: *Moms Raising Sons to Be Men*,
    and *The Marriage Mentor-Becoming the Couple You Long to Be.*

I have known Jon and Ann Dunagan since 1987, and have had the privilege of being their friend, pastor, and fellow worker in the kingdom. Jon and Ann are people of integrity and I have confidence that God will continue to use them greatly in this generation.

— **PASTOR NELS CHURCH**, director of REAP International,
    and missionary to the Philippines

We sincerely appreciate the Dunagan's willingness to help raise the voice of the persecuted church.

—**MYRTLE DODD**, The Voice of the Martyrs

The Dunagan's writing is for those who want a heavy emphasis on world missions. This book was not whipped up by novices. The authors are international mission evangelists and homeschooling parents of seven who have ministered all over the world. They know their stuff!

—**VIRGINIA KNOWLES**, Hope Chest Newsletter

Jon and Ann, may the Lord bless you in the publishing of this needed book. We are truly hoping that the Lord will open our children's eyes and hearts to the tremendous harvest field that they may be called to work in someday. I know that living in a Third-World country broadens our perspectives and helps us to see the bigger picture of God's redemptive plan, so that's what we're praying for our children.

—**VALERIE SHEPARD,** pastor's wife and homeschooling mother, and daughter of Jim and Elisabeth Elliot

I resonate with the thoughts in this book. I have always considered that God's mission includes everyone: men, women, boys, and girls. In fact, when families make God's mission a central focus, their individual gifts and callings grow together. I also love the energy that Jon and Ann bring in these pages. The Dunagan family exemplifies what it means to be a family on mission. This book gives you and your family a great kickstart to move in the direction of God's heart.

—**DAVID JOANNES**, missionary in Bangkok, Thailand, host of Missions Pulse podcast, and author of *The Mind of a Missionary*

Raising our young people to live on mission for God encapsulates so much of what we as parents need to be doing in the raising of our families. Our friends Jon and Ann Dunagan possess a contagious enthusiasm that will ignite within your heart a passion for raising a mission-minded family. In *Mission-Minded Families*, Jon and Ann cast vision for why our families need to be actively pursuing kingdom work and also provide many powerful practical helps including exciting biographical stories of great Christians. Not only will this resource excite you with fresh vision for how God can use your family to expand His family, it will also give you many practical ideas for how to disciple your family towards God's kingdom purposes.

—**MATT & RUTH ADAMS**, parents of seven children, authors, podcaster of Legacy Homeschool Reflections, and parenting speakers

Wow! This resource is such a God-send! Jon and Ann Dunagan understand family. They understand God's heartbeat for all peoples of the world. And it is evident, they possess an anointing from God to communicate and equip families to have the mind of Christ- a missions mind. From the practical easy-to-use tools to the inspirational faith-filled stories, this compilation will fuel your entire family with compassion to live out the great commission! Having just started using this material with my family, I see the flickering fire that has been ignited in the eyes of my children already!

—**ESTHER MORGAN**, raised as a MK (missionary kid) in China, mother, nurse, Bible teacher, and global missions advocate

Did you know that God has a kingdom purpose in mind for your family? He does—and no one knows that better than Jon and Ann Dunagan. For more than thirty years, the Dunagans have been on a mission to help families become more Gospel-centered and mission-minded. In *Mission-Minded Families*, you'll get more than a simple how-to for becoming a mission-minded family; you'll learn to understand the theology of missions. If you've been wanting to help your family learn to confidently engage the world around them, with the hope of the Gospel, Mission-Minded Families is a resource you can't do without.

　　—HEIDI ST. JOHN, mother of 7, grandmother, speaker, podcaster, author of *Becoming MomStrong* (Tyndale), founder of MomStrong International, and co-founder of Firmly Planted Family

Unparalleled passion for families and missions, but first and foremost, love for Jesus—Jon and Ann Dunagan don't just write from their hearts; they gift us with unique wisdom, years of knowledge and vast life experiences from homeschooling their seven children while serving for decades in global missions. Every family member will see missions with new eyes and children will be raised with fresh passion from an early age as they live out God's heart-cry to all to, "Go into all the world and preach the Gospel to all nations" (Mark 16:15).

　　—JEN AVELLENEDA, mother, writer, blogger, speaker and orphan advocate (with a passion for foster care and adoption)

God calls families! From the youngest to the oldest, this book will contagiously compel and inspire every member of your family that the Great Commission is for all. For years, the two original books (*The Mission-Minded Child* and *The Mission-Minded Family*) have been treasured resources in our family library. Within these pages, now in one Mission-Minded Families volume, you will find a wealth of wisdom and such practical applications for instilling in your children a love for sharing the Gospel of Jesus. Your family will be eternally enriched and spiritually equipped to be about God's mission throughout the earth.

　　—JOYE DICHARRY, cofounder of Commission Mankind, missionary family of nine

"At no [other] time
is there greater capacity for devotion
or more pure, uncalculating ambition
in the service of God."

HUDSON TAYLOR'S PARENTS
[SPEAKING OF CHILDHOOD]

"When I am a man,
I mean to be a missionary
and go to China."

HUDSON TAYLOR (AGE FIVE)

The
MISSION-MINDED CHILD

Raising a New Generation to
Fulfill God's Purpose

PART 1

*Discovering the "Why" of World Missions
while making disciples at home*

A PASSION FOR SOULS

A missions poem and hymn, by Herbert G. Tovey, 1888

Give me a passion for souls, dear Lord,
A passion to save the lost;
O that Thy love were by all adored,
And welcomed at any cost.

Jesus, I long, I long to be winning
Men who are lost, and constantly sinning;
O may this hour become of beginning
The story of pardon to tell. . . .

How shall this passion for souls be mine?
Lord, make Thou the answer clear;
Help me to throw out the old life line
To those who are struggling near.

Contents

The Mission-Minded
Child Features

/ Missions Poems and Hymns

(These are all appropriate for memory work and oratorical practice.)

Missions Selections

🧍 Mini Missionary Biographies

(those marked with an asterisk include a "Mission-Minded Monologue Skit")

👫 From My Children's Perspective

🎙 Teaching Opportunities

How to Use This Book

This book is simply a tool to help you, as a Christian parent (or teacher), impart to the next generation a passion for Jesus Christ and a heart for God's mission to our world. It's not just information; it's inspiration!

- **Get inspired!** Browse through the pages for motivating missions stories, songs, poems, and examples to renew your own passion for the lost and God's eternally minded purpose for teaching and training your child.

- **Get missions facts!** Use it to reaffirm your missions foundation, to remember the world's need and our call to reach the lost, and to research a biblical basis for *why* we should share God's love with the nations.

- **Look things up!** This book is a quick missions resource manual, with mini missionary biographies, famous world mission quotes, and a helpful guide to locate great kid-friendly resources with mission-minded vision.

- **Find practical ideas!** Are you looking for easy-to-use missions ideas? This book includes sections on giving to missions, encouraging missionaries, and promoting missions in your local church, plus creative ideas for making missions fun!

- **Teach with a heart for missions!** This book is filled with ideas to incorporate a heart for world missions into nearly every subject. For English, there are missions selections to read aloud, classical excerpts for memory and oratorical practice, plus ideas to spark your child's creative writing. For geography and social studies, there are world maps, missions songs, and funny international stories. For a biblical foundation, there are Scripture verses to learn, prayer projects, and many practical ideas to encourage your child in solid Christian discipleship.

Note: Nearly all of the following mission stories and excerpts can be used for reading aloud to a child, although a few examples (due to difficult or graphic language) may be more appropriate to save until your child has grown into his or her teenage years. As a parent or teacher, please use your own judgment regarding the maturity of your child; and, in any case, let these stories and excerpts challenge *you*, as a mission-minded adult!

When I Was a Child . . .

I was eight years old when I first felt God's "call" to world missions.

I'll never forget the moment. It was a typical summer morning at Christian Renewal Center, a small family camp nestled in the midst of tall evergreens and majestic waterfalls. A teacher had encouraged my class to go out into the woods to pray and to ask God to simply "speak" to us from His Word.

So, taking my tattered children's Bible, I marched down a familiar dirt trail, sat down on a log, and began to pray.

Lord, is there anything you want to tell me?

I was quiet . . . but I didn't "hear" anything, except a small stream rippling beside me. *Would God ever talk to a young child like me?*

I tried to listen.

Just then, a strong thought came to my mind: *Look in Jeremiah.*

Gazing up through the trees, I wondered, *Was that from You, God?*

I knew "Jeremiah" was a book from the Old Testament, but it was in a part of the Bible I usually didn't understand. I assumed it would probably just be full of a bunch of "so-and-so begat so-and-so" type of verses.

But the thought didn't go away. *Look in Jeremiah, chapter one.*

Tentatively, I opened my Bible, found Jeremiah, and began to read. The verses started off like I had imagined they would—with big words and confusing names—but by the time I reached the fourth verse something of God's Holy Spirit began to well up inside me. As I continued reading, it felt like God Himself was talking directly to me.

> Then the word of the LORD came to me, saying: "Before I formed you in the womb I knew you; before you were born I sanctified you; I ordained you a prophet to the nations."
>
> Then said I: "Ah, Lord GOD! Behold, I cannot speak, for I am a youth."
>
> But the LORD said to me: "Do not say, 'I am a youth,' for you shall go to all to whom I send you, and whatever I command you, you shall speak. Do not be afraid of their faces, for I am with you to deliver you," says the LORD.
>
> Jeremiah 1:4–8

Two years later . . .

I was tagging along beside my mom at a Christian women's meeting when a lady came over and asked if she could pray for me. This woman didn't know me at all, but as she laid her hands on my head and started praying, she began quoting those same verses—"my" verses—from Jeremiah!

I was only ten years old, but once again it felt as if God was "speaking" directly to me—drawing me closer to Him and to the nations.

Tears welled up, as I began to cry. Inside, I just *knew* God was real, and those verses from Jeremiah *were* for me.

Thirty years later . . .

Not too long ago I was earnestly praying about this book, searching my motives, and trying to discern God's will. Unless I felt this project was something really "birthed" from the Lord for my life, I didn't want any part of it. In all honesty, I wasn't willing to sacrifice the time and energy I knew it would take if it could be better invested in my own children, in our home church, and in our missionary work.

But I kept feeling a stirring—and urgency—to challenge other parents and teachers that "we must instill a vision for missions in the next generation!"

I sought counsel and prayer and was shocked when my husband actually began encouraging me to write. (Years before, my writing had become consuming, and neither of us wanted *that* again!) Our pastor also prayed with us and felt a strong affirmation about my pursuing this project.

In my prayer journal, I poured out my heart to the Lord: "Father, if this idea for 'The Mission-Minded Child' is not of You, I'm willing to just let this 'baby' die. Please show me, Lord. Not my way, but Your way; not my plans, but Your plans."

Soon afterward I attended a church baby shower. During the refreshment time, I felt drawn to ask a certain elderly woman to pray for me. I didn't know much about her; I just knew she was a woman who prayed. As we talked by the punch bowl, she asked me to share more about my idea.

"It would be a book to impart a passion for world missions in parents and teachers," I explained, "to help raise a new generation of children and young people to fulfill God's Great Commission."

This precious lady then caught me by surprise. "Didn't you know?" she began. "World missions has been my life." She started to share a few of her stories. For nearly fifty years this amazing woman had served God as a missionary in Brazil. She had founded an orphanage, cared for 777 children, and placed them all in families. (And I had thought raising *seven* children was an accomplishment; I was in total awe of this woman's life!)

Right at that moment, our hostess (this woman's grown daughter, who I had just learned was one of the children from this orphanage) came over and asked if she could pray for me. Although she barely knew me, she believed God had shown her something in prayer several months earlier; but she had never felt a peace about sharing it with me—until now.

"As I've been praying for you, I feel like there's been a dream in your heart," the missionary's daughter began. "There's something you deeply wanted and worked on very hard, even through the middle of the night. For years you willingly laid it down—out of submission to your husband and out of submission to God; but now, I believe God is beginning to give it back to you." Then she began quoting the exact verses from Jeremiah that meant so much to me as a little girl!

Before I could stop myself, I unexpectedly burst into tears. The Lord's presence was so strong, I literally sobbed.

Surrounding me and supporting me—like midwives—were three godly women from around the world: the elderly missionary and her daughter (once an abandoned Brazilian orphan), plus a wonderful intercessor from Samoa (who had just arrived in our area that day and was the grandmother of the woman to whom we were giving the baby shower). Together we prayed for this book and interceded for God to raise up a new generation for missions.

Hours later, my husband said he had never seen me so overtaken by emotion—other than when I had given birth—and, spiritually speaking, that is almost what it felt like. I had been willing to totally surrender this idea; but, ironically, at an actual baby shower God confirmed in my heart that this "baby" was really "birthed" of Him.

The whole experience felt like a dream; and once again, I *knew* God was real. Those Jeremiah verses were not just for me, after all! God is calling a new generation of children and young people to the nations.

INTRODUCTION

What Is a Mission-Minded Child?

The famous missionary explorer David Livingstone once said, "This generation can only reach this generation." But will we raise our children to reach effectively *their* generation for Jesus Christ?

We should answer "Yes!", and *The Mission-Minded Child* is a motivational resource to help. We need to focus on God's calling for our lives and work *with* Him to help raise a new generation of young people totally committed to His plans. Every follower of Jesus (including every Christian child) should have a "life mission" aimed at finding God's purpose and fulfilling His potential.

Parents (and Christian teachers), do you realize how important you are? You have been placed in a strategic position to impact the next generation. Parenting children is more than a "duty," and educating children is more than a "job." If your vital role is perceived from God's perspective and fulfilled with a focus toward the Lord and those who aren't Christians yet, multitudes of mission-minded children could be motivated to live a God-centered life. Perhaps this book will even inspire you to reach your potential as well. Your child (and you!) could become today's Christian leader and tomorrow's world-changer.

The Mission-Minded Child is a Christian parent's (and teacher's) guide to world missions. It's filled with practical ideas and information. Included are mini missionary biographies, motivational missions stories, classic poems, international songs and hymns, and hundreds of easy-to-use ideas. Hopefully, it will become a resource you'll want to refer to again and again.

Yet *The Mission-Minded Child* is even more! It's filled with passion, zeal, and inspiration. Within these pages, you'll be encouraged to recognize God's potential in your child. You'll be challenged to release your child to God for His purposes, then motivated to effectively raise your child for God to fulfill His specific mission (whatever that may be).

Often an adult may ask a child, "What do you want to be when you grow up?" But as mission-minded parents and teachers, our typical question could have the potential of directing a child toward total obedience to God and complete surrender to His purposes. We *should* say, "Oh, I wonder what exciting plans God has prepared for your life? When you grow up, will you do whatever *God* wants you to do?"

A Mission-Minded Child

A mission-minded child . . . dreams of fulfilling God's destiny.

A mission-minded child . . . may want to become a missionary—or a teacher or a doctor or a newspaper reporter or a state governor or a pastor or a businessperson or an airplane pilot or an author or a florist or a mother—as long as it's what *God* wants!

A mission-minded child . . . prays for that next-door neighbor.

A mission-minded child . . . is not a picky eater!

A mission-minded child . . . takes home a photo magnet from the visiting missionary family and puts it on the kitchen refrigerator.

A mission-minded child . . . is healthy, active, and adventurous!

A mission-minded child . . . spends a summer night sleeping outside on the trampoline, gazes up at a sky filled with twinkling stars, and realizes God's plan is infinitely bigger than his or her own backyard.

A mission-minded child . . . imagines rollerblading on the Great Wall of China!

A mission-minded child . . . recognizes the names of David Livingstone, Amy Carmichael, Hudson Taylor, and Loren Cunningham.

A mission-minded child . . . knows how to use chopsticks.

A mission-minded child . . . has a reputation for thoroughly enjoying the Bible sword drills and memory verse contests at church.

A mission-minded child . . . puts extra money in the monthly missions offering and feels extra good inside.

A mission-minded child . . . thinks it could be fun to sleep in a mud hut in Africa!

A mission-minded child . . . reads all the way through the Bible by the age of ten (or eleven or twelve)—and is excited to start again!

A mission-minded child . . . stares at the photos in the new geography textbook or magazine and imagines climbing to the top of that Egyptian pyramid, snorkeling in those tropical-blue waters, and giving a new outfit to that poor boy with the ripped-up shirt.

A mission-minded child . . . befriends the new kid at school.

A mission-minded child . . . thinks beyond the "box" of what's merely expected and hopes to do something big, or something little, for God.

A mission-minded child . . . wants to obey (even when no one is looking).

A mission-minded child . . . loves Jesus!

🎤 TEACHING OPPORTUNITY

Creative Writing Idea—Mission-Minded Statements

Read aloud the "A mission-minded child . . ." statements above and talk with your child about what it means to have a mission-minded heart. Encourage your child to write his or her own "A mission-minded child . . ." statements that share a heart for God and for His love for people all throughout the world.

CHAPTER 1

Releasing Your Child to God

As Hannah embraced her little Samuel one last time, what thoughts must have filled her mind? As she placed his timid fingers into the hands of the old priest, Eli, . . . and let go, . . . what questions did she surrender to the Lord?

As Hannah looked back toward her home, what did her mother's heart feel? How could she walk away from the answer to all her prayers? How could she release this dream she had so desperately longed for—this dream that was now a real little boy looking up at her with questioning eyes and a quivering lip, trying to obey her loving instructions, and trying to hold back his tears?

If only Hannah could have known at that moment how the story looks from *our* perspective. We know her Samuel would soon hear the audible voice of God, he would impact the entire nation of Israel, and this very act of her obedient surrender would be recorded and recalled for generations.

But Hannah didn't know the future. She only knew it was time to say goodbye and go home—childless once again. She must have turned her face quickly so Samuel wouldn't see her mixed emotions.

As Hannah walked away, she released her little one into the mighty hand of God and chose to worship. As she did, God's plan began to unfold. For this child was not just Hannah's dream; he was God's dream. At the time, the nation of Israel desperately needed a new spiritual leader, and God had found a mother desperate enough for Him to willingly yield to His plans.

As parents or Christian teachers, we don't always realize the importance of our vital role in the kingdom of God. Will we equip our children to fulfill God's purposes and to reach for God's potential? Will we train our children to reach their world for Jesus?

Through this book I desire to light a spark for world missions that will grow into a fire for the unsaved like you've never had before. I want God's love for unreached people to burn so strongly inside you that it will start spreading to others, specifically to your own children and to the young people you come in contact with.

Over the years I've seen many of our world's appalling needs. I've had opportunities to travel and minister in dozens of countries. However, in this particular season of my life I'm primarily called to be at home. I love being a mother, raising a family, and teaching children. But sometimes, I admit, I get frustrated.

Many days I wonder if I am "doing" anything of significance and I often struggle with a horrible "striving" mentality in my flesh. When I hear of "big needs"—like the "big need" for world missions—I feel a striving to want to do something "important" (for God, of course!).

I want to be busy!

I want to go!

But sometimes it feels like I'm meeting only insignificant "little needs"—like sweeping the kitchen floor over and over, reading that naptime story (again!), and simply watching my children grow.

Yet, deep inside, I *do* know the truth. Raising and training children *is* important! "Striving," or mere "busyness," is not the same as "fruitfulness," and all God *really* requires is for me to stay close to Him and obey Him, day by day.

Today the Lord is simply showing me to be faithful—that is, to love God and to support my husband here at home; to be fruitful—to be a mother and to teach and train our children in the ways of the Lord; and to keep my eyes on the future—to eagerly anticipate the Lord's return and keep living in His joy.

As parents and teachers, we must "train up a child in the way he should go" (Proverbs 22:6), and in the Great Commission; Jesus said the way we should go is "into all the world and preach the gospel" (Mark 16:15).

David Livingstone said, "God had only one Son, and He made Him a missionary." Jesus came as our missionary to earth. He relinquished everything in heaven to provide the way for us (and all people) to come into relationship with Him. He knew the cost before Him, and the price He paid was beyond anything we could imagine.

In Hebrews 12:2, the Bible says we are to look to Jesus, "the author and finisher of our faith, who for the joy that was set before Him endured the cross, despising the shame." Jesus' incredible love compelled Him to the cross. His burning desire was to fully obey the will of the Father, providing a way for humanity to be reconciled back to God. Jesus was willing to sacrifice whatever it took: His position in heaven, His unsurpassed riches and glory, His reputation, and even His very life. Jesus was whipped, beaten, tortured, and despised—all for the *joy* that was set before Him.

Isaiah 9:2–3 describes the joy of harvest as a light shining through darkness. There is rejoicing when a lost coin is found! There is joy when a shepherd finds a lost sheep or when a prodigal finally comes home! Luke 15:7 tells us that "there will be more joy in heaven over one sinner who repents than over ninety-nine just persons who need no repentance."

This is the joy that led Jesus to the cross.

How many of us are so captivated by God's love that we would be willing to lay down everything to follow Him?

We should take a moment to consider our lives and our priorities from God's eternal perspective:

- As we teach and train our children, what are we hoping they will achieve?

- As we steward God's resources, what are we saving toward?

- As we influence the next generation, what dreams are we instilling?

- As we talk to God, what is the primary focus of our prayers?

As Christians, we must realize that God's love, His passionate love, resides in us. Are we willing to allow this love to flow through us (and through our children) to the world? Second Corinthians 5:14–15 says, "For the love of Christ compels us . . . that those who live should live no longer for themselves, but for Him who died for them and rose again."

Like Hannah, we must realize that our child is actually God's child—entrusted to us for only a short time. We need to release our child to God and then follow His guidance to raise His child for His divine purposes!

My prayer is for the simple words in this book to penetrate deep into your soul and spirit. I know you don't need more information; but we all need more inspiration. I pray that God's love for the world will someday explode in your heart like a blast of dynamite. I hope you will begin to be moved by the things that move God's heart and that you will allow God's precious Holy Spirit to impart this heart into your child.

We've all heard the famous saying, "The hand that rocks the cradle rules the world." I say, "May the child in our cradle (or our classroom) *reach* the world . . . for the One who rules it all!"

CHAPTER 2

Raising Your Child for God

*"Train up a child in the way he should go
[and in keeping with his individual gift or bent],
and when he is old he will not depart from it."*
—*Proverbs 22:6 (AMPLIFIED)*

Missions is not an isolated "subject" to study, but an attitude and an exciting (although challenging) way of looking at our entire world! Just as Christianity influences every aspect of our lives, so also should God's heart for the lost completely change our outlook and our priorities.

Hudson Taylor was very young when his parents imparted to him a passionate heart for Jesus and a lifelong commitment to missions. Speaking of childhood, Taylor's parents said, "At no [other] time is there greater capacity for devotion or more pure, uncalculating ambition in the service of God." At only five years of age, Hudson Taylor often said, "When I am a man, I mean to be a missionary and go to China." Was it merely a coincidence that this little boy grew to become one of China's greatest missionaries? No, this childhood dream was God's purpose, diligently nurtured by godly parents.

It's a great responsibility to "train up a child in the way he should go." We begin by training our little one to walk and talk; as our child grows older, we help with reading and writing; and as the years go by, more and more aspirations are added to our agenda—as diverse as encouraging academics and musical skills to cheering at athletic events and monitoring young friends. All along the way, we work hard to instill in our child a deep love for the Lord. We want our child to be a young person with godly character, to have a heart of purity, to desire God's specific plan, and to fully obey Him in whatever way He leads.

I want to challenge you in this calling. The purpose for this book is to provide a practical and encouraging resource. I hope to inspire you to a deeper personal level of commitment to God's Great Commission and to equip you to impart effectively His heart to your child.

Around the world, the need for the gospel is beyond what most of us can even comprehend. Most of us are usually so bogged down with busyness and unending responsibilities that it's an accomplishment just to keep afloat here at home. The idea of traveling across the seas to "rescue souls" is something we try not to think about, but maybe we need to think about the real boys and girls and men and women who have yet to hear about Jesus Christ.

Q. Are you a Christian parent?

- **Public (or Private Non-Christian) School Parents**—Nearly every parent wants to raise his or her child to succeed in life and to find true purpose. For many Christian families, a public (or private non-Christian) school education is the path chosen to reach this goal. Yet a Christian child's true purpose or "mission" will not be found in any book or in any school. True success in God's eyes will come only from a child's personal devotion to God and a practical obedience to His will.

  Beginning in the early educational years, many God-loving children embark on their first "missionary adventure" by going to school. Sometimes, however, impressionable children are influenced for evil more than their peers are influenced for good. We need to guard our child in order to withstand the predominantly non-Christian worldviews within many school systems. As mission-minded parents, we need to provide a strong prayer covering and make sure that our child has a steadfast commitment to Jesus Christ and a sincere concern for those who don't know Christ yet.

By encouraging our child's faith and strengthening our child's own relationship with the Lord, he or she will more easily find God's mission—and fulfill it!

- **Christian School Parents**—If your child attends a Christian school you are likely investing a great deal of money each month to provide your child with a biblically based education. As a Christian school parent, you obviously care deeply about your child receiving godly instruction; yet you can't delegate the ultimate responsibility for your child's spiritual training to anyone else. God places the primary child-raising responsibility on the parents, so it is necessary to take time to check up on your educational investment and ensure that the spiritual training your child is receiving at school and at church is supplemented with a strong biblical foundation from your own home.

Q. Are you a home educator?

All throughout the world today, millions of children are being taught at home. A majority of these homeschooling families are Christians, and many of these parents strongly desire to teach with a biblical worldview. This makes for an excellent foundation for mission-minded training.

One of the greatest challenges many missionary families encounter is the education of their children, but homeschoolers are already prepared! If the Lord would call a homeschool family to foreign missionary service, their children's education could continue nearly the same as before (simply exchanging their kitchen table at home for one overseas). And if the Lord would call a homeschooled child to missionary work, a parent could specifically tailor that child's education to help him or her prepare. Even the idea of world travel sets a homeschooling parent's mind racing with exciting opportunities for international field trips and hands-on geography lessons!

In addition, homeschool families are accustomed to making sacrifices in many areas of life. They're already considered "a little radical" for going against the flow of traditional education; they often think "outside the box" of what's possible; and they're usually spending hours together as a family—reading, exploring new ideas, and continually seeking God's will. Homeschooling and a heart for world missions can make a great combination!

Each Christian family must earnestly seek God's will for the education of their children and obey God's direction—whatever that may be. Strong mission-minded children can be found in Christian schools, in public schools, and in home-based schools.

Q. Are you a teacher in a church or Christian school?

If so, God needs you!

God needs mission-minded educators in every Christian school, in every church program, and in every Sunday school! A heart for world missions should be a vital part of every Christ-centered classroom and included in every child's spiritual training.

As a Christian teacher, your potential in the kingdom of God is great! Year after year, classroom after classroom, you are in a position of leadership that can influence the hearts of many children. Through you, or through one young person you train, God could someday transform a community, city, or nation.

Q. Are you even the "missions type"?

"World missions" is something I am passionate about. A portion of this book was actually written in Tanzania and Uganda while I was on a missionary outreach in Africa. In the midst of children's ministry and women's seminars, visiting village churches, and helping with city-wide evangelistic meetings, I was thinking about this book—and you, the reader—and praying for ways to effectively impart God's compassion for the world.

In light of that, some of you may have compartmentalized me into some stereotypical missionary box in your mind and think that you and I have nothing in common. You may not consider yourself the "missions type" at all.

But please let me redefine "missions." You (and your child) are specially designed by God, who has an individualized "mission" for your life. There is absolutely no one else just like you; and no one else can fulfill the unique God-given mission He has planned just for you. As followers of Jesus Christ we are all called—every one of us—to the mission of expanding God's kingdom.

How "missions" looks in your life—or how it will look in the life of each child—may be very different than how it looks in my life. Or perhaps it may look similar.

You may even discover that you and I have more in common than you realize. In day-to-day life, I actually consider myself a very "normal" Christian:

- I'm a follower of Jesus, and I love my Lord.

- I'm a parent, and I love my children.

- I'm a teacher, and I love to teach. (Well, most of the time!)

Perhaps like you, my daily "missions adventures" include many not-so-glamorous expeditions—such as battling bedroom disasters, tackling insurmountable laundry piles, celebrating a successful potty-training moment, or attacking a stack of schoolwork that needs to be graded. I've had exciting and encouraging teaching experiences, but I continue to struggle with daily disciplines and feelings of inadequacy—especially when homeschooling my teenagers!

Over the past twenty years, God has graciously provided opportunities for my husband and me (along with our children) to travel and minister in many international outreaches all across the globe. By seeing the world's needs for ourselves, our perspective has simply changed—and these experiences have drastically impacted our philosophy of raising and teaching children.

Our Lord's Great Commission is much more than an isolated memory verse. Loving Jesus and reaching those who don't have a relationship with Him is the central core of all we do.

As you read this book, may God begin to unveil His incredible love for the unreached and help you impart a new zeal for missions into the heart of your child. Whatever purpose God has planned—whether your child is called to be a medical doctor, a political leader, a successful businessperson, a teacher, a missionary, or a parent—may each child God entrusts to you be raised as His mission-minded child.

🌐 TEACHING OPPORTUNITY

Missions Memory, Oratorical Practice, and Object Lesson (Life Line)

Encourage your child to read the classic missions poem and hymn, "A Passion for Souls." Look up words your child might not be familiar with (such as *passion*, *adored*, and *pardon*), and explain the concept of a lifeguard who throws a "life line" to a person who is drowning. (For an object lesson, you could give your child a LifeSavers® candy or hold up a life preserver, life jacket, or blow-up flotation device as you teach this point.) Have your child memorize this poem and practice reciting it with clear enunciation as he or she speaks every word with feeling and conviction.

"A KID'S HEART FOR MISSIONS"

By Joshua Dunagan, at age seven

I wrote this letter and drew this picture about ten years ago when I was about seven years old. My spelling and handwriting is embarrassing, but it does show how God can give a vision for missions—even to a kid.

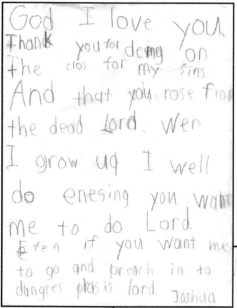

God, I love you.

Thank you for dying on the cross for my sins. And that you rose from the dead Lord.

When I grow up, I will do anything You want me to do Lord. Even if you want me to go and preach into dangerous places, Lord.

Joshua

"Missions is not just for missionaries; God's CALL is for ALL."

JON & ANN DUNAGAN
MISSION-MINDED FAMILIES

CHAPTER 3

Our Call

For many Christians, "missions" is, at best, a necessary responsibility. For hundreds of years the church has always "supported the missionaries," and so tradition continues—yet often without God's heart and passion or even a compelling purpose to win boys and girls, men and women to faith in Jesus Christ.

No wonder, then, when many of us think of a missionary, strange images come to mind!

You may picture some young adventurer—clad in khaki safari clothes—trudging through the jungles with a machete. Perhaps you imagine him (or her) meeting a group of dark-skinned natives, dancing around mud huts and a raging fire, all moving to the beat of a pounding tribal drum. Or maybe your only view of a missionary is of some strange older couple, in outdated clothing, presenting never-ending blurry slides or a shaky home video for some "special" Sunday evening service. Completing this picture are uninspiring stories of terrible food and awful living conditions, ending with that dreaded drawn-out plea for money.

Perhaps, for the sake of our children, it's time to change our pictures of missions today.

Q. Is there still a need for world missions?

The word *mission* brings to mind synonyms such as *goal, vision,* and *purpose.* As Christians, what is God's purpose for our lives? What are His goals and vision?

- **Our primary calling** . . . is to know and love the Lord. But if that were all, God could have taken us to heaven the moment we received Jesus Christ.

- **Our primary mission** . . . is to glorify God in and through our lives and to help make God known throughout the earth.

With our primary mission clearly in view, it's obvious we need to help proclaim the gospel of Jesus Christ and obey God's words to "Go into all the world." We need to ask ourselves if we really believe the Bible is the true and inspired Word of God. Do we honestly believe people must be saved, or "born again," as Jesus said in John 3:3, and can we comprehend the eternal reality of heaven and hell? If we do, these beliefs should radically impact our lives.

Think for a moment about how different your life would be if you were born in a land isolated from God and filled with extreme poverty, sickness, and disease. What would it be like if you were born in an area where praying to an idol or giving homage to an ancestor was your only hope? What if constant fear of evil spirits consumed your life? Wouldn't you want someone to share God's life-giving message of salvation with *you*?

We have received God's light, but it is not just for us. We're called to shine God's light in the darkness.

For those of us who live in developed countries, we need to realize how much God has blessed us.

- **We are blessed!** Every day we enjoy clean, hot running water—without a thought.

- **We are blessed!** Our typical meals often include ingredients from all around the world: fruit from California and the Polynesian islands, olive oil from Italy and the Middle East, and perhaps coffee from Columbia (just try looking at your food labels for a few days). We eat better than the ancient kings!

- **We are blessed!** Most of us, with only a few quick calls to a credit card company and a local travel agency, could likely travel next month to any destination in the world if we really wanted to (not that I'm advocating debt, but if reaching people is our priority, our budgets can be made to accommodate).

God has given us the greatest "Good News" of all time and a job description to "Get this news out!" He has given us an abundance of resources to accomplish the task and a challenge that "To whom much is given, from him much will be required" (Luke 12:48).

 TEACHING OPPORTUNITY

Creative Writing Idea—List God's Blessings

Have your child make a list of some of the blessings God has given. Encourage your child to try to list one item for each letter of the alphabet. Another idea is to look through magazines and cut out pictures of typical blessings that we sometimes take for granted.

Q. Why go overseas when we have so many needs in our own country?

Missionary evangelist Oswald J. Smith answered this question with another: "Why should anyone hear the gospel twice before everyone has heard it once?"

We do have needs, but ours pale in comparison, according to the *World Christian Encyclopedia*:

- **The missions need:** In North America there are more than one million full-time Christian workers (one full-time Christian leader for every 230 people), while in many places there is only one missionary for every 500,000 people!

- **The missions need:** Out of all the finances given to the Christian church worldwide, 96.8 percent is spent on those who have already received Christ (Christians spending money on Christians), 2.9 percent is spent on those who have heard but rejected the gospel, and only 0.3 percent is spent on reaching those who have never once heard God's Good News.

- **The missions need:** Since the invention of the printing press in 1450, 85 percent of all Bibles ever printed have been printed in English—yet only 9 percent of the world speaks that language! An estimated 80 percent of the world's population has never owned a Bible, while in the United States, for example, there is an average of four Bibles in every household.

- **The missions need:** Many of us hear the gospel again and again, while approximately 1.6 billion people are still waiting for their first opportunity to hear.

- **The missions need:** Even among Christian missionaries, only 15 percent of all missionary finances are used for gospel work among "unreached" people. *Revolution in World Missions* states that nearly 80 percent of all missionaries are involved primarily in social work, not in proclaiming the gospel, winning souls, or establishing churches. For heaven's sake—literally—what did Jesus call us to do?

Q. Aren't all cultures equally valid? Why should we try to change other people's cultures?

The core issue of this question stems from a false application of "multiculturalism"—one that is politically correct, educationally encouraged, and sounds nice. But leaving people trapped in sin and isolated from God's hope of salvation isn't the "considerate" option.

As Christians, we bring the cross-cultural, life-changing message of Jesus Christ and His forgiveness for sin. Our purpose is not to propagate our own cultural standards, but to present the gospel in a redeeming yet culturally sensitive way to all people we meet. Eliminating the beautiful uniqueness of international culture is not the purpose of missions; at times, however, sinful elements of a particular culture may need to change.

I will never forget an interview I had with an outstanding Christian teenager who attended a public high school. This young man led a lunchtime "Bible Club" and worship time that grew to reach 250 of his fellow classmates. He was writing a school research paper on Christian missionary work and, specifically, he was trying to support his thesis that "modern missionaries do not attempt to 'change' foreign cultures."

I understood this young man's heart. He was trying to explain how today's Christian missionaries are different—more culturally appreciative and sensitive—than some of the old-time colonial missionaries (who attempted to expand all aspects of Western civilization throughout the world). But I still disagreed with his conclusion.

I asked this young man a pointed question. "But don't you try to 'change the culture' of the people you are trying to reach? Just look at the typical 'culture' of the teens in your high school before they come to Jesus Christ! Look at the way they dress! Listen to their music, their foul language, and the way they address their teachers! What about the videos they watch and the movies they sneak into? What about typical teenagers involved in sexual impurity or the girls who've had abortions? Aren't all of these a part of teen 'culture'?"

I went on to explain to him, "Culture is *life*! When you share Jesus Christ in your high school, of course you don't want your friends to stop being teenagers—that's who they are! But you *do* want Jesus Christ to totally transform the way they live and the way they make their decisions!"

Around the world, societies that have developed isolated from God's laws and the gospel are filled with sinful cultural elements:

- tribal hatred, ancestral worship, and idolatry

- immoral sex, adultery, and prostitution

- drug addiction, drunkenness, and witchcraft

- abuse and neglect of women and children

As Christians, our job is to bring the light of Jesus to every precious culture. Through His Word and His Holy Spirit, God will show people the changes they need to make to redeem their cultures back to Him.

Q. Why go to those remote foreign tribes? Wouldn't they probably be "better off" just left as they are?

My answer to that question is a loud "No! No! No!" The unreached are never better off without Jesus Christ! Often we are blinded to this fact by a movie-world version of a "tropical native paradise." Some influential films and books portray remote tribes living in "peaceful bliss and harmony" until some "big, bad missionary" comes on the scene. But this paradise is only an illusion!

By God's grace I have personally ministered throughout Latin America and the Caribbean, North America, Eastern and Western Europe, Asia, Africa, and Australia—from remote villages to crowded inner cities. Throughout these missionary travels I have never seen this "tropical native paradise"! At times, the land and beaches *are* beautiful and people may be warm and friendly; yet lives without God are always filled with misery.

- **In the Philippines** . . . I remember walking through a squatters' village and seeing streams of human waste flowing openly down a path. I was horrified to watch a group of Filipino children toss a bucket of garbage into an already dirty river, jump in the middle of it, and start throwing the garbage on each other. These poor children were just playing, oblivious to the filth and potential for disease. Although yes, it was tropical, it was so far from God's garden of Eden!

- **In Costa Rica** . . . I saw people crawl on bloody bare knees in penance for their sins. In Guatemala, I sadly watched as crowds of poor, devoted people surrendered large sums of money just to carry a religious icon. These people were desperate for God's forgiveness, but as I looked into their faces I saw no joy and no assurance of salvation.

- **In Uganda** . . . My husband and I once ministered to a tribe of people who actually worshiped a large tree. These Africans were aware of their sins and even the need for the shedding of innocent blood; yet their religion gave them no hope. They blindly offered animal sacrifices to this tree and, as I was told, at times, even the human sacrifices of their young children.

- **In Tanzania** . . . In 1995 my husband and I were ministering in a remote city when one morning we heard horrifying news. Radical Muslims had bombed the city grounds where we were scheduled to sing, preach, and show the *JESUS* film. In the process, these terrorists destroyed a primary school—killing eight precious children and seriously wounding eighty others (most who eventually died)—all to protest the message of Christianity.

- **Across the globe** . . . Throughout history—in places such as Nazi Germany, Rwanda, Bosnia, Ethiopia, and Iraq— government systems have planned for the elimination of entire people groups. Twisted religious beliefs (such as the Hindu reverence of the cow and the rat) have caused self-inflicted food shortages and starvation. Many isolated people groups are bound by fear, controlled by witchcraft, or filled with tribal hatred.

All over the world, individuals without Christ are separated from God by sin and are destined to spend eternity even further separated from Him—unless they hear and respond to God's Good News! Our Lord Jesus Christ came to destroy this barrier of sin. He surrendered His life on the cross and sacrificed His perfect, sinless blood so that all people could have access to God's eternal life in heaven.

The entire message of the Bible can be summarized in words we all likely know by heart: "For God so loved the world that He gave His only begotten Son, that whoever believes in Him should not perish but have everlasting life" (John 3:16).

Q. Are the "lost" *really* lost?

In one of my favorite movies, *Anne of Avonlea*, I've often replayed the scene where two elderly friends, Marilla Cuthbert and Rachel Lynde, are knitting together on the front porch of Anne's house, Green Gables. As Mrs. Lynde refers to some "heathenness" murder trials from a Boston newspaper, she declares, "Can you imagine that new minister, going on about how he doesn't believe that all the heathen will be eternally lost? The idea! If they won't be, all the money we've been sending to the foreign missions will be completely wasted, that's what!"

It's a simple excerpt, but a big issue. As Christians, what we believe about the spiritual and eternal condition of those who don't have a relationship with God greatly affects our attitude toward world missions.

Today the word *heathen* has a negative connotation and is considered an outdated term; yet this word's meaning delves deep into our core theology of world missions. The term refers not only to people who are unsaved but specifically to "unreached people who have *never* heard the gospel." Is our true motivation for missions to share the Good News of Jesus Christ with those who have yet to hear it, or do we merely want to help poor people live a better life? What makes *God's* calling to reach the world any different than a government assistance program or a secular benevolence outreach? The bottom-line distinction is our belief about the lost and especially our convictions about these people who have never heard the gospel.

Are these lost people *really* lost, or does God have an "alternative way" for them to be saved? The question makes us very uneasy and very uncomfortable. We wonder, "How could a good God send people to hell just because they've never heard the gospel?"

It seems so unfair. But to answer this question we need to look beyond what *we think* and what *we feel* about fairness to what *we can know* from God's Word.

First of all, people are not separated from God because they have never heard the gospel; people are separated from God because of sin. This sin includes both the sins we ourselves commit and the "sin nature" that has been passed down to all humanity ever since Adam and Eve's fall in the garden of Eden. Isaiah 53:5 states, "He was wounded for our transgressions, He was bruised for our iniquities." When Jesus Christ died on the cross, He totally paid the penalty price for both our sins and our human sin nature.

The lost in foreign countries are not innocent. They have sinned and will be judged before our absolutely perfect holy God. We can trust God to judge righteously, and we can trust what He has shown us in His Word. The Bible tells us, "For all have sinned . . ." (Romans 3:23); and deep down, everyone knows it. Even without knowledge of God's laws and the gospel message, a person inwardly knows that he or she has done wrong things. Everyone has violated the inborn, God-placed convictions of his or her own conscience (although some have violated these convictions so many times that their hearts may have become calloused and they no longer feel remorse or guilt). This inborn realization of sin is one of the primary reasons why much of humanity is so religious. All around the world people are desperately trying to do something about their sin (even if they are only desperately trying to ignore God's tug on their hearts).

So are those without the Good News *really* lost, or can a person's "ignorance" of the gospel exempt him or her from the consequences of sin? Consider the second alternative: If total ignorance (of the message of

God's salvation through Jesus Christ) was an alternative way to heaven, why wouldn't it be best to keep everyone ignorant? With this reasoning, if everyone was ignorant, everyone could be spared! Why not take it a step further and destroy all Bibles and eliminate evangelism? Then the entire world could be "saved" through this "guaranteed-ignorance exemption."

But obviously, this is not God's way.

If before the gospel came everyone was "ignorant" (but on their way to heaven), and after the gospel came everyone would have "knowledge" of God's salvation (but could then be condemned to hell), then wouldn't the Good News message actually be Very Bad News to a previously unreached people group? But Jesus Christ knew—more than any of us could ever know—that salvation through His perfect sacrifice was (and is) humankind's only hope. The night before Jesus was crucified, he desperately cried to His Father in the garden of Gethsemane, "If it is possible, let this cup pass from Me; nevertheless, not as I will, but as You will" (Matthew 26:39).

If there was any other way for human beings to be saved, then why did God allow Jesus to go to the cross? It is because there was (and is) no other way.

Without God's salvation—on His terms and only through the cross of His only Son—the "lost" are desperately and completely lost. Only the blood of Jesus Christ can eliminate our record of sin and pay the price that the consequence of sin requires before God. Remember the words of the old hymn: *What can wash away my sin? Nothing but the blood of Jesus!*

This fact led Jesus to the cross. This fact motivated early missionaries to leave their homelands with no hope of return; this fact was a passionate force behind the sacrificial giving of previous generations; and this fact motivates millions of Christians today. It's a vital missions fact that we must instill—with conviction—in the hearts and minds of the next generation.

The fact is: without Jesus Christ, the lost *are* lost.

And although Jesus' death was sufficient to pay in full the penalty price for every person's sins, not everyone is saved, or redeemed. Each person is required to come to God individually through faith in Jesus Christ and claim God's gift of salvation for himself or herself.

🎙 TEACHING OPPORTUNITY

Mission-Minded Object Lesson (Coupons)

Have you ever received a package of grocery coupons or a free gift certificate? Just because you possess a coupon for something does not necessarily guarantee that you will ever receive the product. Hold up a grocery store coupon as you read this analogy about God's gift of salvation.

• ***Free Doughnut Coupons:***

Suppose a nationwide grocery store chain decides to promote a certain new brand of doughnuts. The company produces millions upon millions of "free doughnut coupons" and pays the postal service to deliver coupons to every resident in the country. Each person would be eligible for a dozen doughnuts; to receive a free box of doughnuts, however, each person must go to the grocery store and "redeem" his or her coupon. Those who don't redeem their coupons won't get any doughnuts, and thus their unused coupon is worthless.

Unfortunately some people, for one reason or another, do not have a coupon. Perhaps the mailing never reached their home. Perhaps some international residents didn't understand English and were unable to read their coupon. Perhaps some people were too busy and their coupon got lost. Perhaps others couldn't care less about a free box of doughnuts and simply threw their coupon away.

The reasons really don't matter. The point is, unless a person receives a coupon, he will likely know nothing about the special offer; and unless a person takes her coupon to the store to get it "redeemed," she will not get any doughnuts.

The lost must hear.

This fact should compel us to our knees and draw us to the nations.

Is it fair? No.

Is it fair that Jesus had to die in our place? No.

Is it fair that we go to our churches week after week . . . and year after year . . . when multitudes have never even heard once that Jesus came?

Is it fair that we sit on padded pews and critique our pastor's polished sermons, while over 1.6 billion people have never heard even one simple gospel message?

No. It is not fair. But God is totally good and holy and just. He has never been "obligated" to save the lost, and He was not even "obligated" to save us! It is only because of God's great grace that He offers us His salvation, and it is only because of God's great love that He now passionately urges and compels us to proclaim this salvation—God's great news.

🌐 TEACHING OPPORTUNITY

Object Lesson and Mission-Minded Prayer Project (Clock)

Second Peter 3:9 tells us that God is "not willing that any should perish but that all should come to repentance." And He has given us the job of sharing His message of hope and Good News. To help explain this need to your child, emphasize Christ's love and His sacrifice on the cross for the sins of the world. To set a more serious tone, you and your child could watch a second hand on a clock for exactly one minute as you share how every sixty seconds (according to current statistics) nearly one hundred people die (which totals about 150,000 people every day), and the vast majority have not received God's salvation through Jesus Christ. Emphasize the importance of having God's heart for the lost, and then encourage your child to pray for people who don't know Jesus. Use the clock again to pray—fervently and compassionately—for exactly one minute for God to send missionaries to these people who need Jesus.

A HUNDRED THOUSAND SOULS***

Unknown

A hundred thousand souls a day
Are passing, passing fast away,
In Christless guilt and gloom;
Oh Church of Christ, what wilt thou say,
When in the awful Judgment Day,
They charge thee with their doom?

*** Author's Note: These vital mission concepts of death, dying, hell, and the unsaved (along with this classic mission poem) will likely be too traumatic for a younger child. Parents and teachers should seek the Lord's discretion and guidance to know when these biblical truths should be appropriately introduced.

> "Every man, woman, and child in heathen darkness
> is a challenge to the church."
>
> S. E. TAYLOR

 THE LITTLE STARFISH

A mission story to read aloud to children

One day an old man was walking along the beach at low tide. Across the sand he could see thousands upon thousands of starfish drying in the sun. He knew they would soon die, but he thought nothing of it.

As he continued to walk he noticed, far ahead, a child throwing something into the water. Coming closer, the man could see a young boy hurriedly tossing starfish—one by one—into the ocean waves.

"Why are you working so hard?" the man asked the boy. "Can't you see how many starfish are still on the sand? What difference could it make?"

The boy looked down at the starfish in his hand, and then looked up. "Well, Sir," he humbly responded, "it'll make a difference to this one."

And with that, he threw the little starfish into the water.

TEACHING OPPORTUNITY

Mission-Minded Discussion (Starfish Story)

Read the story of "The Little Starfish" with your child and discuss the importance of doing what we can to help others. We will never be able to meet *every* need in the world, but with God's help we can make a difference in the lives of some people, one by one.

Discussion Questions:

1. What does this story about the little starfish represent?
2. Do you know anyone like the little boy? Or like the old man?
3. Who should we be more like?
4. How can we be "starfish savers"?
5. Can you think of a specific person we can help?

"You can only export what you grow at home."

JON & ANN DUNAGAN
MISSION-MINDED FAMILIES

THE GREAT COMMISSION IN EVERY GOSPEL

Jesus came and spoke to them, saying, "All authority has been given to Me in heaven and on earth. Go therefore and make disciples of all the nations, baptizing them in the name of the Father and of the Son and of the Holy Spirit."

Matthew 28:18–19

He said to them, "Go into all the world and preach the gospel to every creature."

Mark 16:15

He said to them, "Thus it is written, and thus it was necessary for the Christ to suffer and to rise from the dead the third day, and that repentance and remission of sins should be preached in His name to all nations, beginning at Jerusalem. And you are witnesses of these things."

Luke 24:46–48

Jesus said to them again, "Peace to you!
As the Father has sent Me, I also send you."

John 20:21

He said to them, "It is not for you to know times or seasons which the Father has put in His own authority. But you shall receive power when the Holy Spirit has come upon you; and you shall be witnesses to Me in Jerusalem, and in all Judea and Samaria, and to the end of the earth."

Acts 1:7–8

CHAPTER 4

Our Biblical Basis

Matthew 28:19–20 and Mark 16:15 are often referred to as "The Great Commission." These final words of Jesus to "Go therefore and make disciples of all the nations . . ." and to "Go into all the world and preach the gospel . . ." are often memorized and sometimes overly familiar; but the biblical basis for world missions reaches far beyond these two verses! God's heart for the world—and our obligation as His followers to take the gospel to the ends of the earth—is a central theme throughout the entire Word of God.

World Missions from Genesis to Revelation!

We can see God's compassion for *all* people in Israel's invasion of Jericho which was led by Joshua. By faith, a prostitute in Jericho named Rahab believed in God and extended a scarlet cord through her window on the wall. By faith, she and all her loved ones gathered in her house were saved from destruction.

I don't think it was just a coincidence that the color of Rahab's rope was red. I see this "scarlet cord" as a powerful object lesson of God's grace and mercy that extends to all people—and as a recurring illustration of God's truth that is intertwined throughout the Bible, from Genesis to Revelation, and ultimately fulfilled in our Lord Jesus Christ.

We see our first glimpse of this "scarlet cord" when God clothes Adam and Eve with the skins of an innocent animal after sin enters the world. We see it during the Passover deliverance as God saved the Israelites by instructing them to put the blood of the lamb over their doorways and specified a way for the "strangers" (or Gentiles) living among them to celebrate the Passover (see Exodus 12:48). We see it in the book of Daniel as God reveals Himself to the mighty kings of Babylon and Persia, and we see it interwoven throughout the prophecies of Isaiah and Jeremiah. This "scarlet cord" is found in God's unrelenting call to Jonah and the people of the wicked city of Nineveh and throughout many of David's psalms.

Jesus' Heart for All Nations

It's true that a person's last words are important, but God's heart and focus did not suddenly change as Jesus Christ ascended into heaven. As He rose into the clouds, it wasn't as if Jesus dropped some last-minute change of plans on His followers: "Oh, by the way, there's just one major thing I forgot to tell you. . . ."

When Jesus came to earth, His birth was announced to Jews (the shepherds) and to Gentiles (the wise men) as an angel brought "good tidings of great joy which will be to all people" (Luke 2:10). As Jesus was dedicated in the temple, Simeon's prophetic word included, "My eyes have seen Your salvation which You have prepared before the face of all peoples, a light to bring revelation to the Gentiles" (Luke 2:30–32).

During Jesus' first recorded sermon, in the city of Nazareth, He included two Old Testament examples of God's heart for the Gentiles: Elijah's provision for a widow of Zarephath and Elisha's healing for Captain Naaman of Syria. Along with these examples, Jesus read a prophecy from Isaiah and then said, "Today this Scripture is fulfilled in your hearing" (Luke 4:21). He was claiming to be the Messiah—of both Jews and Gentiles—a concept totally contrary to Israel's preconceived ideas of nationalistic patriotism. For generations the Jewish people had longed for a Messiah to deliver them and bring them glory. It's no wonder that the people of Nazareth wanted to throw Jesus over that cliff!

Throughout His earthly ministry, Jesus revealed God's heart for all people. Yes, He was sent first to the lost sheep of Israel; but He also ministered to a Samaritan woman, healed a Roman centurion's servant, delivered a Gadarene demoniac, and fed four thousand people in a Gentile area. Even while on the cross, one of Jesus' final acts of ministry was to offer God's salvation to an undeserving thief.

Jesus taught with stories and analogies that conveyed God's love for the whole world. He called for laborers in the harvest. He commanded His disciples to launch deep and fish for men. He challenged His followers to welcome more guests to the wedding. Jesus told of a shepherd earnestly searching for a lost sheep, a woman stopping everything to look for a lost coin, and a father embracing a prodigal son.

Jesus said, "There will be more joy in heaven over one sinner who repents than over ninety-nine just persons who need no repentance" (Luke 15:7). If lost sinners matter *that much* to God and to the angels in heaven, they should matter to us.

Throughout the New Testament we see God's "scarlet cord" of salvation—from Philip preaching to the Samaritans and the Ethiopian in Acts 8, Peter bringing the gospel to Cornelius and his friends and family in Acts 10, in Paul's letters to churches comprised of both Jews and Gentiles, and concluding with John's end-time vision of "a great multitude which no one could number, of all nations, tribes, peoples, and tongues" worshiping together before the throne of God in heaven (Revelation 7:9).

Even in the map section in the back of most of our Bibles there are usually several pages highlighting early missionary journeys. It's not hard to find a biblical basis for world missions; it's hard *not* to see it.

Missions Theme	Reference	Bible Verse/Paraphrase
Since the time of Adam and Eve, all people have sinned and all need a Savior.	• Genesis 2:17 • Genesis 3:6 • Psalms 14:3 • Romans 5:12 • Romans 3:10	When you eat of its fruit, you will surely die. Eve ate its fruit; Adam ate it also. No one does good, not even one. Through one man sin entered the world. There is none righteous, no, not one.
From the beginning, God required innocent blood to be shed for the guilty.	• Revelation 13:8 • Genesis 3:21 • Leviticus 17:11 • Hebrews 9:22	"Lamb slain from the foundation of the world" God made garments of skin for Adam and Eve. It is the blood that makes atonement. Without shedding blood there is no forgiveness.
All people descend from Adam and Noah.	• Acts 17:26 • Genesis 10:32	From one man, Adam, God made every nation. From Noah's sons the nations spread over earth.
God is no respecter of persons.	• Romans 10:12 • Acts 10:34-35 • James 2:1-9	There is no distinction between Jew and Greek. God accepts men from any nation who fear Him. Be like God–don't show partiality.
God revealed His love for the Gentiles in the Old Testament Law and Passover.	• Exodus 12:48 • Leviticus 16:29 • Leviticus 19:10 • Leviticus 22:18 • Numbers 9:14 • Numbers 15:14	"Strangers" are invited to celebrate Passover. "Aliens" can participate in Day of Atonement. Leave fallen grapes for the poor and the alien. Strangers are permitted to offer sacrifices. Passover regulations for foreigners Sacrificial regulations for strangers
God promised that through Abraham and his descendants all families on earth would be blessed.	• Genesis 12:1-3 • Genesis 18:18 • Acts 3:25	In you all families of the earth will be blessed. All nations will be blessed through Abraham. In Abraham's seed all peoples will be blessed.
Through signs and wonders, many nations heard of God's power and gave Him honor and glory.	• Exodus 7:5 • Exodus 15:11-14 • Exodus 18:10-11 • 2 Kings 5:15	The Egyptians will know that I am the Lord. The nations will hear and tremble. "The Lord is greater than all gods" (Jethro) "There is no God except in Israel" (Naaman)
The Old Testament prophets revealed God's heart for all nations.	• Isaiah 45:22-23 • Jeremiah 1:5 • Jeremiah 16:19 • Ezekiel 39:21 • Daniel 2:28 • Joel 3:9-14 • Zechariah 8:20-23	Turn to Me and be saved, you ends of the earth! I ordained you a prophet to the nations. O Lord, the Gentiles shall come to You. I will display My glory among the nations. God has revealed the future to Nebuchadnezzar. Proclaim this among the nations . . . Many peoples and nations will seek the Lord.

Missions Theme	Reference	Bible Verse/Paraphrase
Notice God's love for all nations as expressed in the Psalms.	• Psalm 18:49 • Psalm 22:27 • Psalm 33:8,12 • Psalm 57:9 • Psalm 67 • Psalm 96:2-3 • Psalm 117	I will give thanks to You among the Gentiles. All the families of the nations will worship You. Let all the people of the world revere Him. I will praise You, O Lord, among the nations. Oh, let the nations be glad and sing for joy! Declare His glory among the nations. Praise the Lord, all you Gentiles.
God was glorified in the sight of other nations through Old Testament leaders and characters.	• Genesis 45:8 • Exodus 7:5 • I Kings 10:1-9 • Daniel 3:28 • Daniel 6:25-27	God lifted up Joseph before Pharaoh. God showed His power in Egypt through Moses. Queen of Sheba saw God's wisdom in Solomon. Example of Shadrach, Meshach, and Abednego All commanded to fear God because of Daniel.
Old Testament Gentiles who had faith in God were saved.	• Joshua 2:8-21 • Ruth 4; Matt. 1:5 • Jonah 4:2 • I Kings 17:7-24 • 2 Kings 5	Rahab, a sinful woman, is saved at Jericho. Ruth, a woman of Moab, joins Jesus' lineage. The wicked city of Nineveh is saved. God provides for a Gentile widow. Namaan, a Syrian captain, is healed of leprosy.
Through Jesus' birth, God proclaimed His salvation for all people.	• Matthew 2:1-12 • Luke 2:8-14 • Luke 2:25-32	Wise men from the East come to worship Jesus. "news of joy to all people" (angel to shepherds) "a light of revelation to the Gentiles" (Simeon)
Through His ministry and preaching, Jesus demonstrated God's heart for all people.	• Luke 4:25-27 • Luke 8:26-37 • John 4:1-26 • Matthew 8:5-13	Jesus' first sermon lauds two Gentiles. A Gentile man is set free from demons. Jesus offers a Samaritan woman "living water." Jesus affirms a Roman centurion's "great faith."
In His final words (recorded in all four Gospels and in Acts), Jesus gave us His Great Commission.	• Matthew 28:19 • Mark 16:15 • Luke 24:47 • John 20:21 • Acts 1:8	Go and make disciples of all the nations. Go into all the world and preach the gospel. Repentance will be preached to all nations. As the Father has sent Me, I also send you. You will be My witnesses to the end of the earth.

Missions Theme	Reference	Bible Verse/Paraphrase
When Jesus died, His blood was shed for all people on earth. Only through His blood can people be saved.	• John 1:12 • John 3:16 • John 1:29 • Colossians 1:19-20 • Revelation 5:9	"as many as received Him . . ." Whoever believes in Him shall not perish. "The Lamb who takes away the sin of the world" God has made peace through Christ's blood. You have redeemed us by your blood.
There is only one way to heaven: through salvation in Jesus Christ.	• John 14:6 • John 3:1-7 • John 3:18 • Acts 4:12	No one comes to the Father except through Me. You must be born again. He who does not believe is condemned already. No other name by which we must be saved.
Without Jesus, the heathen are lost, separated from God, and will spend eternity in hell.	• Romans 3:23 • Romans 6:23 • Romans 10:14-15 • Galations 5:19-21	All have sinned and fall short of God's glory. Wages of sin is death; gift of God is eternal life. How will they hear without a preacher? Those who live like this won't inherit kingdom.
God places in all people knowledge of God their Creator and a consciousness of sin, so that all are without excuse.	• Eccesiastes 3:11 • Psalm 19:1-3 • John 1:9 • Romans 1:18-20	God has put eternity in their hearts. "no speech or language where they aren't heard" "the true Light which gives light to every man" God's attributes are clear; we are without excuse.
It is God's desire for everyone to be saved.	• Ezekiel 33:11 • John 3:16 • John 3:17 • 2 Peter 3:9 • Romans 10:13	I take no pleasure in the death of the wicked. God so loved the world, He gave His only Son. God sent Jesus to save, not condemn, the world. The Lord is not wanting anyone to perish. Whoever calls on the Lord will be saved.
The early church believers were active in missionary work.	• Acts 8:4-6 • Acts 8:26-39 • Acts 10 • Acts 10:34-35 • Acts 16:9-10 • Romans 1:16	Philip went to preach in Samaria. God led Philip to an Ethiopian. God led Peter to Cornelius and fellow Gentiles. "I realize that God shows no partiality" (Peter) Paul's "Madedonian call" Paul preached salvation for Jew and Gentile.
In the Bible, the world is as a field "ripe for harvest." We must reap these souls now, before they are lost.	• Proverbs 10:5 • Joel 3:13-14 • Matthew 9:37-38 • Luke 10:2 • John 4:34-36	He who sleeps in harvest is a disgraceful son. Swing the sickle, for the harvest is ripe. The harvest is plentiful, but the laborers are few. Pray the Lord of the harvest to send out laborers. Look at the fields! They are ripe for harvest.
In Revelation, all tribes, tongues, peoples, and nations worship the Lamb.	• Revelation 5:9-10 • Revelation 7:9-10 • Revelation 14:6 • Revelation 21:24	"redeemed of every tribe, tongue, people, nation" "a great multitude from every nation, tribe . . ." "the eternal gospel to preach to every nation . . ." The nations will walk by its light.

CHAPTER 5

Our Historical Heritage

*"We speak God's wisdom in a mystery, the hidden wisdom,
which God predestined before the ages to our glory; the
wisdom which none of the rulers of this age has understood;
for if they had understood it, they would not have crucified the
Lord of glory." 1 Corinthians 2:7–8 (NASB)*

History is not just a random assortment of dry facts, dates, and wars. It's more than mandatory memorizations or an unending list of boring dead people. If viewed from a biblical perspective, history can become an adventurous mystery, full of God's eternal purposes and exciting action!

World history is the study of *real* people whom God loved—people with *real* feelings, desires, and dreams (much like ours) who simply lived in another time.

What is our purpose for studying history? As mission-minded parents and teachers, how can we incorporate a fervent heart for today's world into learning about the past? As we encourage our children in this area, we can instill an appreciation for God's amazing guidance, providence, and enduring love throughout time.

As your child considers an important historical moment, he or she can be challenged to make a positive difference in today's world. Timeless truths can be applied to present situations, and your child's character and thinking skills can be encouraged by asking specific questions. For example, you could ask your child:

- *What would it have been like to serve God as an Israelite in ancient Egypt?*

- *When Jesus was about your age, what was a typical day like?*

- *Did anything good happen because the early Christians were persecuted?*

- *What were some big challenges for early missionary pioneers in America?*

- *What would it have been like to travel across Africa with David Livingstone?*

As Christians, it's especially important to see the relationship between history and God's heart for our world. As you and your child look at a particular event, consider how the Lord was preparing the way for His future plan. Examine how people responded to God's call (if they had a chance to hear it). Focus your discussion on God's enduring love.

Ultimately, God orders the events of human history to accomplish His overall plans. Through every political change, God always remains the same.

No news shocks Him. No event alters His direction.

Just look at the correlation between these two "13:8" verses: Hebrews 13:8 tells us that "Jesus Christ is the same yesterday, today, and forever," and Revelation 13:8 speaks of Jesus as "the Lamb slain from the foundation of the world."

From the very beginning, God knew that Adam and Eve (and all of humanity) would sin and that the Son of God would have to die. Yet God still *chose* to create us and to save us.

But why?

That is one of the greatest mysteries of the Bible and human history. From our perspective, it doesn't add up; but somehow, from God's eternal and heavenly viewpoint, it made sense.

We need to realize that God was *never* obligated to create us or to save us—but He still did. And because of His amazing grace (and because of who He is), we owe Him everything. So when God gives us a glimpse of *His* purposes, or reveals an insight into a passion of *His* heart, we need to pay attention!

God's Secret Plan

Throughout the ages, God has always had a "secret plan" to provide people with access to a wonderful "endless treasure" He wants us to have.

For many generations, God kept His wonderful plan hidden from the devil. At the same time, He revealed insight about His plan to His *own* people—through sneak previews (prophecies) and secret clues (hints of God's plan)—so His treasure would be obviously recognized after it finally was revealed.

So what was God's "secret plan" and what is His "treasure" (and how does this relate to how we can help our child with history)?

God's highest prize (goal or treasure) for us is simply this: *knowing and loving God*—and being able to enter into a personal relationship with Him for all of eternity. In Philippians 3:14, Paul says, "I press toward the goal for the prize of the upward call of God in Christ Jesus"; and in verse 10 we see that this goal is to "*know Him* and the power of His resurrection" (emphasis mine).

Every historical event, every book of the Bible, and every God-purpose for people is connected to the critical moment when God's plan was carried out and His treasure was made available—at the death and resurrection of Jesus Christ.

God's strategy was incredible! At the cross, the devil thought he had finally outsmarted God. But in reality, God had totally outwitted the enemy, as the devil fell for God's ultimate trap! As Jesus died on the cross, His sacrifice paid the price for sin's penalty; and as Jesus rose from the dead, His triumph over death provided the way for all people to access His eternal life.

At the absolute center of human history is the cross of our Lord Jesus Christ. The cross is the transition point between the Old Testament and New Testament. It's the transition point in our dating system between BC (Before Christ) and AD (*anno Domini*, Latin for "In the year of our Lord"). It's the transition point in our own lives (as we respond to Christ's sacrifice) between our own spiritual death and God's eternal life!

🎙 TEACHING OPPORTUNITY

Mission-Minded Overview of World History

"The Hidden Mystery of History" is a brief overview of world history from a mission-minded perspective.

As you read this outline, take time to *discuss* the questions with your child. I pray you will *discover* more of God's secret plan through time (the cross), *dig deeper* for more of God's treasure (a personal relationship with Him), and then begin to *distribute* God's mystery to others (by sharing the gospel).

The Hidden Mystery of History

To read aloud and discuss with your child

Do you know what a "mystery" is?

A mystery is a hidden secret someone is trying to find.

Like a detective looking for secret clues . . .

Or like an explorer hunting for buried treasure . . .

We're going to be searching for God's *hidden mystery of history.*

In the Bible, God tells us about a "mysterious plan" and an "endless treasure" that can help us to understand how all of world history works together to fulfill God's plans. Listen carefully for clues that point to God's plan.

> God himself revealed his secret plan to me. As you read what I have written, you will understand what I know about this plan regarding Christ. God did not reveal it to previous generations, but now he has revealed it by the Holy Spirit to his holy apostles and prophets.
>
> And this is the secret plan: The Gentiles have an equal share with the Jews in all the riches inherited by God's children. Both groups have believed the Good News, and both are part of the same body and enjoy together the promise of blessings through Christ Jesus. By God's special favor and mighty power, I have been given the wonderful privilege of serving him by spreading this Good News.
>
> Just think! Though I did nothing to deserve it, and though I am the least deserving Christian there is, I was chosen for this special joy of telling the Gentiles about the endless treasures available to them in Christ. I was chosen to explain to everyone this plan that God, the Creator of all things, had kept secret from the beginning.
>
> Ephesians 3:3–9 NLT

The Beginning of God's Story

The first four words of the Bible say, "In the beginning God . . . ."

In the very beginning, before there was any time and before there was any history, God—the Father, Son, and Holy Spirit—already existed.

God has *always* been around. He never had a start, and He will never have an end. God is *absolutely* powerful, He can do *anything* He wants, and He knows *everything* there is to know! God can be *anywhere* or *everywhere*, *whenever* He wants. He isn't limited in time (like we are): God has the ability to see the *entire* story of the universe in one glance. And God not only sees this story but is in charge of putting it all together; so all the details of history—or "His Story"—will turn out just the way He wants.

He is *completely* good, *totally* perfect, and *entirely* holy. And God is so full of love that He *is* love; and He is *absolutely* wonderful.

What are the first four words of the Bible and what do they tell us about God? ("In the beginning God . . ." teaches us that God has always existed!) Here are some big words to describe the amazing characteristics of God. Can you remember them? "Omnipotent" means all-powerful; "omnipresent" means being present everywhere at once; and "omniscient" means all-knowing.

The Beginning of Evil

Some may wonder, *Why then—if God is so good* (or *if there really is a God)—is there evil in the world? And where did the devil come from?*

God directs and rules the universe from a place called heaven, and He has an incredible throne surrounded by angels. Long ago a beautiful and powerful angel, named Lucifer, became so full of pride that he wanted all of heaven to worship *him* (instead of God). So Lucifer rebelled against God; but he was humiliated and cast from heaven (see Isaiah 14:12–15; Ezekiel 28:12–19).

Since then the devil (as Lucifer is now called) has been at work on the earth: trying to make God look bad, trying to tempt people to turn away from God's purposes, and trying to make God's heart sad by people doing evil.

Where did the devil come from and why is there evil in the world? (Originally, God created a beautiful angel named Lucifer, but he rebelled against God and became the devil.) What does John 10:10 tell us about the purposes of the "thief" (who has the same motives as the devil), and how does this compare to the purposes of Jesus? (The thief comes to steal, kill, and destroy; but Jesus comes to give life more abundantly!)

God's Design for People

All along, God has had a special purpose for people. As God's unique creation, people would be designed differently than the animals (or even the angels)—being made in God's own image (Genesis 1:27). People would be created to relate to God in a personal way and to work *with* God to help fulfill His plans. People would have an ability to create and make things, to enjoy beauty, to organize and plan, to imagine and dream. And very importantly, people would be created with a free will to choose whether or not they wanted to follow God's plans and purposes.

God knew it would be a very big risk to give people a free will. God could see into the future, so He knew way ahead of time that Adam and Eve would disobey Him and that all of their children and grandchildren and great-grandchildren (all of humanity) would inherit their sinful hearts. God could see all the evil, hatred, and selfishness that would come and separate people from His perfect holiness; and God definitely knew the very big cost He would have to pay (at the cross) to take care of this problem.

If God had wanted to, He *could* have designed people with preprogrammed minds that would only do what He wanted. But God didn't want people to be like mechanical robots or puppets. Instead, God wanted people to choose to love and serve Him by their own free will. God wanted a special relationship with people—like a relationship between a parent and a child or between best friends.

TIME PERIOD	DATE	HISTORICAL EVENT
BC/AD	• 4-6 • 26-28 • 29-31 • 29-31	**THE MESSIAH COMES** Birth of Jesus Christ Jesus enters the ministry The Cross and Resurrection Ascension/Great Commission

50 AD
 	
100 AD
	• 64
	• 67
	• By 100
	• 117
	• 313
	
	• 375
	
	• 397-395
		THE EARLY CHURCH
		Persecution from Nero begins
		Martyrdom of Peter and Paul
		New Testament is written
		Height of the Roman Empire
		Constantine's Edict of Milan
		   Christianity now legal
		Christianity official and only
		   religion of Rome
		Emperor Theodosius I begins to
		   persecute all other religions
		   forcing "Christianity" on all

500 AD
 	
1000 AD
	• 395
	• 395
	• 400-1300
	• 432
	• 476
	
	• 500
	• 400-1300
	• 432
	• 476
	
	• 1095
		THE DARK AGES
		Rome divided
		Mohammed/beginning of Islam
		Attack of Vikings and barbarians
		Patrick arrives in Ireland
		First German openly rules Rome
		   Western Roman Empire falls
		The "MIDDLE AGES" begin
		Boniface leaves on first mission
		Emperor Leo III - forbids idols
		Council of Constantinople
		   image veneration resumed
		Holy War Crusades begin

1500 AD	• 1181 • 1320-1384 • 1415 • 1431 • 1450 • 1454 • 1478 • 1495 • 1492 • 1508 • 1515 • 1522 • 1536 • 1542	**RENAISSANCE & REFORMATION** Francis of Assisi is born John Wycliffe John Huss burned at stake Joan of Arc burned at stake First printing press invented Gutenberg prints the first Bible Spanish Inquisition begins DaVinci paints *The Last Supper* Columbus sails to Americas Michelangelo begins his work on *The Sistine Chapel* Martin Luther's *Ninety-five Thesis* *Zwingli breaks from Rome* John Calvin publishes teachings Francis Xavier in India

Persecution and Dispersion

During the time period of the early church, first the Jewish religious leaders and then the Roman government began to persecute Christians. If people believed in Jesus, they would get in trouble—perhaps being thrown in prison or even killed. But God used these bad things for His good purposes. Because of danger in Jerusalem the disciples started to flee to other areas, and the gospel began to spread.

In Acts chapter 8 we learn about Philip the evangelist. When persecution arose in Jerusalem, Philip went to Samaria to preach God's Good News. The entire city was filled with joy as multitudes received Jesus Christ. But then God told Philip to leave this mighty revival to go into the desert. There Philip preached to one important man—a government official from Ethiopia.

Do you see how God used this terrible persecution to begin spreading His Good News? (Because of persecution, the gospel went from Jerusalem to Samaria and, through the Ethiopian man, even to Africa. According to tradition, the apostle Thomas also took the gospel to India.)

Cornelius and the Call to the Gentiles (Acts 10)

The Jewish believers thought that God's plan of salvation was only for them, but God gave the apostle Peter a vision that explained His plan for the Gentiles. Peter saw a large sheet coming down from heaven, filled with all sorts of animals God had forbidden the Jews to eat in the Law of Moses. God said, "Rise, Peter; kill and eat."

Peter said, "Not so, Lord! For I have never eaten anything common or unclean."

This happened three times, and the Lord said, "What God has cleansed you must not call common."

TIME PERIOD	DATE	HISTORICAL EVENT
1500 AD	• 1580	**EXPLORATION/COLONIZATION**
		Sir Francis Drake - completes
		circumnavigation of world
	• 1596	Mercator publishes world map
	• 1597	Japan expels west. missionaries
1600 AD	• 1611	KJV Bible published
	• 1620	Pilgrims arrive at Plymouth Bay
	• 1646	John Elliot to Native Americans
1700 AD	• 1732	Moravians sent to Virgin Islands
	• 1743	David Brainerd begins work
	• 1776	US Declaration of Independence
	• 1793	William Carey arrives in India
1800 AD	• 1816	Moffat begins missionary work
	• 1835	Whitmans - Oregon Trail
	• 1841	Livingstone arrives in Africa
	• 1861	Telegraph stretches across US
	• 1865	Hudson Taylor founds CIM
	• 1876	Bell displays the first telephone
	• 1890	The Evangelical Alliance Mission
	• 1895	African Inland Mission founded
1900 AD	• 1903	Wright brothers - first airplane
	• 1903	Ford makes the auto affordable
	• 1910	CT Study arrives in Africa
	• 1914	US opens the Panama Canal
	• 1914	World War I begins
	• 1917	Collapse of Russian Czars
	• 1918	Birth of Billy Graham
	• 1922	Founding of USSR
	• 1927	Lindberg's Cross-Atlantic flight
	• 1930s	The Great Depression
	• 1936	First regular TV broadcasts
	• 1939	World War II begins
	• 1945	Missionary Aviation Fellowship
	• 1950	Founding of World Vision
	• 1956	Auca Massacre in Ecuador
	• 1960	YWAM founded
		(shift to short-term missions)
	• 1974	First Operation World published
	• 1991	Breakup of Soviet Union
2000 AD	• 2000	New Millennium - rise of Internet
	• 2001	Sept. 11th attack on America
	• 2020	Global COVID Pandemic
	• 2020	JESUS Film seen by over 6 billion
		(shift toward national missions)
	• TODAY	GOD CAN USE YOU

Just when Peter was wondering what this vision meant, a messenger—sent by Cornelius, a Roman centurion who was known for being good and generous—arrived at the house where Peter was staying. An angel had told Cornelius to invite Peter to come and speak to him. So Peter went, and this Gentile man and his family and close friends became Christians.

Why was it so hard for the Jewish people to understand that God's Good News was also for the Gentiles? What did Peter's vision mean? (The Jews, who had always been God's "chosen people," did not understand that God's plan included non-Jews as well. Peter's vision meant that salvation was for everyone.)

The Holy Roman Empire

Oddly enough, it was actually when a Roman emperor named Constantine (who lived about three hundred years after Jesus) made Christianity not only legal but the *official and only religion* that history entered a period of time known for its spiritual darkness. God wanted people to have a free will to choose Him, but when the Holy Roman Empire tried to force everyone to become Christians, God's salvation message was distorted. Sometimes huge crowds were baptized all together—without a choice, and without even believing in God! "Christianity" and the "church" became tools for expanding a human empire, as religious leaders began using their power to gain money and military victory.

What can we learn from this time period? How does God want His gospel spread to others? (God uses difficult times to make us stronger. When the Christians were persecuted, they grew in numerical and spiritual strength; but when Christianity was forced on people, the message was confused. God wants us to choose to come to Him.)

The Dark Ages

The Middle Ages has often been referred to as the "Dark Ages." Only a few groups of monks and friars were allowed to read the Bible, they lived in isolated places called monasteries, and worship services were held in the Latin language (which most people couldn't understand). Religious Christianity was the center of this medieval age, but the true light of the gospel was so dim that it was nearly extinguished.

During this time, German barbarians and Viking invaders from the north came to conquer Europe; as a result, they were influenced by this "religious" Christianity, and knowledge of Jesus spread into northern Europe and Scandinavia. Through medieval art—largely sponsored by the church—many people learned about Jesus. (Even today, medieval paintings—which typically focus on Jesus and the Bible—fill museums throughout the world.)

Why was this time period spiritually "dark"? Was God's plan for people to have religious rituals or to have a personal relationship with Him? (Most people couldn't read God's Word for themselves, so they didn't understand God's plan. What God really wants is for us to have a personal relationship with Him.)

The Crusades and Holy Wars

During the "knights in shining armor" days, the church in Europe began the Great Crusades to try to win the land of Israel from the conquering Muslims (who had declared their own jihad, or holy war). Through the use of force the Christian religion began to spread, for a short time, into the Middle East. Other warriors used military force to try to convert the "heathen" in other areas to Christianity as well; but this type of Christian "expansion" left a negative effect on the world.

*Can you force people to become Christians? (When people are forced to become Christians, their belief is not sincere—you can't be saved just by **saying** you believe; you have to actually believe.)*

Early Catholic Missions

The Roman Catholic Church began to expand throughout the world (mostly for political purposes) into places such as India and Africa. During this time, God had a small group of people who continued to keep His Word and His truth alive. Through the missionary efforts of these people who loved God, such as Ulfilas, Boniface, Francis of Assisi, Francis Xavier, and others, many heard the message of Jesus.

Monks and Scripture

All through the Dark Ages, many monks worked diligently—all by themselves for many years—to protect and hand copy God's Holy Scriptures.

Many Christians were put in prison for their faith in Jesus Christ and some were even martyred (killed) for their beliefs. As Christians were brought to trial, religious leaders often heard powerful testimonies and God's message of salvation. Even though most of the religious leaders rejected this truth of salvation, God was still at work, and His kingdom could not be destroyed.

Can you see the "secret clues" of what God was doing during this hard time? How was God working behind the scenes to prepare for His Good News to spread? Why was it so important for the Word of God to be copied so diligently? (God used special people to make sure the Bible survived. They copied it carefully so that we can read the Bible just like it was written thousands of years ago!)

Reformation and the Printing Press

People began searching for knowledge and the truth both outside and inside the church, which led to the Renaissance and the Reformation (a time of spiritual awakening). As spiritual leaders such as Martin Luther and Ulrich Zwingli discovered the importance of salvation by faith, the light of God's Good News began to spread again. Through others such as John Calvin, people learned about the need for evangelism as the fire of the gospel began to spread.

With this new desire to "know things" came new discoveries and inventions, such as the printing press by Johann Gutenberg. The first book ever printed was the Holy Bible, and this invention of the printing press enabled the average person to have access to many books and teaching materials, especially God's Holy Word.

Can you imagine what it would have been like to hear God's Word for the very first time? How has God used the printing press to help spread His Good News? (Printing is much faster than copying by hand. Now more people can read the Bible for themselves.)

The Mongolian Empire

A mighty Asian leader, Genghis Khan, united the tribes of Mongolia and founded a kingdom that became the largest (geographically) in the entire world, stretching from northern China to eastern Europe and bordering Russia and Persia. During the golden years of this vast empire, the father of Marco Polo traveled to Mongolia and was able to share about Christianity with the great Kublai Khan. At that time, Khan requested of Polo, "Bring to me one hundred teachers of the Christian faith, able to show me that the law of Christ is best. If persuaded, I and all under my rule will become His followers."

Unfortunately, Polo found only two willing missionaries; and because of travel difficulties, they turned back . . . and Mongolia turned to the Buddhist religion.

The fact that no missionaries responded to this request was a missed opportunity in missions history; but God allowed this mighty Mongolian ruler at the height of his reign to hear the gospel of Jesus Christ! What lesson can we learn from this example? (God can help even the most important and powerful people in the world know about Him!)

Exploration and Evangelism

As people began to learn more, they gained an increased desire to explore and discover the world, as evidenced by famous explorers such as Christopher Columbus and Sir Francis Drake. Europeans began to travel across the ocean to faraway places in Latin America, India, and the Caribbean to trade with foreign lands. Stories about these distant lands began to spread across Europe. Christians came to realize the importance of sharing God's truth, and thus the gospel message began to spread.

As European countries started trading with other countries, many leaders in Europe began to establish permanent colonies in various areas. As European Christians traveled, their desire to spread God's gospel message to the unreached people in these faraway lands grew.

The colonial attitude was often bossy and controlling, but God worked through colonial efforts and early colonial missionaries to bring His message of truth and love to India, Africa, America, and Asia.

Do you see how God worked though people's natural curiosity and desires to learn about unknown places? How did God use empire expansion to spread the Good News of Jesus? (As people began to travel more, they carried the message about the Good News to people who had never heard about Christ.)

God is pursuing with omnipotent passion a worldwide purpose of gathering joyful worshipers for Himself from every tribe and tongue and people and nation.

He has an inexhaustible enthusiasm for the supremacy of His name among the nations.

Therefore, let us bring our affections into line with His, and, for the sake of His name, let us renounce the quest for worldly comforts and join His global purpose.

- John Piper

Great Missionary Heroes

Great missionaries began not only to *go*, but to *return* and excitedly share about the urgent need for foreign missions. Leaders such as William Carey, Hudson Taylor, and Amy Carmichael influenced many people—not only in "foreign" countries but also in their homelands, as many Christians finally began to understand the importance of Jesus' Great Commission.

How was God preparing the way for the future? Why did these missionaries take the time to share about the need for missions? (The missionaries knew how important it was to tell everyone in the world about Jesus. They wanted to get as many helpers as they could.)

Early Pioneers

In Canada, the United States, and Australia early pioneers began to move across their continents—to the west and to the interior. Some went because they wanted religious freedom or financial opportunity, while others were driven by adventure. Through these advances, the gospel began to spread to native tribes and to interior areas.

How did God use this attitude of adventure to spread the news of the cross? (As people reached further into unknown places, they met new kinds of people who also needed to hear about the Savior. This helped the Good News continue to spread.)

Nationalization

In recent years many countries have changed from being controlled by foreign colonial powers to being led by their own national governments. This switch has influenced the spread of Christianity! Now instead of just coming in and taking over, many missionaries focus on training local pastors, encouraging national churches, and developing national leadership.

Can God's Good News spread faster when more people are involved? (Yes!)

Specific Ministries and Multiplication

Across the world, specific global ministries are working together like never before. The *JESUS* film is available in nearly a thousand languages; Wycliffe Bible Translators is continuing to translate God's Word in unreached languages; YWAM and many youth ministries are mobilizing short-term and long-term mission teams; Missionary Aviation Fellowship is transporting ministers into remote areas; international evangelists are preaching to multitudes; children and orphans are being effectively sponsored; ministries like Samaritans Purse are assisting the poor; and missions books such as *Operation World* are helping us see the big picture.

As ministries have focused on specific areas, how has this helped God's secret plan to spread quicker? Why is it good for ministries to work together? (When we take care of someone's specific need, they are more ready to hear us share about Jesus. God wants all Christians to work together to help people in need and to share the Good News.)

New Advances for a New Generation

In recent years new advances have impacted our world in unprecedented ways. We can hop on a plane and fly across the world; we carry cell phones; we text message our friends; we send e-mails to the other side of the globe. We design international websites, access unlimited information on the Internet, and view live video footage from across the planet. All of these advances are merely tools that can help us take God's message of the cross to the nations.

Even now God is searching the earth for a new generation—to help write the final chapters of "His Story."

How can modern advances help spread the gospel to our generation? Can you see the clues of what God is doing on the earth today? (Computers, cell phones, and other modern inventions have helped us communicate better and given us a way to reach people who couldn't be reached without these inventions.)

The End . . .

How will "His Story" end? In the last book of the Bible, God describes an incredible scene in heaven where people from "all nations, tribes, peoples, and tongues" are worshiping the Lamb of God (Revelation 7:9–10). God's divide-and-conquer strategy is working, and the message of the cross will reach the ends of the earth.

We don't know how long "His Story" will continue; but we do know that Jesus said, "This gospel of the kingdom will be preached in all the world as a witness to all the nations, and then the end will come" (Matthew 24:14).

Reading these verses about heaven and the end times is like skipping ahead to the last page of a book and seeing how "His Story" ends. Will the message of the cross ultimately reach all people? (Yes!)

Conclusion:

Can you recognize God's *hidden mystery of history*?

- What was God's "secret plan"? (The cross.)

- What was God's purpose for the cross? (God wanted to give us His "endless treasure." Read John 3:16.)

"... but the people who know
their God shall be strong,
and carry out great exploits."

Daniel 11:32

Chapter 6

Our Missionary Heroes

In each generation, God has called men and women to rise up and be "missionaries" for Him: to go into another culture or nation to share God's love. From yesterday's martyrs to today's global ministries, our heritage is great!

Many believers sacrificially gave of their lives so we could have the gospel, and now it is our turn. We have the honor and responsibility to convey this godly heritage to the next generation. We need to instill in our children an admiration for servants of God who lived for His purposes instead of their own.

📹 TEACHING OPPORTUNITY

Mini Mission Biographies and Mission-Minded Monologue Skits

This chapter includes mini-biographies of many prominent mission-minded heroes. These brief summaries can serve as a quick missionary reference guide. Included are recommendations for great kid-friendly resources (to help introduce your child to the lives of these men and women of God), mission stories to read aloud, classic excerpts (primarily to challenge *you* to have a deeper passion for the lost), and ten enjoyable "Mission-Minded Monologue Skits" for your child, or someone else, to perform.

IGNATIUS

Early Christian martyr (AD 35–107)

Kid-Friendly Resources:

*   Christian Hall of Fame
    (www.Christianhof.org): Ignatius

*   Mission-Minded Monologue Skit (below)

Mission-Minded Monologue Skit #1

Costume: *Have Ignatius dressed in a simple Bible-time robe*

Setting: *Inside the catacombs, the underground tombs where early believers worshiped (To create this setting, simply turn off all the lights and use a lantern.)*

IGNATIUS: Welcome to this underground place called the catacombs. This is a secret place where we—as followers of Jesus Christ—can meet together. This dark meeting room is filled with tombs, but it is a safe place for us to come for worship and prayer.

My name is Ignatius, and I am a church leader (they call me a bishop) here in the city of Antioch. I like to encourage Christian believers to pray for people who do not yet know Jesus. One time, in a letter I sent to believers in another city called Ephesus, I wrote, "Pray ye without ceasing on behalf of other men. For there is in them hope of repentance, that they may attain to God."

I was born a few years after our Lord rose from the dead and ascended to heaven, so I never met Jesus in person; but John, one of our Lord's twelve apostles, was a close friend of mine. John was one of the three closest disciples of Jesus Christ (along with Peter and James); John saw Jesus glowing brightly on the Mount of Transfiguration; he was called "the disciple Jesus loved"; and he was the only disciple with our Lord on that terrible (but wonderful) day when Jesus died on the cross. John the apostle shared many of his personal experiences with me, and he helped me to know Jesus Christ for myself.

I have lived during a very frightening time, as Roman soldiers have often captured believers and put them in prison. And many of my close friends have been thrown to the lions and killed just because they believed in Jesus.

Even now my life is in danger. But I will always follow my Lord, Jesus Christ. In fact, *I would rather die for Christ than rule the whole earth. I say, Leave me to the beasts that I may by them be a partaker of God. Welcome nails and cross. Welcome broken bones and bruises. Welcome all diabolical torture, if I may but obtain the Lord Jesus Christ.*

NARRATOR: When Ignatius was seventy-two years old, he was thrown to the lions and eaten alive. He is an early Christian hero because of his love for the lost and his steadfast faith in our Lord Jesus Christ.

"I would rather die for Christ than rule the whole earth."

– IGNATIUS

POLYCARP

Last Christian leader to know the original apostles (AD 69–155)

Kid-Friendly Resources:

*   Christian Hall of Fame (www. Christianhof.org): Polycarp

- Mission-Minded Monologue Skit (below)

Mission-Minded Monologue Skit #2

Costume: *Have Polycarp look like an old man with a long white beard and a Bible-time robe*

Setting: *Inside an old Roman prison*

POLYCARP: It has been over a hundred years since Jesus lived on the earth. Although I never saw our Lord in person, I was taught by the apostle John, and Ignatius was my friend.

Now I am a very old man, and I am known as the last individual on earth who personally talked with eyewitnesses of Jesus Christ.

I was born in the city of Smyrna, and later I became the bishop (or church leader) of this area. But I was arrested for my faith; and now I am condemned to die in a flaming fire. I know that soldiers will tell me to turn away from my faith in Jesus. But how could I do that? I say, *Eighty-six years have I served Him and He hath done me no wrong. How can I speak evil of my King who saved me?*

I remember the Old Testament story about Shadrach, Meshach, and Abed-Nego. They were threatened with the fiery furnace of King Nebuchadnezzar but were determined to stand firm for God—not knowing if God would deliver them or not. These three young Hebrew men were saved from that furnace. However, many of my friends also had great faith . . . yet they died and are now in heaven.

I do not know what will happen when they throw *me* into the fire. But no matter what, I am determined to stand in faith for my Lord Jesus, until the very end.

NARRATOR: Because of his steadfast commitment to his Lord, Jesus Christ, the old man Polycarp was thrown alive into a raging fire. According to tradition, his body would not burn—so soldiers killed Polycarp with a sword and then burned his body.

> "Eighty-six years have I served Him and He hath done me no wrong. How can I speak evil of my King who saved me?"
>
> POLYCARP

ULFILAS

Missionary to Gothic people (c. AD 311–381)
One of the earliest Bible translators (in the area of modern-day Romania)

Kid-Friendly Resource:

• Mission-Minded Monologue Skit (below)

Mission-Minded Monologue Skit #3

Costume: Have Ulfilas dressed in a simple priest-like robe

Setting: Ulfilas is sitting beside several old Bibles and many stacks of papers

ULFILAS: Greetings! My name is Ulfilas, and I have been a Christian missionary for forty years among a barbarian Gothic tribe.

Let me tell you a little about myself. I was born nearly three hundred years after Jesus lived on the earth. My mother was from a Gothic tribe; and although my father was a Christian, he was captured by Gothic raiders. So when I was young, I did not know Jesus. Instead, I was raised in a very pagan, non-Christian home.

Thanks to God, I became a Christian and joined the church. In time I also became a minister, a priest in the church. After becoming a follower of Jesus, I began to have a great burden for the people who had captured my father. I left the Roman Empire to come to this remote tribe; and here

I have lived and conducted evangelistic work for forty years, sharing with people about Christianity.

It has not been easy. Throughout my ministry I have faced many hardships and much persecution. I am one of the very first people who ever translated the Bible into another native tongue, and it has been difficult work. I even had to develop my own alphabet for this unwritten Gothic language.

Right now the church and the government of Rome (the Holy Roman Empire) are one and the same, so Rome primarily sees my mission work as a way to expand the empire. But ever since I came to know the Lord Jesus Christ my heart's desire has been to expand God's kingdom—to translate His Word and to spread His Good News.

JOHN WYCLIFFE

Preacher and Bible translator (1320–1384)

Kid-Friendly Resources:

- *John Wycliffe: Man of Courage* (By Faith Biography Series), Ambassador-Emerald International

- See also Wycliffe Bible Translators (www.wycliffe.org), named in Wycliffe's honor

John Wycliffe was born in England and spent the first part of his life preaching the gospel to the poor and the lost instead of only to the wealthy in high places.

Wycliffe was once asked, "How must the Word of God be preached?"

He answered, "Appropriately, simply, directly, and from a devout, sincere heart."

Later in his life, the bishop (church leader) of London told Wycliffe that he could no longer preach openly about Jesus. So Wycliffe devoted his life to ministry through writing and Bible translation work. Today he is mainly remembered for translating the Holy Bible from Latin into English.

Thirty-one years after his death, the church protested Wycliffe's work by ordering all of his books to be burned. His bones were also dug up and burned, and his ashes were scattered on the Thames River.

Today, because of Wycliffe's sacrificial ministry, Wycliffe Bible Translators is named in his honor, and multitudes of missionaries are following his example and translating the Bible into many other languages.

MARTIN LUTHER

Leader of the Reformation (1483–1546)

Kid-Friendly Resources:

*   "Martin Luther: Giant of the Reformation," in *Hero Tales*, Vol. 1, by Dave and Neta Jackson, Bethany House

*   *Spy for the Night Riders: Martin Luther* (Trailblazer Books), by Dave and Neta Jackson, Bethany House

*   *Martin Luther: The Great Reformer* (Heroes of the Faith Series), by Daniel Harmon, Barbour Publishing

Martin Luther is known as the "Great German Reformer" and a major leader of the Protestant Reformation.

As a Roman Catholic priest and monk, Luther worked hard to try to attain God's righteousness—even attempting to clean sin from his life through self-denial and self-torture. But after reading Romans 1:17, Luther discovered that the *only* way he could receive personal salvation and righteousness was by faith in Christ's sacrifice. From that time on, Luther began to recognize many wrong church practices, which he then condemned.

On October 31, 1517, Martin Luther attached a paper, called his "Ninety-Five Theses," to the door of the Castle Church in Wittenberg, Germany. This paper summarized major problems in the church, especially highlighting the practice of selling "indulgences" as a way of supposedly "buying" forgiveness. Luther was charged with heresy (teaching beliefs contrary to those held by the church) by the "diet" (or general assembly) that took place in the town of Worms. The emperor of the Holy Roman Empire, Charles V, issued the Edict of Worms, which was in effect a death warrant, though it was never carried out.

Later, Luther spent about twenty years translating the New Testament into German, as well as composing many beloved hymns, including "A Mighty Fortress Is Our God."

Martin Luther primarily taught that a person is justified by faith alone, every believer is a priest with direct access to God through Jesus Christ, and the Bible (not tradition) is the sole source of faith and authority for Christians.

Despite his great influence, Luther's theology was not faultless. His teachings against the Jews had a negative impact on many people throughout history. Also, Luther was so certain of Christ's return that he saw no need for missions and taught that the Great Commission was only for the New Testament apostles. (Later, the Lutheran Church realized the importance of international mission work and became an active force in world evangelism.)

Through Martin Luther's leadership, boldness, and influence, many people through history have been led to find true faith in Jesus Christ.

His life helped spread the true Christian message of faith throughout Europe and the world.

"The just shall live by faith" (Romans 1:17).

MARTIN LUTHER'S THEME

COUNT ZINZENDORF

Founder of the Moravians (1700–1760)

Kid-Friendly Resource:

* *Count Zinzendorf: Firstfruit* (Christian Heroes: Then & Now Series), by Janet and Geoff Benge, YWAM Publishing

Nicolaus Ludwig von Zinzendorf was born into a wealthy German family in the year 1700. As an adult, he once saw a painting of Christ with a crown of thorns and the inscription, "All this I did for you; what are you doing for Me?" Zinzendorf was greatly moved and proceeded to found the Moravian Church, which became a worldwide missionary movement that was unprecedented throughout the eighteenth century.

In 1727, the Moravians began a prayer vigil that continued, uninterrupted, twenty-four hours a day, seven days a week, for over one hundred years. As a result of this prayer movement—combined with Moravian missionary evangelism—a tremendous revival began. The Moravians helped spread Christianity throughout the world.

DAVID BRAINERD

Evangelist to Native Americans (1718–1747)

Kid-Friendly Resources:

*   *The Life and Diary of David Brainerd*,
    by Philip E. Howard, edited by Jonathan
    Edwards, Baker Books

*   Wholesome Words website, Children's Corner, Missionary
    Heroes: "David Brainerd: Missionary to the Indians at
    Twenty-Four" http://www.wholesomewords.org

David Brainerd grew up in Connecticut, in colonial America, as
one of nine children. His father died when he was eight years old and
his mother died when he was fourteen. Despite his difficult childhood,
Brainerd studied with an elderly minister, and in 1742 he was offered
missionary support by a Scottish mission society.

Brainerd began traveling to many Native American tribes but was
initially discouraged by their poor response. He eventually led his
national interpreter (and this man's wife) to Christ, and they began to
see tremendous ministry results. Throughout New Jersey, the Native
Americans were very open to Christianity and would often come from
miles away just to hear Brainerd preach.

During the summer of 1745 (during the time of the Great Awakening),
revival began to break out among Native Americans. As Brainerd shared

the gospel, he witnessed God's touch on their lives. "Many of them were then much affected, and appeared surprisingly tender," Brainerd testified, "so that a few words about their souls' concerns would cause the tears to flow freely, and produce many sobs and groans."

Brainerd had hoped to marry a woman named Jerusa, but he became sick with tuberculosis. Although Jerusa nursed him for nineteen months, Brainerd died before they could be married—at the young age of twenty-nine. The following Valentine's Day, Jerusa died of tuberculosis (which she had apparently contracted from him).

Although Brainerd's ministry lasted only five years, his mission work was significant to Native American people.

> "I would not have spent my life otherwise for the whole world."
>
> DAVID BRAINERD

GEORGE LIELE

America's first foreign missionary
(1752–1828)

Kid-Friendly Resource:

* Mission-Minded Monologue Skit (below)

Mission-Minded Monologue Skit #4

Costume: Have Liele (with black hair and a beard) in a three-piece suit with a bow tie

Setting: In a tropical setting, perhaps next to a palm-like tree

LIELE: It is God who brings freedom, and it is God who set me free to preach the gospel of Jesus Christ—first in America and then here in my new homeland of Jamaica.

I am George Liele. I was born in 1750 as an African slave in Virginia. My master was a Baptist minister, and he brought me to live in Georgia. There, when I was in my early twenties, I became a Christian and began preaching to my fellow slaves. My master saw my devotion to the Lord and my ability to explain the Scriptures, so he decided to free me to become a preacher.

I began preaching to other slaves in plantations along the Savannah River, and then I became the pastor of the First African Church in Savannah.

When the American Revolutionary War began in 1776, the British soldiers offered freedom to all slaves who would go to them for refuge. So when the British entered Georgia and captured our city of Savannah, most of my church members fled to them for freedom.

At the end of the war, thousands of these freed slaves were afraid they would be forced back into slavery; so many of them followed the British soldiers into Canada. I had led David George, a good friend of mine who was a former slave, to the Lord and trained him to have a fervent passion for missions. He fled to Canada and then traveled to West Africa to preach the gospel.

But I decided to sell myself as an indentured servant to a British colonel who was sailing to Jamaica. I had felt a calling to preach the gospel to the people here in this land, and this seemed to be God's way for my family and me to reach this island. We left thirty-three years before the Judson family left for India; so we were actually America's first foreign missionaries. The Judsons have the title, but God knows the truth.

I gave up my freedom for a time because I wanted to surrender to God's direction for my life. After I paid off my debt, I was again free to preach the gospel. I started a church here on the island—and from that, a Jamaican Baptist movement.

Yes, it is God who brings freedom; and true freedom only comes through total obedience to our Lord Jesus and His purposes.

NARRATOR: The church Liele founded in Jamaica continued to grow, often combining a zeal for spreading the gospel with expansion in education. By the 1840s, many Jamaican believers were sent to the African nation of Cameroon as missionaries.

WILLIAM CAREY

Missionary and Bible translator (1761–1834)

Kid-Friendly Resources:

- *William Carey: Bearer of Good News* (Heroes for Young Readers Series), by Renée Meloche and Bryan Pollard, YWAM Publishing

- *William Carey: Obliged to Go* (Christian Heroes: Then & Now Series), by Janet and Geoff Benge, YWAM Publishing

- *William Carey: Father of Missions* (Heroes of the Faith Series), by Sam Wellman, Barbour

- Wholesome Words website, Children's Corner, Missionary Heroes: "William Carey: The Consecrated Cobbler" www.wholesomewords.org

William Carey is known as the "father of modern missions." He was born in England, and although his family was poor, he had a great desire for learning. By the age of twenty, young William had mastered five foreign languages: Dutch, French, Greek, Latin, and Hebrew. He became a minister; and from the very beginning he focused his preaching primarily on the importance of foreign missions.

When William Carey shared his burden for reaching the lost at a minister's meeting, he was reprimanded with these words, "Sit down, young man. When God sees fit to convert the heathen, He will do so of His own accord."

Despite this opposition, Carey believed strongly in the need to reach the lost and wrote a small book entitled *An Enquiry into the Obligations of Christians to Use Means for the Conversion of the Heathens*. Soon afterward, he preached a powerful message on missions. Using Isaiah 54:2–3 as his text, Carey challenged others to "Expect great things from God; attempt great things for God!"

Because of William Carey's leadership, an English missionary society was founded. Later, Carey traveled to India to serve in missionary work. During Carey's forty-two years of ministry, he and his coworkers translated the entire Bible into twenty-six languages and the New Testament (or parts of it) into twenty-five more. He developed several native language dictionaries and was actively involved in mission evangelism.

> "Expect great things from God;
> attempt great things for God."
>
> WILLIAM CAREY

 ## OUR OBLIGATION

An excerpt from William Carey's book on missions, in contemporary language:

Just as our blessed Lord has told us to pray for His will to be done on earth as it is in heaven, it is obvious that we should not just *talk* about that desire. We need to *take action* and do whatever we can—and to use every lawful method—to spread the knowledge of His name.

In order to do this, we must try to understand the spiritual condition of our world. This should be something we should want to do—not only because of the gospel of our Redeemer, but also because of our own feelings.

We often *feel* naturally "drawn" toward helping others and that is one of the strongest proofs that we *should*. God has given us His grace, and God has given us His heart and His spirit to care for those in need. We want to help other people because that is obviously the character of God.

DAVID LIVINGSTONE

Great missionary explorer (1813–1873)

Kid-Friendly Resources:

*   *David Livingstone: Courageous Explorer* (Heroes for Young Readers Series), by Renée Meloche and Bryan Pollard, YWAM Publishing

*   *David Livingstone: Africa's Trailblazers* (Christian Heroes: Then & Now Series), by Janet and Geoff Benge, YWAM

*   Wholesome Words website, Children's Corner, Missionary Heroes: "David Livingstone: Over Thirty Years Missionary to Africa"   www.wholesomewords.org

*   *David Livingstone: Missionary to Africa* (By Faith Biography Series), Ambassador-Emerald International

*   Mission-Minded Monologue Skit (see following page)

Mission-Minded Monologue Skit #5

Costume: Khaki clothes, a safari-style helmet, a dark mustache, a few props
(such as a rope over the shoulder, a machete, and a well-worn
journal), and an old-English accent

Setting: As Livingstone enters, it seems he is in the middle of an exploration,
slashing imaginary jungle leaves with his machete and breathing
hard.

LIVINGSTONE: Whew! Getting through this jungle is quite an adventure—with so many valleys and mountains, fierce lions, and, ah yes, those dreadful mosquitoes! But I tell you, "The mission of the church is missions!"

I'm David Livingstone, and I have a heart for Africa. I'm a missionary explorer, and I like to share the gospel of Jesus Christ, especially in remote tribal areas.

It's actually quite remarkable that I could get all the way here, since I was born into a humble family near Glasgow, Scotland. When I was a boy I had to work in a textile mill from six o'clock in the morning until eight o'clock at night. That was hard! But I was a determined young lad. And do you know what I bought with my very first paycheck? A Latin grammar book! You see, I wanted to learn all about the world.

My family always went to church, and I was converted to Christ during my youth. Then a preacher named Robert Moffat (who is now my father-in-law) told me about his adventures in Africa. One time he said, "On a clear morning, the smoke of a thousand villages could be seen where the name of Christ had never been heard." That really challenged me—so much so that I've spent my whole life traveling across the interior of Africa, covering over fourteen thousand miles and one-third of the continent! I've learned all kinds of things—about animals, plants, places, and people—but most importantly I've been able to share with unsaved people who had never heard of Jesus.

My life has been very difficult at times. I've been attacked by a lion; I've been sick; and people close to me have died. But I must keep sharing God's Good News of salvation, because *This generation can only reach this generation.*

And even now, I must *go*; and like I've written in my journal, I will go *anywhere, provided it be forward!*

"The mission of the church is missions!"
"Anywhere, provided it be forward!"
"This generation can only reach this generation."

DAVID LIVINGSTONE

DID NOT YOUR FOREFATHERS KNOW?

A classic missions excerpt, from David Livingstone's journal

I was from the first struck by his intelligence, and by the special manner in which we felt drawn to each other. This remarkable man has not only embraced Christianity, but expounds its doctrine to his people. . . .

On the first occasion in which I ever attempted to hold a public religious service, Sechele (the tribal chief and a new convert) remarked that it was the custom of his nation to put questions when any new subject was brought before them. He then inquired if my forefathers knew of a future judgment.

I replied in the affirmative, and began to describe the scene of the Great White Throne, and Him who shall sit on it, from whose face the heaven and earth shall flee away.

"You startle me," he replied; "these words make all my bones to shake; I have no more strength in me; but my forefathers were living at the same time yours were, and how it is that they did not send them word about these terrible things sooner? They all passed away into darkness without knowing whither they were going. . . ."

HUDSON TAYLOR

Missionary to China (1832–1905)

Kid-Friendly Resources:

- *Hudson Taylor: Friend of China* (Heroes for Young Readers Series), by Renée Meloche and Bryan Pollard, YWAM Publishing

- *Hudson Taylor* (Men and Women of Faith Series), Bethany House

- *Hudson Taylor: Deep in the Heart of China* (Christian Heroes: Then & Now Series), by Janet and Geoff Benge, YWAM Publishing

- "Hudson Taylor: Englishman with a Pigtail," in *Hero Tales*, Vol. 1, by Dave and Neta Jackson, Bethany House

- *Shanghaied to China: Hudson Taylor* (Trailblazer Books), by Dave and Neta Jackson, Bethany House

- *Hudson Taylor: Founder, China Inland Mission* (Heroes of the Faith Series), by Vance Christie, Barbour Publishing

- Mission-Minded Monologue Skit (see following page)

- "Man of Mission—Man of Prayer," a classic missions excerpt (see following page)

Mission-Minded Monologue Skit #6

Costume: *Oriental-style pajamas, round-rimmed eyeglasses, white hair, and a beard*

Setting: *As Taylor enters, he approaches a simple table with a candle, matches, a Bible, and an old-fashioned clock. He sits down, lights the candle, and opens the Bible.*

TAYLOR: "Delight thyself in the Lord, and He shall give thee the desires of thine heart."

Yes, that Bible promise is true, as we focus and delight in the Lord—not in the ministry, not on the tremendous needs here in China, and not even on my exciting missionary experiences.

I'm Hudson Taylor, and I love to pray. Right now it is two o'clock in the morning; from this time until about four o'clock is my usual time to pray and study the Bible. During this early morning time, I'll be undisturbed as I wait upon God.

For many years I've ministered throughout China, because I believe *The Great Commission is not an option to consider, but a command to obey.* Sometimes my family and I have traveled with just a simple cart and wheelbarrow; sometimes we stay in the poorest of inns. But missions is so rewarding. Usually I eat, dress, and talk like the Chinese people; I've translated the Bible into the Ningpo dialect; and through our China Inland Mission, God has established over 200 mission stations, 800 missionaries, and 100,000 witnessing Christians.

And this is what I've always wanted to do.

Even when I was just five years old, I was known to say, "When I am a man, I mean to be a missionary and go to China." Back in England, my father was a minister who had always wanted to be a missionary to China. But when he couldn't go, he prayed that I, his son, would be able to go in his place. Growing up, I was weak and frail; but as a young man I wanted to come here so badly that I once said, "I feel I can not go on living unless I do something for China." And now, here I am!

But after all these years as a missionary in China, I've learned that my most important work is not translating the Bible, recruiting missionaries, or even converting Buddhists to Jesus Christ. Instead, my primary mission and calling is simply to pray.

I've found that maintaining a prayerful Bible study can be the hardest part of missionary work. I've often said, "Satan will always find you something to do, when you ought to be occupied about that, if it is only arranging a window blind." But when I spend time with the Lord, by His grace He fills me with His power and joy.

So now I will focus on this most-important work. I will "delight myself in my Lord"; and yes, "He will give me the desires of *His* heart."

> "I feel I can not go on living unless
> I do something for China."
> "The Great Commission is not an option to consider,
> but a command to obey."
>
> HUDSON TAYLOR

 ## MAN OF MISSION—MAN OF PRAYER

A classic missions excerpt, by Dr. and Mrs. Howard Taylor (Hudson Taylor's son)

God was first in Hudson Taylor's life—not the work, not the needs of China or of the Mission, not his own experiences.

It was not easy for Mr. Taylor to make time for prayer and Bible study, but he knew that it was vital. Well do the writers remember traveling with him month after month in northern China, with the poorest of inns at night. Often with only one large room they would screen off a corner for their father and another for themselves, with curtains of some sort; they then, after sleep at last had brought a measure of quiet, would hear a match struck and see the flicker of candlelight which told that Mr. Taylor, however weary, was poring over the little Bible in two volumes always at hand. From two to four in the morning was the time he usually gave to prayer; the time when he could be most sure of being undisturbed to wait upon God. That flicker of candlelight has meant more than all they have heard on secret prayer; it meant reality, not preaching but practice.

Because he did this, Hudson Taylor's life was full of joy and power, by the grace of God.

When over seventy years of age, Hudson Taylor paused, Bible in hand, as he said to one of his children, "I have just finished reading the Bible through today, for the fortieth time in forty years."

And he not only read it, he lived it.

AMY CARMICHAEL

Missionary to India (1867–1951)

Kid-Friendly Resources:

- *Amy Carmichael: Rescuing the Children* (Heroes for Young Readers Series), by Renée Meloche and Bryan Pollard, YWAM Publishing

- *Amy Carmichael: Rescuer of Precious Gems* (Christian Heroes: Then & Now Series), by Janet and Geoff Benge, YWAM Publishing

- "Amy Carmichael: Dohnavur Fellowship, India," in *Hero Tales*, Vol. 1, by Dave and Neta Jackson, Bethany House

- *The Hidden Jewel: Amy Carmichael* (Trailblazer Books), by Dave and Neta Jackson, Bethany House

- *Amy Carmichael: A Life Abandoned to God* (Heroes of the Faith Series), by Sam Wellman, Barbour Publishing

- Mission-Minded Monologue Skit (below)

Mission-Minded Monologue Skit #7

Costume: *Have a woman wear a long Victorian-style dress with a high collar and puffed sleeves, and with her hair pulled up loosely*

Setting: *Miss Carmichael walks in slowly, with very proper posture, toward a globe or a world map on a table. Have her point to the country of India as she begins. Ideally, she should speak with an Irish accent.*

CARMICHAEL: India. Yes, this faraway land is my home.

My name is Amy Carmichael, and for over fifty years I have been a missionary to the children of India. (Have her point to Ireland on the map.) I was born here in Northern Ireland. My family was quite wealthy. As the eldest of seven children, I had much responsibility—especially after my mother died when I was just eighteen years old. I helped my father a great deal, especially with the children.

In 1892, when I was twenty-four years old, the Lord called me to missions—specifically to India. It was not easy to travel back then. I went on a boat to Japan and Ceylon, came home for a brief time, then I set sail for this land of India.

This country is a strange place, so different from where I grew up. The streets are crowded with people and the air smells of smoke and burning incense. Most of the Indian people are Hindu, and they worship millions of idols and statues. They are so lost and so desperately need Jesus. In fact, the need in this land is so great that I have never returned home. So many of the children—especially little girls—were being abused in Hindu temples, and God has called me to rescue them. That is what I have done throughout my life. I have rescued hundreds of children, and I have worked hard to inspire others to come and help me.

I love to write; I often try to convey the need for missions to the people back in Europe.

One time I had a very vivid dream, which I wrote down. In this dream I heard tom-tom drums thumping all night as I stood on a grassy field next to a cliff that dropped down into infinite darkness. Then I saw people walking toward me and toward the horrible cliff. They were stone blind as they marched toward the cliff. I tried to warn the people, but no one could hear me. Though I strained, not a sound could come. Then, in my dream, my friends and family called me to come back home. They said they needed me for something important, so I went; but all we did back home was to sit peacefully on the grass and make daisy chains. One day, as I sat there in my dream, I thought I heard a cry of a little girl far away, falling off a cliff; but as I stood to go help her, my friends pulled my down. "You really must stay here with us and help us to finish our daisy chains," they told me. "It would be so selfish of you, if you made us finish this work alone."

As I woke up, I realized that God was speaking to me about the need to reach the lost with the gospel of Jesus Christ. And for all these years, I have stayed here in India to help as many people as possible, especially children. I continually pray, "Give me the love that leads the way . . . the passion that will burn like fire."

May God give us all more of His love for the lost.

> "Give me the love that leads the way . . . the passion that will burn like fire."
>
> AMY CARMICHAEL

MARY SLESSOR

Missionary to Africa (1848–1915)

Kid-Friendly Resources:

- *Mary Slessor: Forward into Calabar* (Christian Heroes: Then & Now Series), by Janet and Geoff Benge, YWAM Publishing

- *Mary Slessor: Queen of Calabar* (Heroes of the Faith Series), by Sam Wellman, Barbour Publishing

- *Trial by Poison: Mary Slessor* (Trailblazer Books), by Dave and Neta Jackson, Bethany House

- Wholesome Words website, Children's Corner, Missionary Heroes: "Mary Slessor: Mission Africa" www.wholesomewords.org

- Mission-Minded Monologue Skit (below)

Mission-Minded Monologue Skit #8

Costume: Mary is barefoot. Her red hair is up in a messy bun, and she is dressed in a simple African style with bright sheets wrapped around her.

Setting: She comes in and sits on the ground. If possible, have a few African-style items, such as an African drum or some simple baskets.

SLESSOR: My name is Mary Slessor, and I will go anywhere for Jesus.

While I was growing up, my mother instilled in my brother and me a big heart for world missions. She used to dream about my brother, John, becoming a missionary. But when I was twenty-five years old, something very sad happened: John died. Right then, even though I was young, I was determined to take my brother's place.

I had heard about David Livingstone and his adventures and explorations throughout Africa, so that's where I decided to go. Back then most single women missionaries only stayed at the established mission bases, where it was safe—but not me! My idea of missions was exciting adventure and exploration! I wanted to take the gospel to precious people in Africa who had never heard of Jesus. I've always been willing to go anywhere—even to places where the men couldn't survive!

I've always lived and dressed like the African people, but with my bare feet and native African clothing (and untamed red hair!), I've often been criticized. Some of the missionaries want me to wear fancy Victorian dresses, because they think my clothing is scandalous. But I just want to reach these African people, and I don't want my clothing to be a distraction to them.

It has been wonderful to serve the Lord as His missionary these many years. I've never been married or had children, but my life has been very full. I've traveled to remote villages. I've supervised schools and helped African children with their education. I've dispensed medicine and helped the poor. And most importantly, I've preached the gospel of Jesus Christ.

NARRATOR: After being called to Africa as a young woman, Mary Slessor spent the rest of her life in African as a missionary. She died in her simple mud hut. After her death, many missionaries (including those who had been critical of her) honored her as a great woman of God.

JOHN AND BETTY STAM

Martyred in China in 1934

Kid-Friendly Resources:

- "John and Betty Stam: They
  Lived—and Died—for Christ," in
  Hero Tales, Vol. 4, by Dave and
  Neta Jackson, Bethany House

- A missions prayer, by Betty Stam (see following page)

When John Stam attended a prayer meeting for missions at Moody Bible Institute, he met Betty, a daughter of missionaries in China. The two were attracted to each other, but their desire for marriage came second to their desire to obey God's call.

In the fall of 1931 Betty sailed for China, while John stayed for his final year of school. At his graduation, John spoke of advancing the Great Commission despite America's depressed economy: "Shall we beat a retreat and turn back from our high calling in Christ Jesus, or dare we advance at God's command, in the face of the impossible? Let us remind ourselves that the Great Commission was never qualified by clauses calling for advance only if funds were plentiful and no hardship or self-denial involved. . . . We are told to expect tribulation and even persecution, but with it victory in Christ."

After graduation, John also went to China. Betty went to Shanghai for medical reasons, and the two unexpectedly met. The surprise reunion led to an engagement, and soon the two were married. In 1934 they had a baby girl, Helen.

John and Betty worked with China Inland Mission (now Overseas Missionary Fellowship) and were assigned to an area where missionaries had been evacuated. Although assured of no "Communist danger" in the area, within a few weeks after their arrival John and Betty were captured, forced on a grueling march, and executed. A week later, little Helen was miraculously delivered in a rice basket across a mountain to the home of a missionary family. A Chinese evangelist had found the baby abandoned in a house about thirty hours after the execution.

The Stams' devotion and commitment to Jesus Christ still inspires people today.

 A PRAYER

"Lord, I give up all my own plans and purposes,
All my own desires and hopes,
And accept Thy will for my life.
I give myself, my life, my all,
Utterly to Thee, to be Thine forever.
Fill me and seal me with Thy Holy Spirit.
Use me as Thou wilt,
Send me where Thou wilt,
Work out Thy whole will in my life
At any cost, now and forever."
—Betty Scott Stam

 **TEACHING OPPORTUNITY**

Missions Challenge and Handwriting Exercise

Encourage your child to carefully read this prayer by Betty Stam and then copy it in his or her own handwriting. Your child may even want to write this prayer on the front page of a Bible. This prayer is a big commitment; but as we surrender our own plans and purposes, God can have His way in our lives—and God's ways are always best!

Did you know?

When Elisabeth Howard (Elisabeth Elliot) was only ten or eleven years old, she copied this prayer by Betty Scott Stam into her Bible and then signed her name. Elisabeth grew up to become a famous missionary and author.

GLADYS AYLWARD

Missionary to China (1902–1970)

Kid-Friendly Resources:

*   *Gladys Aylward: The Adventure of a Lifetime* (Christian Heroes: Then & Now Series), by Janet and Geoff Benge, YWAM Publishing

*   "Gladys Aylward: The Small Woman," in *Hero Tales*, Vol. 1, by Dave and Neta Jackson, Bethany House

*   *Gladys Aylward: For the Children of China* (Heroes of the Faith Series), by Roy Lessin, Barbour Publishing

*   *Gladys Aylward: Daring to Trust* (Heroes for Young Readers Series), by Renée Meloche and Bryan Pollard, YWAM Publishing

- *Flight of the Fugitives: Gladys Aylward* (Trailblazer Books), by Dave and Neta Jackson, Bethany House

- *The Inn of the Sixth Happiness:* a classic film, starring Ingrid Bergman

- "The Small Woman": a book excerpt, by Alan Burgess (below)

The story of Gladys Aylward is an inspiring missions testimony that appeals to both boys and girls. Even though she was small in size, rejected by a mission agency, and lacked money and education, Gladys was determined to obey God's call. Her adventure of faith and courage in China included stopping a prison riot, escaping a war-torn city, and rescuing hundreds of orphans.

For oral reading, I highly recommend *The Small Woman* by Alan Burgess; and for a heartwarming mission-minded movie, I recommend the classic film *The Inn of the Sixth Happiness*, starring Ingrid Bergman. (Though this movie is not totally accurate and Aylward was disappointed by a romantic scene that did not occur, it is a very inspirational film for the whole family.)

 THE SMALL WOMAN

A classic missions excerpt to read aloud, by Alan Burgess

Gladys Aylward was twenty-six when she made up her mind that more than anything in the world she wanted to be a missionary in China. Fortunately she was a very determined person; otherwise she could never have overcome all the difficulties that stood in her way.

She was working as a parlor maid in London at the time. How, out of her very small wages, was she going to earn enough money to pay for the frighteningly long journey to China? As she lacked the education to pass the examinations to become a missionary, she could expect no help in getting the money for her fare. She had to do it entirely on her own, but at last Gladys had saved up three pounds. With that in her pocket, she went to a travel agency.

The clerk there was amazed when Gladys told him what she wanted to do. He patiently explained to her that the cheapest route to China was overland through Russia to Tientsin via the Trans-Siberian Railway. It cost forty-seven pounds, ten shillings, but it was quite impossible to go that way because of the undeclared war between Russia and China.

"I couldn't really care about a silly old war," Gladys said. "It's the cheapest way, isn't it? Now if you'll book me a passage, you can have these three pounds on account and I'll pay you as much as I can every week." The clerk looked at her carefully. Then, defeated, he picked up the three pounds.

Gladys hardly knew what she would be able to do when she arrived in China without a penny in her pocket, and understanding not one word of the language. But she could at least learn to become a preacher.

"I must learn to talk to the people," she said to herself. So in every moment of spare time she went to Hyde Park, where she mounted a soapbox and preached, often to a jeering audience. Tired Londoners going home in the evenings were startled to find themselves being told to turn to God by a small girl, only five feet tall, in a black dress.

Then Gladys had her first piece of luck. From a friend she heard of Mrs. Jeannie Lawson. Mrs. Lawson was seventy-three, and still working as a missionary in China. She had written that she wanted a younger woman to carry on her work. When Gladys heard this, her mouth dropped open in astonishment, and she whispered weakly, "That's me! That's me!" She wrote to Mrs. Lawson at once: Could she join her in China?

Now it was tremendously important to save the money for the train ticket. In the house where she worked she was willing to do anything. She also besieged employment agencies, offering to work on her days off, and at night too, serving at banquets. Then came that wonderful morning when a letter bearing brightly colored Chinese stamps arrived. It told her that if she could manage to get to Tientsin, a messenger would guide her from there to Mrs. Lawson. The excitement! She would get her passport at once! She would soon make the money to finish paying for her ticket! "I'm going to China!" she said to all her friends.

JIM ELLIOT, PETE FLEMING, ED MCCULLY, NATE SAINT, AND ROGER YOUDERIAN

Missionaries martyred in Ecuador (1956)

Kid-Friendly Resources:

- *Jim Elliot: One Great Purpose* (Christian Heroes: Then & Now Series), by Janet and Geoff Benge, YWAM Publishing

- *Nate Saint: On a Wing and a Prayer* (Christian Heroes: Then & Now Series), by Janet and Geoff Benge, YWAM Publishing

- *Jim Elliot: A Light for God* (Heroes for Young Readers Series), by Renée Meloche and Bryan Pollard, YWAM Publishing

- *Nate Saint: Heavenbound* (Heroes for Young Readers Series), by Renée Meloche and Bryan Pollard, YWAM Publishing

- "Jim Elliot: A Modern Martyr for Stone-Age Indians," in *Hero Tales*, Vol. 2, by Dave and Neta Jackson, Bethany House

- *The Fate of the Yellow Woodbee* (Trailblazer Books), by Dave and Neta Jackson, Bethany House

- *End of the Spear* is a film that highlights these famous missionaries. It is too graphic for most children but is an excellent resource for teens and adults.

With Nate Saint as their MAF (Missionary Aviation Fellowship) pilot, five devoted young men—Nate, Jim Elliot, Pete Fleming, Ed McCully, and Roger Youderian—devised a plan, called "Operation Auca," to share the gospel of Jesus Christ with the Aucas, a remote and unreached tribe in Ecuador.

For several months the missionaries airlifted various gifts to these people, such as clothing, knives, and life-size pictures of themselves. On one occasion, the Aucas sent back a gift, including a live parrot and a smoked monkey. Because of this gesture, the men decided it was time to land. After one peaceful visit, the five missionaries landed together on the Auca's "Palm Beach." All five were brutally killed with wooden spears, leaving behind five young widows. *Time* and *Life* magazines both reported the incident; and although many believed it was a tragic waste of young lives, multitudes of Christians were (and continue to be) inspired by their sacrificial devotion to Christ and their desire to reach unreached people.

 ONLY THE GRACE OF GOD—SPEAR-WIELDING KILLER NOW CHURCH ELDER

An excerpt from *The Missions Addiction*, by David Shibley

Not long ago I met Mincaye, a member of the spear-wielding Huaorani (Auca) killing party who massacred Jim Elliot, Nate Saint, and three other gallant missionaries in 1956. Today, Steve Saint, Nate's son, lives with his family among the Huaorani. Mincaye is now an elder in the Huaorani church. And the man who killed Steve's dad is now referred to as "grandfather" by Steve's children. Only the grace of God can accomplish that.

Before thousands of evangelists at Amsterdam 2000, Mincaye gave this testimony:

"When I killed Steve's father, I didn't know better. No one told us that he had come to show us God's trail. My heart was black and sick in sin, but I heard [that] God sent His own Son, His blood dripping and dripping. He washed my heart clean. . . . Now I see you God-followers from all over [the world]. I see well my brothers and sisters that God's blood has washed your hearts, too. Go speak [about God] all over the world. Let's take many with us to God's place in heaven."

"He is no fool who gives what he cannot keep to gain what he cannot lose."

JIM ELLIOT

ELISABETH ELLIOT

Missionary and author (born 1926)

Kid-Friendly Resources:

- Elisabeth's Mission-Minded Family (see following page)

- For teen girls, I highly recommend Elisabeth Elliot's book *Passion and Purity*

- See also the recommended resources for Jim Elliot above.

Elisabeth Howard was born in 1926 in Brussels, Belgium, where her parents served as missionaries. She attended Wheaton College and then became a missionary in Ecuador. After much prayer and seeking the Lord, in 1953 she married her former classmate, Jim Elliot. They worked together on translating the New Testament into the language of the Quichua Indians.

Jim and Elisabeth's daughter, Valerie, was born in 1955. Only ten months later, Jim was massacred while attempting to bring the gospel of Christ to the Huaorani people (known then as the Auca tribe).

Elisabeth has no regrets about the events that led to her husband's death, saying, "This was not a tragedy. God has a plan and a purpose in all things." Elisabeth continued to have a strong heart for the Auca people; so at the invitation of Rachel Saint, Elisabeth and four-year-old Valerie lived and ministered among these primitive people.

Together Elisabeth and Rachel worked to translate the Bible and to share God's message of salvation with the very people who had killed their loved ones. Their courage and love has inspired many in missionary work. Today Elisabeth Elliot is a highly respected woman of God. She was widowed a second time, and then married Lars Gren. Her daughter, Valerie Shepard, is a pastor's wife, a missionary in the Democratic Republic of Congo, and a homeschooling mother of eight. Elisabeth Elliot has written many outstanding books on missions, family life, and purity.

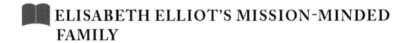

"God has a plan and a purpose in all things."

ELISABETH ELLIOT

📖 ELISABETH ELLIOT'S MISSION-MINDED FAMILY

Elisabeth Howard was raised as a mission-minded child. While growing up, her father, Philip E. Howard Jr., led the family in daily times of prayer, which included singing hymns together and reading the Bible.

Elisabeth's parents viewed hospitality as an issue of Christian obedience. They also believed that it benefited their family; for by opening their home their children could meet believers from different backgrounds, ask specific questions, and hear real-life testimonies of God's faithfulness. The family's hospitality (especially toward other missionaries) was often expected by their church; however, instead of feeling the weight of such an obligation, Elisabeth's mother, Katherine, told young mothers, "You don't understand what you're missing out on. You're missing out on some wonderful things!"

Of the six children in her mission-minded family, Elisabeth and four of her siblings became missionaries.

RACHEL SAINT

Bible translator (1914–1994)

Kid-Friendly Resource:

*   *Rachel Saint: A Star in the Jungle* (Christian Heroes: Then & Now Series), by Janet and Geoff Benge, YWAM Publishing,

*   See also the recommended resources for Nate Saint above.

Rachel Saint was trained by Wycliffe Bible Translators and began her missions career in Peru. Later she helped her brother, Nate Saint, with his missions work in Ecuador. With the help of a young Huaorani (Auca) woman named Dayuma, she learned their language and began translating the Bible. After her brother and the other missionaries were tragically killed by the Huaorani people in 1956, Rachel began traveling and sharing about the mission need of this tribe. She spoke on television and shared at Madison Square Garden with Billy Graham.

At Dayuma's invitation, in 1959 both Rachel Saint and Elisabeth Elliot went to live among the people who had killed their loved ones, and they succeeded in evangelizing and planting a church among these people (which is still going strong). Over the years, Rachel Saint's name became nearly synonymous with "Bible translation," since she helped relay the importance of this ministry.

WILLIAM CAMERON TOWNSEND

Founder of Wycliffe Bible Translators (1896–1982)

Kid-Friendly Resources:

- *Cameron Townsend: Planting God's Word* (Heroes for Young Readers Series), by Renée Meloche and Bryan Pollard, YWAM Publishing

- *Cameron Townsend: Good News in Every Language* (Christian Heroes: Then & Now Series), by Janet and Geoff Benge, YWAM Publishing

- See Wycliffe Bible Translators at www.wycliffe.org

- Mission-Minded Monologue Skit (below)

Mission-Minded Monologue Skit #9

Costume: Have Cam Townsend dressed in a simple 1920s suit and tie, with slicked-back hair and round wire-rimmed glasses

Setting: Sitting at a writing table with a stack of Bibles and many papers

TOWNSEND: Hi! I'm Cameron Townsend, and I really love God's Word, the Holy Bible.

I grew up in a poor family in California; and when I was just a teenager I heard about the need for world missions. In 1917 I joined the

Student Volunteer Movement and headed to Latin America as a young missionary.

My first assignment was selling Spanish Bibles in remote areas in Guatemala, but I soon realized that many of the Cekchiquel people had no understanding of Spanish. I became deeply burdened for the hundreds of thousands of people who had no Bible translation of their own. (Could you imagine if the only Bible *you* had to read was written in a foreign language, like Russian or Japanese?) Well, as I was trying to distribute these Spanish Bibles, one of these Cekchiquel nationals asked me, "Why, if your God is so smart, hasn't He learned our language?"

Wow. I took that as a challenge.

For over fifty years I devoted my life to Bible translation work—personally translating the Bible, helping others to learn foreign languages, and motivating Christians to realize the importance of Bible translation. I founded a ministry called Wycliffe Bible Translators, which was named in honor of another missionary, John Wycliffe, who long ago translated the Bible into English and was killed because of his work.

The greatest missionary is the Bible in the mother tongue. It never needs a furlough, is never considered a foreigner.

Everyone should be able to have the Word of God in his or her own language, and that's why we need more Bible translators. Even today, there are still many people who have never heard of Jesus and whole people groups who do not yet have a Bible in their own language. We need to take that as a challenge. What are we going to do about it?

Please pray that God will continue to call people to work on translating the Bible into other languages. It's a lot of work, and the process takes a long, long time. But it's so necessary. And when you see your own Bible, realize what a blessing it is to be able to have God's Word in your own language. The Holy Bible is God's Word to us. We need to read it and study it. And we always need to remember to pray for people throughout the world who are still waiting for God's Good News in *their* language.

Well, I'd better get back to my translation work. Thanks so much for letting me share. Who knows, maybe *you* will someday help translate the Bible into a new language!

"The greatest missionary is the Bible in the mother tongue. It never needs a furlough, is never considered a foreigner."

CAMERON TOWNSEND

🌐 TEACHING OPPORTUNITY

Explore Bible Translation Work

Find a Bible verse written in a foreign language (search online or look in the front of a Gideon Bible, which has John 3:16 printed in many languages). Have your child attempt to write the foreign letters and words perfectly. Discuss with your child what it would be like if these strange letters and symbols were the only way you could ever read the Bible.

Check Wycliffe Bible Translators (www.wycliffe.org) for current statistics on languages that still need a translation of the Bible. (Wycliffe has many excellent missions resources available for children.) Pray with your child for God to provide missionaries and national ministers who can help meet this need, and for God to call children who can meet this need in the next generation.

ERIC LIDDELL

Olympic gold medalist and missionary to China (1902–1945)

Kid-Friendly Resources:

- *Eric Liddell: Something Greater Than Gold* (Christian Heroes: Then & Now Series), by Janet and Geoff Benge, YWAM Publishing

- "Eric Liddell: Olympic Champion and Missionary to China," in *Hero Tales*, Vol. 2, by Dave and Neta Jackson, Bethany House

- *Eric Liddell: Gold Medal Missionary* (Heroes of the Faith Series), by Ellen Caughey, Barbour Publishing

- *Chariots of Fire*, the popular 1981 film

- Mission-Minded Monologue Skit (below)

Mission-Minded Monologue Skit #10

Costume: *Liddell is wearing a plain white T-shirt and baggy white shorts, with black running shoes and no socks*

Setting: *Have Liddell looking at a medal or a trophy*

LIDDELL: Greetings! I am Eric Liddell, and I am a missionary here in China. I'm wearing my running clothes because in a few minutes I will lead some athletic events for the Chinese students at this school. I'm going to show these boys a few of my athletic medals, because I want them to listen to me share the gospel.

I was born in China, and this is where I lived until I was five years old. When I turned six, my brother and I were brought to England to attend a missionary boarding school; and my parents and sister, Jenny, went back to China. While I was growing up I only saw them a few times, just when they came to Scotland on furlough (to visit and to share about their work in China), but we loved each other very much.

I used to be known as the "Flying Scotsman," because during my years at school and at the University of Edinburgh I enjoyed playing rugby and running fast. When I was at the University of Edinburgh I became a champion athlete, and many newspapers said I was a potential Olympic winner. No one from my country had ever won a gold medal. Sometimes, because of athletics, I was chosen to speak to large crowds, and I enjoyed the opportunity to share about my faith in the Lord.

In 1924 I was selected to run in the Olympic Games in Paris. It was a tremendous honor to represent Scotland; but first of all, I was God's representative. When I learned that my qualifying race was going to be held on a Sunday, I had to make a very tough choice between running the race and following God's will for my life. I knew I couldn't run on the Lord's Day, which meant I had to surrender my Olympic dream. But God made a way: I was able to switch to a different race, and then God helped me win an Olympic gold medal!

Less than a year later I came here to China, where I've been working with my family and China Inland Mission. I teach and help with athletics at this school, and I serve as the Sunday school superintendent at the church where my father is the pastor. In 1934 I got married to a young woman, named Florence, from a Canadian missionary family and we now have three little girls.

The political situation between China and Japan is getting tense, so I don't know what is ahead for me. But no matter what happens, I will serve God and follow His will for my life.

NARRATOR: With the outbreak of World War II, the political situation in China became worse, so in 1941 Liddell sent his wife and children to Canada. Liddell was later arrested by the Japanese and sent to a prison camp. Even in this terrible camp, he continued to minister and help people—but food and medical supplies were very limited. Eric Liddell died in this prison camp, shortly before World War II ended. His sudden death brought shock and sadness to the Christian world, but his testimony has inspired many.

> "I know God made me for a purpose
> —for China. But He also made me fast;
> and when I run, I feel God's pleasure."
>
> ERIC LIDDELL, IN *CHARIOTS OF FIRE*

OSWALD J. SMITH

Missionary evangelist and spokesman (1889–1986)

Kid-Friendly Resources:

* *The Challenge of Missions*, by Oswald J. Smith, Eternal Word Ministries reprint edition (a missions classic for older children)

* "Dr. Duff's Appeal," an inspiring excerpt from *The Challenge of Missions*, by Oswald J. Smith (see following page)

At age sixteen Oswald J. Smith was saved at an evangelistic meeting, and he soon had a great burden for world missions. While still young Smith applied for missionary service, but he was turned down due to poor health since childhood. Longing to make an impact, Smith determined to start a missions-oriented church to send others throughout the world. He founded and served as the pastor of People's Church in Toronto, Ontario. This grew to become a large and influential congregation, sending missionaries and raising large amounts of funds for missions.

Smith's "faith promise" strategy enabled his church and many others to give multiplied millions of dollars to world missions. He established a ministry to northern Canada, a mission to reach Jewish people, and a gospel tract distribution outreach. Throughout his life (despite the warnings concerning his health) he traveled all around the globe as a mission evangelist, always returning home to inspire and encourage others. Oswald Smith is probably best known for his missions writings, including 1,200 poems and hymn lyrics (with over 200 of them set to music). His books include *The Passion for Souls* and the missions classic, *The Challenge of Missions*.

DR. DUFF'S APPEAL

A classic missions excerpt to read aloud, from *The Challenge of Missions*, by Oswald J. Smith

Dr. Alexander Duff, that great veteran missionary to India, returned to Scotland to die, and as he stood before the General Assembly of the Presbyterian Church, he made his appeal, but there was no response. In the midst of his appeal he fainted and was carried off the platform. The doctor bent over him and examined his heart. Presently he opened his eyes.

"Where am I?" he cried. "Where am I?"

"Lie still," said the doctor. "You have had a heart attack. Lie still."

But in spite of the protests of the physician, the old warrior struggled to his feet, and, with the doctor on one side and the moderator of the assembly on the other side, he again mounted the steps of the pulpit platform, and, as he did so, the entire assembly rose to do him honor. Then, when they were seated, he continued his appeal. And this is what he said:

"When Queen Victoria calls for volunteers for India, hundreds of young men respond; but, when King Jesus calls, no one goes." Then he paused. There was silence. Again he spoke:

"Very well," he concluded, "then, aged though I am, I'll go back to India. I can lie down on the banks of the Ganges and I can die and thereby I can let the people of India know that there was one man in Scotland who loved them enough to give his life for them."

In a moment, young men all over the assembly sprang to their feet, crying, "I'll go! I'll go!" And after the old white-haired warrior had been laid to rest, these young men, having graduated, found their way to dark benighted India, there to labor as his substitutes for the Lord Jesus Christ.

My friend, will you go? Has God spoken to you? Have you heard His Call? Will you not answer, "Lord, here am I, send me"? And if you cannot go, will you not send a substitute? It is for you to decide. Why should anyone hear the Gospel twice before everyone has heard it once?"

"I have seen the Vision and for self I cannot live;
Life is less than worthless 'till my all I give."

"Why should anyone hear the Gospel twice
before everyone has heard it once?"

OSWALD J. SMITH

BILL BRIGHT

Founder of Campus Crusade for Christ
(1921–2003)

Kid-Friendly Resources:

- The *JESUS* film (available in over 900 languages)

- The *JESUS* film for Children

- "The Four Spiritual Laws"

- "Good News Comic Book" (a booklet for children)

- "The Man in the Clouds," a *JESUS* film story (see following page)

Throughout his life of ministry, Bill Bright was "fueled by his passion to present the love and claims of Jesus Christ to every living person on earth" (www.billbright.ccci.org/public). He founded and directed Campus Crusade for Christ, an interdenominational ministry, which has grown to become one of the largest Christian outreaches in the world—with 26,000 full-time staff members, over 225,000 trained volunteers, and ministry locations in 191 countries.

In 1947 Bill Bright received a vision from the Lord to produce a film on the life of Christ. He realized that a large majority of the world's unreached people were unable to read and considered how effective a movie about Jesus could be if it was created specifically to be translated into many different languages. Although he did not have the financial backing, Bright commissioned the *JESUS* film in 1979. God brought together producers, supporters, and professional people to make this dream a reality, including one couple who were willing to finance the entire original cost.

The result of this vision is the *JESUS* film, currently translated into over 900 languages. This ministry is directed by Paul Eshleman, who worked with Bright since the early development of this project. The *JESUS* film ministry has thousands of missionaries and national ministers working on this project throughout the world, not counting the multitudes of other ministries from all denominations that use this incredible tool. As of 2004, the *JESUS* film has been seen by over five billion people, with over 100 million people registering decisions for Christ!

Bill Bright also wrote "The Four Spiritual Laws," a gospel booklet used by many Christians and Bible-believing ministries throughout the world. This little booklet has been printed in 200 languages and distributed to over 2.5 billion people!

Did you know?

"The Four Spiritual Laws," written by Dr. Bill Bright, is available online in nearly every language (www.greatcom.org/laws/languages.html). This is an excellent resource, especially if you are sharing with someone who speaks a foreign language or are headed to an international restaurant and needing an appropriate witnessing tool. Also available online is Campus Crusade for Christ's "Good News Comic Book" for children.

 ## THE MAN IN THE CLOUDS

A testimony of The *JESUS* Film Project to read aloud
By Paul Eshleman, director of The *JESUS* Film Project

Several years ago in India, a young national missionary couple felt the call of God to take the gospel to a very resistant area in the north. They went with their three-year-old son to live among the Maltos people in a notorious area known as the "graveyard of missionaries."

They labored faithfully for many years without seeing a single person come to Christ. Their every effort to share the gospel was met with opposition. They battled discouragement, depression, spiritual oppression, and polluted water. Often, the entire family was ill.

One day the husband was returning home after seeing the doctor for his severe pain. As he walked through the door of their tiny home he collapsed and died. Distraught, his wife went to check on their sick child. He also had died. Devastated, confused, and with an acute sense of loss, she returned home, seemingly defeated.

A few weeks later, a *JESUS* film team arrived in that exact Maltos area. This time the government officials cooperated. The governor had previewed *JESUS* and instructed that the film be shown and not resisted.

Now, if you have seen *JESUS*, you know there is a moving scene when Jesus is first revealed at His baptism in the Jordan River. The moment Jesus' face appeared on the screen the crowd erupted with shouts and exclamations. The team had no choice but to stop the film and learn what the commotion was about.

"It's Him, it's Him!" they shouted. They could not believe what they were all seeing. "He is the One we saw walking in the clouds!" The team was astonished at their testimony. It seemed that everyone had seen Him. It happened the day the national missionary and his son died. Clouds formed over the hillsides. The vision* of a man, larger-than-life, appeared above the clouds, walking over their hills, shedding tears. The Maltos people suspected that it was a message from God, that He was displeased that they had rejected the gospel.

Now, they were being given a second chance. They were stunned. As the team restarted the projector, the people settled down to continue watching the film. Everyone was transfixed by the story. Then, at the end, the majority of these hard, resistant Maltos people put their faith in Christ!

Other miracles followed. People were delivered from evil spirits. The sick were healed. The deep spiritual hunger of many was met. But the greater miracle is this: where once there were no Christians, there are now 46,000 Maltos believers and hundreds of growing and maturing churches! Today, they are preparing to send out their own missionaries to other unreached people, some of whom will use the *JESUS* film. The "graveyard of missionaries" has become the "vineyard of missionaries"!

* Note by Eshleman: For reasons we cannot understand, on occasion, the Holy Spirit breaks through spiritual strongholds via the use of visions. In this case, it appears that He affirmed the truth of the gospel contained in the JESUS film by allowing the man in the vision to resemble the appearance of the actor who played Jesus.

"The bedrock foundation for our call to world missions is the blood of Jesus Christ."

JON DUNAGAN
MISSION-MINDED FAMILIES

LOREN CUNNINGHAM
MISSION QUOTES:

"You never get bored with God in action!"

"When a critical mass of people have the Bible and
apply what it teaches in their lives, a nation is transformed."

"You're either a missionary
or a mission field."

"Disagreements don't cause disunity,
a lack of forgiveness does."

"If we want to be known in heaven and feared in hell
we must be willing to lose our reputation here on earth."

"The way you discover your gifts is really
by serving not by searching."

LOREN CUNNINGHAM

Founder of Youth With a Mission (YWAM)
(born 1936)

Kid-Friendly Resources:

- YWAM and YWAM King's Kids
  (www.ywam.org)

- *Is That Really You, God?* (Loren Cunningham's
  autobiography), YWAM Publishing

- *Daring to Live on the Edge: The Adventure of Faith and
  Finances,* by Loren Cunningham, YWAM Publishing

- *Loren Cunningham: Into All the World* (Christian Heroes: Then & Now Series), by Janet and Geoff Benge, YWAM Publishing

As a young man, Loren Cunningham had a vision of "waves of young people" moving across the continents to proclaim the Good News of Jesus Christ. His mission plan was rejected by his denomination, but Cunningham stepped out in faith and founded Youth With a Mission (YWAM) as a nondenominational, international ministry.

From a late-night vision given to a 20-year-old in the Bahamas
to a global ministry with over 18,000 workers,
the growth of YWAM is the story of God's inspiration,
God's grace for many mistakes,
and the creativity of the Holy Spirit's leading.

— FROM YWAM'S WEBSITE

Loren Cunningham has personally traveled to every country in the entire world, and through YWAM he has provided missions opportunities for thousands of youth (and those "young in heart"). His life and ministry have greatly influenced world missions. Many give Cunningham the credit for "deregulating missions." He has helped open the door for many more people—of all ages—to participate in the Great Commission.

Are you interested in missions? Take a look at www.ywam.org:

- For children and their parents: King's Kids outreaches
- For young adults: DTS—Discipleship Training Schools
- For college students: University of the Nations
- For older adults and families: Crossroads DTS
- For every age: YWAM books

> ## "To know God and to make Him known."
>
> YWAM'S MOTTO

THE CHRISTIAN MAGNA CARTA

By Loren Cunningham

Everyone on earth has the right to:

1. Hear and understand the Gospel of Jesus Christ.
2. Have a Bible available in their own language.
3. Have a Christian fellowship available nearby, to be able to meet for fellowship regularly each week, and to have biblical teaching and worship with others in the Body of Christ.
4. Have a Christian education available for their children.
5. Have the basic necessities of life: food, water, clothing, shelter, and health care.
6. Lead a productive life of fulfillment spiritually, mentally, socially, emotionally, and physically.

📖 A "BIG MAN" MEETS A "REAL MAN"

A mission challenge to read aloud
By Loren Cunningham

Paul Rader was a big, strapping football player who lived in the early part of the twentieth century. He became an imposing figure on Wall Street, where he headed City Service Oil Company. Then he got saved and obeyed God's call to preach, finding a post as an assistant pastor in Pittsburgh. Paul Rader would have

been appalled if someone had told him there were still false gods in his life.

One week, a visiting speaker came to his church. Paul took one look at the man—a missionary—and shook his head in disgust. First of all, the man was wearing a flimsy-looking suit of wrinkled brown silk. When he began to talk it was in a soft, delicate voice. He seemed a little frail. Not like a real man at all, thought Rader. As he spoke about his work in China, he often dabbed at the corners of his mouth with a handkerchief.

Paul approached the man after the meeting and challenged him. "Sir, why are you so sissified? You call yourself a man of God, but look at the way you're dressed and the way you talk. I don't think you're much of a missionary!"

The man patiently explained. "I'm sorry about this suit, but I have ministered in China for twenty-five years. When it was time to leave, all my western clothes had been worn out for years. The believers in my village pooled their resources to buy the silk to make me this suit, shirt and tie. They didn't have a machine, so they stitched it by hand."

He dabbed at this mouth again and Rader's disgust must have shown on his face, for the missionary continued.

"As for my voice . . . I did a lot of street preaching and was often beaten up. One time, a gang took turns beating me and a man jumped on my throat. My larynx is permanently damaged and I no longer have control of my salivary glands."

Embarrassed now, Rader murmured an apology and hastened to find a place alone. He went down to the church basement, found a pile of coal and stretched out on it face down. He cried out to God begging forgiveness for his attitude. He told the Lord he wanted to serve Him like this man.

From that day on, Paul Rader was a man with a missionary heart. As a pastor and leader in the Christian Missionary Alliance, he influenced many thousands of young men and women to give themselves for missions.

BILLY GRAHAM

International evangelist (1918-2018)

Kid-Friendly Resources:

- *Billy Graham* (Men & Women of Faith Series), by Terry Whalin, Bethany House

- "Billy Graham: Evangelist to the World," in *Hero Tales*, Vol. 3, by Dave and Neta Jackson, Bethany House

- *Billy Graham: The Great Evangelist* (Heroes of the Faith Series), by Sam Wellman, Barbour Publishing

Billy Graham grew up on a dairy farm in Charlotte, North Carolina, and made a personal commitment to Christ at the age of sixteen during a revival meeting held by Mordecai Ham. "I do remember a great sense of burden that I was a sinner before God," says Graham. Later he learned that a businessman who helped plan these meetings had prayed for God to raise up a man from Charlotte to preach throughout the world. This businessman's prayers were definitely answered!

It's hard to talk about the life of Billy Graham without using numbers. He has likely preached the gospel to more people in live audiences than anyone else in history—to over 210 million people, it is estimated, in more than 185 countries and territories—with hundreds of millions more reached through television, video, film, and webcasts. As a result, multitudes of people have made personal decisions for Christ. He has preached in remote African villages and in the heart of New York City, to U.S. presidents and heads of state and to bushmen of Australia and wandering tribesmen of the Middle East.

Fifty times, Billy Graham has been listed by the Gallup organization as one of the ten most admired men in the world—by far the most appearances on the list since the poll began. He has written twenty-five books, including many bestsellers. His ministries include the weekly "Hour of Decision" radio broadcast, heard around the world for over fifty years, writing a weekly newspaper column called "My Answer," and publishing *Decision* magazine. Another ministry is World Wide Pictures, which has produced and distributed over 130 evangelistic films—translated into forty languages and viewed by over 250 million people worldwide.

Note: Billy Graham's concise salvation tract entitled *Peace with God* is a simple and excellent evangelistic tool.

> "My one purpose in life is to help people find a personal relationship with God, which, I believe, comes through knowing Christ."
>
> BILLY GRAHAM

FRANKLIN GRAHAM

International relief worker and evangelist
(born 1952)

Kid-Friendly Resources:

- Operation Christmas Child (www.samaritanspurse.org)

- Dare to Be a Daniel (D2BD) (www.daretobeadaniel.com): an excellent evangelism training program for young people on "How to Win Souls for God"

William Franklin Graham III is the fourth of Billy and Ruth Graham's five children. But just being the son of an internationally famous Christian evangelist was not enough. At the age of twenty-two, after a period of rebellion and world travel, Franklin Graham sat alone in a Jerusalem hotel room and totally committed his life to Jesus Christ.

Soon afterward, Graham was invited on a six-week mission trip to Asia by Bob Pierce, founder of Samaritan's Purse. During this time, he felt a call "to the slums of the streets and the ditches of the world" in areas affected by war, famine, disease, and natural disaster. Following Pierce's death, Graham became the president of Samaritan's Purse, a world relief ministry, which now provides more than $150 million each year in assistance in over one hundred countries—including an excellent missions program for children called Operation Christmas Child, in which shoebox gifts are sent to children in need.

Franklin Graham says, "Evangelistic preaching is what Daddy [Billy Graham] does; I never thought I would." Today he is the president and CEO of the Billy Graham Evangelistic Association and has committed to spend 10 percent of his time preaching and conducting at least five evangelistic festivals each year.

"Just being the son of Billy Graham won't get me into heaven."

FRANKLIN GRAHAM

LUIS PALAU

*International evangelist from Argentina
(1934-2021)*

Kid-Friendly Resources:

- "Luis Palau: The Billy Graham of Latin America," in *Hero Tales*, Vol. 3, by Dave and Neta Jackson, Bethany House

- *Luis Palau: Evangelist to the World* (Heroes of the Faith Series), by Ellen Bascuti, Barbour Publishing

Luis Palau was born in Argentina and grew up in a Christian family. Deeply impressed by his father's faith as a child, Palau says, "One of my earliest memories is of sneaking out of bed early in the morning to watch my father kneel, pray and read the Bible before going to work." After his father's untimely death, Luis worked to support his family, and early in life he found his calling to preach the gospel.

At every opportunity Palau preached on street corners and shared the Good News of Jesus. He went to Portland, Oregon, to study the Bible and later returned to Latin America to build an evangelistic team. Palau began working with other evangelists, including Billy Graham; in the 1970s ministry invitations starting coming from Europe and other parts of the world. By the early 1980s Palau's ministry had made a great impact in Britain. In the 1990s Palau began to minister throughout the United States, at times speaking to crowds of half a million people. He has also ministered in the White House with national political and religious leaders.

Today Palau's focus is primarily on "festival evangelism": leading exciting contemporary city events including popular Christian music, exotic food stands, extreme sports skate parks, children's shows (cooperating with the popular Veggie Tales), and preaching—with no offerings taken from the massive crowds. Through his global outreaches, millions have committed their lives to Jesus Christ.

"A nation will not be moved by timid methods."

LUIS PALAU

RICHARD WURMBRAND

Founder of The Voice of the Martyrs
(1909–2001)

Kid-Friendly Resources:

- The Voice of the Martyrs website (www.persecution.com), which has many excellent missions resources for children

- dc Talk and The Voice of the Martyrs: *Jesus Freaks, Volume 1: Stories of Those Who Took a Stand for Jesus*; *Jesus Freaks, Volume 2: Stories of Revolutionaries Who Changed Their World*; Bethany House

- *Richard Wurmbrand: Voice in the Dark*, by Carine MacKenzie, Christian Focus Publications

In 1945, a year after communists seized power in Romania, thousands of religious leaders gathered for a meeting at the parliament building. One by one, priests and ministers stood to praise communism and declare its unity with Christianity. Finally, Pastor Richard Wurmbrand boldly stood to speak the truth: "Delegates, it is our duty not to praise earthly powers that come and go, but to glorify God the Creator and Christ the Savior, who died for us on the cross."

From then on Wurmbrand was a marked man in the eyes of the communist government, and in 1948 he was captured and imprisoned by the secret police. He was brutally tortured, brainwashed, and placed in underground solitary confinement—separated from his family for a total of fifteen years. All the while, by God's grace he loved those who persecuted him, asking, "What can we do to win these men to Christ?"

Upon his release, Pastor Wurmbrand resumed his ministry among the underground church. After a government ransom was paid, the Wurmbrand family traveled to Scandinavia, Europe, and finally to the United States.

In 1967 Wurmbrand founded The Voice of the Martyrs, a ministry dedicated to serving the persecuted church worldwide and seeing freedoms won in places that persecute Christianity (see www.persecution.com).

> "What can we do to win these men to Christ?"
>
> RICHARD WURMBRAND, SPEAKING OF THE MEN
> PERSECUTING HIM

K. P. YOHANNAN

Founder of Gospel for Asia

Kid-Friendly Resource:

* *Revolution in World Missions*, by K. P. Yohannan   — free at www.gfa.org

K. P. Yohannan grew up in a very poor family in India, but today he directs a large international ministry, Gospel for Asia. This far-reaching mission outreach supports over eleven thousand full-time national missionaries throughout Asia. With ministry training centers throughout India and thousands of current students, Gospel for Asia is one of the most powerful missionary movements working across the nation of India in evangelism and church planting.

Every year, Gospel for Asia produces nearly 50 million pieces of gospel literature to supply national missionaries as they preach the gospel and win people to Christ. More than 14,000 fellowships and more than 3,230 fully established churches have been planted. Other ministry areas include radio and film outreach, ministry to Muslims, ministry in slums, and providing national missionaries with vehicles and ministry tools.

In his exciting and fast-moving book, *Revolution in World Missions*, Yohannan shares how God brought him from his remote Indian village to become the founder of Gospel for Asia.

"Walk away from your own preoccupations to the harvest fields of Asia—and see the perishing multitudes through the eyes of Jesus."

K. P. YOHANNAN

God Can Use Anyone—Including YOU!

Around the world today, God is working mightily through willing individuals. Some missionaries are getting older, but others are young, daring, and full of adventure . . . some missionaries are even little children! Some have fair skin, but multitudes of today's missionaries have dark-colored skin. Some missionaries travel around the world on commercial airline jets or small Missionary Aviation Fellowship bush planes, but many travel by motorcycle, or bicycle, or even on foot. Some are well-known and even famous.

CHAPTER 7

Training Your Child in Biblical Christianity

We need to train ourselves and our children in the important foundations of our faith. This chapter can be used as a reference tool to help effectively train a new generation to be "rock solid" for Jesus Christ. Never underestimate the ability of your child to learn God's Word! As your child matures, he or she will build upon the early foundational training received. Even a little child can be well-grounded in sound biblical doctrine and well-established in a meaningful relationship with the Lord.

TEACHING OPPORTUNITY

Foundational Bible Verses to Memorize

Share the gospel with your child—and teach your child to share it! Go through these basic foundations of faith with your child, and make sure he or she understands what it means to be saved and how to share the gospel with others. Encourage your child to check off each verse as he or she memorizes it.

One of life's greatest privileges is being able to lead a child into a genuine, personal relationship with Jesus Christ. I always want to remember to keep this focus, because every child will someday stand before God. As parents and teachers, our number one priority should be to make certain that each child we are influencing has an opportunity to receive Jesus Christ as his or her personal Lord and Savior.

Q. What does it mean to be "saved"?

Many people who call themselves "Christians" (including many children) have no understanding of what it really means to be saved. Just because someone is a basically good person does not mean that he or she is in right standing with God and will someday go to heaven. The Bible teaches us that people cannot get to heaven merely by being good, by being born into a religious family, or even by believing there is a God (in James 2:19, the Bible says, "You believe that there is one God. You do well. Even the demons believe—and tremble!").

Q. How are we saved, or "born again"?

There is only one way to be saved and that is through receiving God's salvation through Jesus Christ—by being "born again." We were each born the first time, physically, as a baby; but we must also be born a second time, born again spiritually. God's salvation is by grace (a gift we don't deserve and haven't earned), through faith in Jesus Christ.

Jesus was the first person to use the term "born again" when he said:

❑ John 3:7   "You must be born again."

❑ John 3:3   "Unless one is born again, he cannot see the kingdom of God."

Q. What is sin?

Sin is anything a person does (or neglects to do) that falls short of God's perfect will and His perfect law. Like missing a target, sin is missing God's will for our lives. As a person comes to Jesus Christ, he or she must repent (or turn away) from all sin.

❑ Romans 3:23   "For all have sinned and fall short of the glory of God."

Q. Is there really only one way to God?

Yes! There is only one way a person can receive God's eternal life and that is through God's salvation by His grace that we receive by faith in Jesus Christ! The Bible says:

❑ John 14:6   "Jesus said to him, 'I am the way, the truth, and the life. No one comes to the Father except through Me.'"

❑ Acts 4:12   "Nor is there salvation in any other, for there is no other name under heaven given among men by which we must be saved."

Q. Why do we need God's salvation?

If you were to die right now, do you know without a doubt that you would go to heaven—and how do you know? Someday, when you die, you will stand face-to-face with the perfect, holy, almighty God, and you will be judged (see Hebrews 9:27). God has undeniable evidence of every wrong thing you have ever done and of every bad thought you have ever imagined. On that day there will be no excuses and no way to hide. If you are trusting in yourself, you will be pronounced guilty of sin and of not measuring up to God's perfect law, and not even following the conviction of your own conscience (what you know in your heart is the right thing to do). It will not matter if your sins are many or few, or how many "good things" you did. On God's day of judgment our only hope will be to know that we have received God's salvation and cleansing from sin through the death of Jesus Christ on the cross.

❑ 1 Peter 2:24   "He Himself bore our sins in His body on the cross, so that we might die to sin and live to righteousness; for by His wounds you were healed" (NASB).

Q. How can we know for sure if we're really saved and going to heaven?

We can have assurance (or "know for sure") about our salvation from what God has told us in the Bible. Our salvation is not based on our feelings but on the fact of God's Word.

❑ 1 John 5:11–13 "And this is the testimony: that God has given us eternal life, and this life is in His Son. He who has the Son has life; he who does not have the Son of God does not have life. These things I have written to you who believe in the name of the Son of God; that you may know that you have eternal life, and that you may continue to believe in the name of the Son of God."

Q. How can we receive Jesus Christ?

After you hear and understand God's plan of salvation, you must accept and believe it for yourself, and then confess your sins to God and confess Jesus Christ as the Lord and Savior of your life.

It's as simple to remember as A, B, C: Accept, Believe, and Confess!

A—Accept: God loves you and has a purpose for your life.

❑ John 3:16 "For God so loved the world that He gave His only begotten Son, that whoever believes in Him should not perish but have everlasting life."

B—Believe: Jesus Christ is God's only provision for our sin.

❑ Romans 6:23 "For the wages of sin is death, but the gift of God is eternal life in Christ Jesus our Lord."

Each person must individually receive God's salvation through faith in Jesus Christ. Our salvation is a gift of God's grace.

❏ Ephesians 2:8   "For by grace you have been saved through faith, and that not of yourselves; it is the gift of God."

C—Confess: Completely surrender your life to Jesus Christ! Confess your sins to God, and confess (speak out of your mouth) that Jesus is your Lord and Savior.

❏ Romans 10:9–10   "If you confess with your mouth that Jesus is Lord and believe in your heart that God raised him from the dead, you will be saved. For it is by believing in your heart that you are made right with God, and it is by confessing with your mouth that you are saved" (NLT).

Q. What is an example of a "sinner's prayer"?

The following prayer is an example of a simple prayer to receive Jesus Christ as the Lord and Savior of your life. This type of prayer is often called a "sinner's prayer" because it is a prayer of turning away from sin to receive God's salvation. Your prayer does not have to use these exact words, because God knows your heart. But when praying to receive Jesus Christ as your Lord and Savior, it's good to speak your prayer out loud—"confessing" (or saying) it with your mouth.

Dear Heavenly Father,

I know that I have sinned, and I know that my sin would keep me from You forever. But I thank You, God, for sending Your Son, Jesus Christ, to die on the cross for me and to pay this price for my sins. I don't deserve Your gift of salvation, but I am now turning away from the wrong things I have done and I receive Your Son, Jesus Christ, as my Lord and Savior. Jesus, You are now my Lord! Please come into my life and forgive all my sins. I believe that You are alive, and I thank You for giving me Your new life. Help me live for You all the days of my life. I love You, Lord, and give my entire life to You.

In Jesus' name, Amen.

Ephesians 2:8 – "For by grace you have been saved through faith, and that not of yourselves; it is the gift of God."

2 Corinthians 6:2 – "Behold, now is the accepted time; behold, now is the day of salvation."

Q. What is the Bible all about?

The Bible is the most remarkable book ever written. It is a God-inspired library of sixty-six books—both large and small—including history, poetry, psalms (hymns or songs), letters, teachings, and proverbs (wise sayings). The Bible contains the deepest wisdom and knowledge, yet it is simple enough for a child to understand. The Holy Bible is divided into two main sections:

- **The Old Testament** contains thirty-nine books and was written before the birth of Jesus Christ. It tells of the creation of the world and the fall of humanity through sin, and it contains many prophecies concerning the birth, life, death, and resurrection of the promised Messiah (Jesus Christ). The Old Testament shows us how people could never meet all the perfect requirements of God's law and how we all desperately need a Savior.

- **The New Testament** contains twenty-seven books and was written after the resurrection of Jesus Christ. The first four books, the Gospels, give the history of Christ's life and ministry. The book of Acts tells how Jesus' disciples carried on the work of Christ and how Christianity began. Most of the remaining New Testament books give practical instructions for Christian living and instructions for the church. The final book, Revelation, is a prophetic book, telling us about the end times and the second coming of our Lord Jesus.

Q. How can I know the Bible is true?

- God's Word is alive and life-changing!

  The Bible is never out-of-date on any subject, and its teachings fulfill the spiritual and moral needs of all people, young and old, in all lands, and in any time period. Over and over (some say 3,800 times) the Bible claims to be the actual Word of God; for example, 2 Timothy 3:16 says, "All Scripture is inspired by God and is useful to teach us what is true and to make us realize what is wrong in our lives. It corrects us when we are wrong and teaches us to do what is right" (NLT).

- God's Word fits together like a perfect puzzle!

  Approximately forty writers—all directed and supernaturally led by God—wrote the sixty-six books of the Bible over a period of about sixteen hundred years. These writers lived in many different lands and were from a wide range of social classes: from kings and scholars to prophets, fishermen, and shepherds. Many writers never saw the words of the others, yet the books of the Bible are all totally true and never stray from the Bible's central message of salvation through the promised Savior and Messiah—our Lord, Jesus Christ!

- God's Word is totally accurate!

  The Bible is scientifically accurate and historically correct. Its truths have withstood the test of time, as many biblical details have been proven to be true through archeological discoveries, through factual research in the areas of botany, geology, and astronomy, and through studies of ancient history.

- The prophecies of God's Word come true!

  The Bible contains over five thousand prophecies, many of which were predicted hundreds or even thousands of years before their fulfillment. Most of the prophecies of the Bible have already been completely fulfilled; the rest are being fulfilled now or will be fulfilled in times to come.

- God's Word has changed and impacted the world!

  The Bible has blessed millions of people from generation to generation. Throughout the ages, religions and governments have tried to destroy the Bible, persecuting and even killing all who refused to deny its truth; but God's Word has always survived. The Bible has been translated into hundreds of languages and is the most widely distributed book of all times.

❏ Hebrews 4:12 "The word of God is living and powerful."

Q. What does it mean to grow as a Christian?

Just as a baby needs milk to grow, your newly born spirit needs spiritual food:

❏ 1 Peter 2:2 "As newborn babes, desire the pure milk of the word, that you may grow thereby."

- Read and study the Bible:

  God's Word will help you to know Him and to understand His will and purpose for your life.

- Pray daily:

  God desires to be your closest friend. Take time to talk to God and listen to Him every day.

- Attend church regularly:

  Find a Bible-believing church where you can worship God, learn from a pastor and good Bible teachers, make Christian friends, and be part of God's work in your community.

- Be baptized (if you haven't been baptized already):

  God instructs us to be baptized as a sign to God and others that we have decided to follow Jesus Christ.

- Be led by the Holy Spirit:

  As a Christian, God's Spirit lives in you. Be sensitive to what God wants, and allow God to direct you in every area of your life.

- Tell others about Jesus:

  The gospel (or "Good News") of Jesus Christ is for everyone, and God wants us to share this news with others.

Q. What are common challenges for new Christians?

- What if I can't understand the Bible?

  God will help you to understand and apply His Word to your life. God is the One who led each of the Bible writers to write exactly what He wanted to say. Since God lives in you, as a Christian, He will help you understand what He meant. Other Christians, such as a Sunday school teacher or a pastor, can also help you understand and apply God's Word to your life.

- What happens when I am tempted to sin again?

  When a temptation comes, you have a choice—either to resist the temptation or to sin. As a follower of Jesus, it is very important to stay as far away from evil as possible and to draw closer to God. It's important to avoid places or situations that could tempt you to sin or negative people who could pressure you to do wrong things. God will help you to do what is right, and His Holy Spirit—who is now inside you—will convict your heart (or help you to "know" inwardly) when you have done something wrong.

  When we sin, the Bible says:

❑   1 John 1:9   "If we confess our sins, He is faithful and just to forgive us our sins and to cleanse us from all unrighteousness."

- What about my non-Christian friends?

  God wants us to love everyone, and He wants us to show people how wonderful He is through our love, our kindness, and the way we live. We are to be a light for Jesus and a witness to our friends by sharing our faith in Him.

It is a good thing to train a child in biblical knowledge and help him or her learn biblical facts. But it is even more important to strengthen and motivate the heart and spirit of a child. Encourage your child to have a holy fear of God, a desire to always love and obey the Lord, and a commitment to wholehearted worship.

CHAPTER 8

Preparing Your Child to Be a Prayer Champion

A true heart for world missions is not something that can be *taught* (although we will certainly try!); it is a revelation of God's heart that must be *caught* from the Lord Himself, through His Word, and through prayer. When it comes to praying with your child, I encourage you not to spend all your time talking about prayer needs or even teaching about prayer. The most effective way to train your child in effective prayer is simply to pray!

Q. Is it possible for my child to really *want* to pray?

Your child can become a champion for God in prayer. He or she can be trained to hear God's voice and can learn to pray in boldness and in faith.

When God spoke to young Samuel in 1 Samuel 3, it wasn't some sweet children's message; God spoke to Samuel as if he were a man, with a tough word for the high priest of all Israel. As teachers and parents, our goal should not be to teach our children to pray cute little prayers to make *us* look good. We must realize that the prayers of a child—even the prayers of *our* children—could change lives and impact nations! A child's simple trust may even challenge and encourage us to rise to a higher level of faith.

CHILDREN PRAYED FOR HOURS, WEEPING FOR THE LOST

A testimony of prayer to read aloud to children

One time at a large camp for children, I simply prayed for God to give the children more of His heart and compassion for the lost. After a time of worship, I felt led to invite any children with unsaved parents to come forward for prayer, and I was completely shocked as over a hundred children came to the altar.

Children began to pray for their parents, as other children came forward to support them. Then something like a wave of God's love and compassion began to pour over the campers. The children started to cry, earnestly interceding for the salvation of these parents, and then fervently interceded for the lost around the world.

I had expected the prayer time to last for only a few minutes, but God had something else in mind! For over two hours, hundreds of children fell to their knees weeping, hugging each other, and praying—like I had never seen children pray. By the time we were done, wadded-up, mushy tissue paper covered the chapel floor, and the prayers of children had covered the earth. It was one of the most incredible ministry experiences of my life!

Prayer time with children is not always spectacular, but it always makes a difference. As we train our children to grow in prayer, God also wants us, as parents and teachers, to develop our own personal prayer life. This takes work, time, and an establishment of new habits; but it's exciting to know that we can grow with our children as we learn to pray.

I once spoke with an international minister who had ministered in hundreds of Christian churches of many different denominational backgrounds. When I mentioned this book and my desire to devote one chapter to the importance of prayer, this man encouraged me not to assume that most Christian parents and teachers are already praying. In congregation after congregation he had asked people to raise their hands if they spent thirty minutes in prayer each day, and unfortunately usually less than 5 percent of his audiences could honestly answer yes.

Although faithful, quality prayer time is something that I believe most of us desire, I will not presume that you (or your child) have already established this discipline in your lives. But I want to encourage you that yes, you can pray!

Q. But what if my child won't pray for more than a minute?

Praying *longer* is not necessarily *better*. However, without training and encouragement, I have found that most children will usually pray for only about thirty seconds (unless they go through their entire list of "God bless Uncle Mitch, Aunt Marilyn, Grandpa and Grandma" . . . and everyone they've ever met).

One of the best ways to encourage your child to establish a deeper relationship with the Lord is simply to set aside more time in your child's day for spiritual development—including more time for personal Bible reading and more time dedicated to prayer. A helpful idea is to encourage children to establish personal Bible reading and prayer goals and to keep track of their weekly progress.

For a while, you could even have a special reward each week or month when your child has met a goal. This isn't bribing children to pray but rather is a celebration of an important new discipline! A child might begin with a goal of praying for thirty minutes a week (which is five minutes a day, six days a week—not counting Sunday church time). After a few successful weeks, your child can then raise his or her prayer goal to perhaps an hour a week (ten minutes a day)—and so on.

At our home in the country, we have a ten-minute "prayer trail" around our property. Before school, our older children begin their day by praying for one or more "prayer laps." My little ones aren't old enough to go out into the woods, but they have their own little five-minute "prayer walk" around the outside of our house.

I have sometimes encouraged the parents in our church to actually set a kitchen timer for five or ten minutes and to encourage their children to go off by themselves to a quiet corner and keep praying—out loud, as hard as they can, from their heart—until the buzzer goes off.

☕ TEACHING OPPORTUNITY

Practical Ideas to Increase Your Child's Prayer Time

- Sing worship songs
- Sit quietly and simply think about God
- Thank God for as many specific things as you can
- Review the fruit of the Spirit (Galatians 5:22–23) and the armor of God (Ephesians 6:13–18)
- Say (and pray) favorite Bible verses as they come to mind
- Review (and commit to obey) God's Ten Commandments (Exodus 20:1–17)
- Go through the Lord's Prayer (Matthew 6:9–13) as a seven-step prayer guide

Q. What do I do if my child's prayer isn't answered?

You may be afraid to have your child pray about specific concerns because it might make God "look bad" if your child's prayer doesn't get answered. But don't be afraid. Let God take care of His own reputation—and let us pray! Encourage your child to be specific in his or her prayers and to pray according to God's will as revealed in the Bible.

There may be times when things happen that we don't understand. Perhaps your child prays for a dying grandparent to get better, and yet the grandparent dies. Many times we will not know why things didn't work out as we had prayed. We may not understand ourselves, and we may not have any answers for our children.

Even so, we can't ignore this opportunity for spiritual training. These are vital times to train our children in steadfast faith. If things happen that we don't understand, we can still encourage our children that God is good and loving and worthy to be praised—*no matter what*!

You may want to refer to some of the missionary biographies included in this book. For example, when missionary Jim Elliot was killed by the people he was trying to reach, his wife, Elisabeth Elliot, proclaimed: "This is not a tragedy. God has a plan and a purpose in all things." God can even take what the enemy meant for bad and turn it around for good. (You can read how the men who killed Jim Elliot are now believers in Christ and even church elders in that tribe!)

Agree together as a family (or as a class) for specific needs. Many people pray such vague prayers that they would never even know if God answered them. For example, instead of praying "God bless all the missionaries . . ." you could pray "Dear Lord, we ask You to provide all the finances needed for Mr. and Mrs. Smith and their family in Peru so they will be able to buy that sound system they need. Speak to people's hearts to give to their ministry, and help the Smiths and their mission organization to make the best choices with the money they receive."

It's exciting when you agree together for a specific request and then see the Lord answer it! Seeing specific answered prayer encourages our faith and motivates us to keep praying.

And when you pray, pray in faith. Instead of praying for things you don't even believe can happen, begin by praying for specific things you *can* believe for—and then ask God to increase your faith! At the same time, don't discourage your child if he or she has faith for something that you do not. Your child's faithful prayers may surprise you!

Q. How can I teach my child to use God's Word in prayer?

One key that will help you pray in faith and believe for answers is to find (and memorize) key Bible verses that deal with the particular circumstances about which you are praying. For example, if you are praying for your Uncle Al to receive the Lord, it would be good to find a few verses that relate to the situation, such as:

- "The Lord is . . . not willing that any should perish . . ." (2 Peter 3:9).

- "Believe on the Lord Jesus Christ, and you will be saved, you and your household" (Acts 16:31).

With these verses, your faith in God can be strengthened and you can believe what you are praying when you say:

"Heavenly Father, Your word says that You don't want Uncle Al to perish. We know that You love him—even more than we do! Your Son even died for Uncle Al so that he could be saved! We ask You to open his eyes to see the truth of the gospel. Let him see how much he needs You. Send someone to witness to him today! You have saved us, Lord, and we ask that all of our household would be saved too, especially Uncle Al. In the name of Jesus, Amen."

TEACHING OPPORTUNITY

The Lord's Prayer—As a Child's Seven-Step Prayer Guide

Teach your child to pray effectively by using the Lord's Prayer as an outline.

1. Our Father who art in heaven:

   Thank God that you are His child and that He is your perfect Father!

2. Hallowed be Thy name:

Speak out different names or descriptions of God for every letter of the alphabet. Worship God as you think about how He is awesome! Almighty! Abba, Father! Beautiful! Benevolent! Burden-bearer! Creator! Christ! Comforter!

3. Thy kingdom come, Thy will be done on earth, as it is in heaven:

Pray for God's perfect will to be done in your life—for yourself, your family, your school, your church, your city, your state, your country, and for all the leaders in authority over you. Pray for the world: for missions, the poor, unreached people, specific countries, current news, and your missionaries.

4. Give us this day our daily bread:

Ask God for everything you need and for everything your family needs, including an increased "hunger" for God's Word!

5. And forgive us our trespasses (sins), as we forgive those who trespass (sin) against us:

Spend time being quiet before God. Ask Him to show you if you are doing anything that doesn't please Him, and then ask God to forgive you. Be willing to change. Forgive anyone who has sinned against you or hurt your feelings.

6. And lead us not into temptation, but deliver us from evil:

Ask God to help you stay away from sin and bad things. Pray for God to protect you and to keep you safe in Jesus.

7. For Thine is the kingdom and the power and the glory forever:

End with a time of praise. Commit to live for God and His kingdom for the rest of the day—and for the rest of your life.

Q. Are there tools to help train my child in prayer?

Children don't need expensive prayer books or special journals in order to pray; they only need a desire for God. (And if your child doesn't have that, you can ask God to give him or her that desire!) However, just as you might buy a soccer ball and uniform to encourage physical development or reading books to encourage mental development, you could organize some prayer tools to encourage your child's spiritual development.

TEACHING OPPORTUNITY

Establish a Child's Personal Prayer Spot

You may want to set up a corner of your child's bedroom (or your school or church classroom) as a "prayer spot." This could be a comfortable, welcoming place or perhaps a quiet, hidden place.

The following list of "Quiet Time Accessories" may help you to encourage your child in his or her prayer time.

Quiet Time Accessories:

- Personal Bible (that your child can write in)

- Bible-reading chart

- Prayer-time chart

- Bible promise book

- Prayer journal or prayer diary

- World map on the wall

- Child's book about praying for the world (such as *Window on the World*)

- Posters (such as the fruit of the Spirit, the armor of God, the Ten Commandments, or favorite Bible verses)

- Pictures (of friends, relatives, missionaries, people, etc.)

- Comfortable chair or beanbag

- Little table (or box)

- Audios for Bible verses or worship songs

- Timer (to set prayer time goals)

A Highly Recommended Prayer Resource:

Window on the World, is an Operation World kid's prayer resource. It's like a "ticket to travel around the world" and is an outstanding prayer resource for Christian parents and teachers and highly recommended for every mission-minded child. Filled with stunning full-color glossy photographs, this A to Z overview of one hundred countries and people groups provides an exciting learning experience with many specific ideas to help your child pray for hundreds of prayer needs from all around the world. As a beautiful yet practical hardcover book, *Window on the World* is an excellent resource and my number one choice to help children pray effectively for international needs. (Please refer to the "Recommended Resources" for other great mission-minded prayer tools.)

Q. How can I encourage my child to write in a prayer journal or prayer diary?

A prayer journal is simply a blank notebook used to write thoughts and prayers to the Lord. It provides a context for being open and honest about what the Lord is doing in your life and to express what you are going through. A child can write specific prayers to the Lord or make a list of things to be thankful for.

Some children will enjoy this, and it will become a part of their prayer life. For others, however, it just won't work—and it doesn't have to. My husband is not a "journal person" at all, yet I admire his prayer life more than anyone's. He loves to simply walk outside and pray for hours every day, letting the Lord direct his prayers. We need to encourage our children to pray in a way that works for them.

A prayer journal does not have to be written in every day. You can encourage your child to use a percentage of regular "writing" time (perhaps once or twice a week) to encourage this discipline. But it is important to remember that these journals are for the writer and the Lord only. Personal prayer entries should not be evaluated for correct spelling, grammar, and writing techniques, or even critiqued for proper thinking. Instead, realize this is an opportunity for a child to write simply for personal enjoyment and spiritual growth.

A prayer diary is a tool for keeping a record of day-to-day time in prayer, similar to a daily planner. If you decide to buy a prayer diary, one of the best available is YWAM's *Personal Prayer Diary and Daily Planner*. Along with maps, pictures, a Bible-reading guide, and a daily guide for praying for the world, this resource also includes a weekly calendar and daily schedule organizer with spaces to write down specific daily requests and praise reports. YWAM also has a special diary/journal designed for young people and children entitled *Walking with God*. Both of these prayer tools are highly recommended.

It is very important to teach your child to be flexible and sensitive to the Holy Spirit as you pray each day. It is good to have a plan but even better to be open to God's plans.

When you become aware of a specific prayer request, your child can . . .

- pray about the need right away.

- save the request for dinner or bedtime prayers or a later quiet time.

- write the need in a prayer journal.

- continue praying about the need as God brings it to mind.

When you become aware of a specific answer to prayer, your child can . . .

- say "Thank you, Lord!"

- spend part of his or her quiet time praising God for His faithfulness.

- write the answer in a prayer journal.

- share the great report with others, including both Christians and non-Christians.

Wonderful Memories of Family Prayer Time

All throughout my childhood, my family gathered together before bedtime for a time of family prayers. My parents were amazingly consistent; it didn't matter if we had company with us or even if we were staying somewhere else with friends or relatives. Every evening—the only exception being if we didn't get home until late because of going to a church service—our family came together to pray. Just as some parents yell, "Come and eat!" our family was known throughout the neighborhood for our typical evening call: "Hey kids! It's prayer time!"

This family devotion time was never complicated. My mom usually led us in singing a simple song or two, my dad would read aloud a chapter or two in the Bible, we would go around the room and each of us would thank God for something or pray for specific needs, and then we ended by quoting the Lord's Prayer together. It was our regular evening practice, and it's a heritage of prayer that I've always been thankful for!

TEACHING OPPORTUNITY

Ten Prayer Projects for Your Child

1. Have your child start a prayer journal or prayer diary. For three days, encourage your child to begin writing notes and comments to God for about fifteen minutes a day.

2. Put up a world map in a prominent place and use this as a reminder to encourage your child to pray for other countries and people.

3. Have your child make a photo prayer-collage on a bulletin board, poster board, or in a mini-album. (This doesn't have to be hard. My eight-year-old son, Mark, simply uses push pins to tack photos of various prayer needs around his bed. These pictures remind him, as he drifts off to sleep, to pray for African orphan children, specific missionary friends, and special relatives.)

4. Page through a current newspaper with your child. Find an international need, locate the place on a world map, and then pray together.

5. Make a poster using the Lord's Prayer as a seven-step prayer guide. Draw a large staircase and write each area of prayer on a separate level; then pray through the Lord's Prayer with your child.

6. On the left side of a bulletin board write *Prayer Needs*, and on the right side write *Praise Reports!* Have a stack of 3 x 5 cards for your child to begin writing down specific requests. Pin the cards to the *Prayer Needs* side until they are answered; then have your child write *Answered!* in big red letters across the

card, move it to the *Praise Reports!* side of the bulletin board, and thank God together for His faithfulness.

7. Have your child cut up old magazines to make a poster entitled "Blessed to Be a Blessing!" On one side glue magazine pictures of things to be thankful for (food, clothes, appliances, toys, homes, etc.). On the other side glue pictures of international people in need (gathered from world relief magazines or magazines like *National Geographic* or printed off of mission-oriented websites). Use the poster to encourage your child to thank God for His blessings and to seek Him for how to use these blessings to help others.

8. Make a copy of a one-page world map and then cut it into continental sections. Fold the pieces and place them in a bowl. Have your child select one of the pieces of paper each day and pray for that particular continent. In seven days your child will pray for every continent!

9. Get a stack of *National Geographic* or missionary magazines and have your child cut out faces of people from all over the world. Put these in a box. Have your child pull out a picture and use it as a starting point for prayer—not necessarily for the particular person in the photo, but for general world needs that come to mind (such as the needs of African orphans, or poor mothers in India, or people who worship idols and need to hear the gospel).

10. Organize a special "Prayer Spot" for your child (in a closet, a corner of a room, or some other special place). Put up a world map and photos of people groups to pray for; and have some prayer tools nearby, such as a Bible, missions books, and a prayer journal.

🌐 TEACHING OPPORTUNITY

Prayer Ideas for Your Location and Leaders

As you train your child to pray for other nations of the world, encourage your child to also pray for your own country and your own leaders. As you learn your country's history, learn about the spiritual history (what God has done) in your nation. Find the names of your national and local leaders who are in positions of authority (including teachers, coaches, music instructors, pastors, and children's ministers), and encourage your child to remember to pray for these people.

Our children have also participated in and helped to organize several local open-air meetings (at critical times of need) to pray for local, national, and international leaders—along with publicly proclaiming God's Good News. A mission-minded child is always on the lookout for creative ways to share the gospel!

CHAPTER 9

Missions and Money

"For where your treasure is, there your heart will be also."
—Jesus Christ (Matthew 6:21)

In our family's ministry office, a carved wooden bowl displays simple coins from all around the world. Most of the pieces are dull and worn, while some are new and shiny. Our children often enjoy fingering the various francs from France, pulas from Botswana, and euros from Europe, to mention just a few. My favorite is an intricate gold-and-silver-colored piece from Italy, although, as with most of these coins, I have no idea of its worth. Some of the coins are no longer in circulation; some of the countries they're from no longer exist. All are simply extra pocket change left over from years of past mission trips, each saved as little souvenirs and little reminders that money is only a temporary "little thing." Each coin is (or was) valuable only because some government somewhere determined it would have value.

But money is also a "big thing"—and we can't underestimate the importance of training our children to have a godly perspective toward money and financial stewardship. Our money represents our life: our time, our talents, our education and experiences, and our priorities. In fact, if we really want to find out what is important to us, we can simply look back through our checkbooks and credit card statements over the past few months. Our true priorities are right there in black and white (or red!); and the numbers don't lie.

It's really very simple. If we have a heart for the Lord and for the lost, we will give our resources to glorify Him and to help spread His gospel; and if our children are raised with this perspective, it will affect their bottom-line attitude toward the purpose of money. As mission-minded Christians, we need to come to the realization that our resources are not really "ours" anyway. Both parents and children need to acknowledge regularly that *everything* we have ultimately belongs to God: our life is God's, our home (or bedroom) is God's, our car (or bicycle, or special toy) is God's, our money is God's. We're all simply stewards of God's "stuff."

"I'm not called to go; I'm called to give."

You may have heard this common statement in regard to missions: "Some are called to go, but others are called to pray or to give." I believe this is true—and that *all* of us as Christians are *equally* called to do our unique part in helping to fulfill the Great Commission. Whether we're called to go or to pray or to give, the level of commitment to God's purposes should be the same for all of us; and this is a vital principle to instill in the next generation.

As we train our children, we need to emphasize that God has blessed each of us for a bigger purpose than merely to satisfy our own wants and desires. Like Abraham, God has blessed us to establish His covenant on the earth. If *your* part (or your child's part) in helping to fulfill His Great Commission is to support world missions financially, then you need to trust God to meet your needs, and you need to begin to expand your desire to help others.

If you or your child is called to be a "giver," then begin to think (and dream) about what your money and future financial resources could do for God. Instead of browsing through department stores, catalogs, and eBay, be on the lookout for projects and people that God may want you to support. Of course, we must provide for our personal needs and prepare for our future, but as stewards of God's Great Commission we must be willing to abandon our dreams for God's dream!

One Child and a Few Coins Make a Big Difference

One young boy named Ethan heard of a mission project to sponsor a little Ugandan orphan boy at our ministry's new orphanage. Although he was only eight years old, Ethan wanted to sponsor this child personally; and with his mother's permission, he made the commitment. Right away Ethan began collecting coins from all around his house. He started asking his friends at church if they could donate spare change to help an orphan. And he set up a simple lemonade and cookie stand in a parking lot near his house. With homemade signs covered with marking-pen exclamation points and a photo of his new African friend, Ethan soon raised over six months of full orphan support—all on his own initiative.

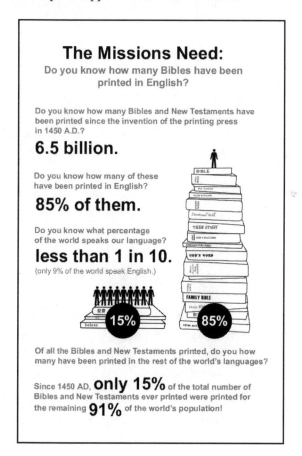

The Missions Need:

Do you know how many Bibles have been printed in English?

Do you know how many Bibles and New Testaments have been printed since the invention of the printing press in 1450 A.D.?

6.5 billion.

Do you know how many of these have been printed in English?

85% of them.

Do you know what percentage of the world speaks our language?

less than 1 in 10.

(only 9% of the world speak English.)

15%   85%

Of all the Bibles and New Testaments printed, do you how many have been printed in the rest of the world's languages?

Since 1450 AD, **only 15%** of the total number of Bibles and New Testaments ever printed were printed for the remaining **91%** of the world's population!

As he presented his first donation, this young boy was so excited to make a big difference in the life of an African orphan. His family and friends were inspired by his generosity, and many other people (including both adults and children) were so challenged by his testimony that they wanted to step out in a greater way to do something for others.

── 👫 FROM OUR CHILDREN'S PERSPECTIVE

"KIDS CAN RAISE MONEY FOR MISSIONS!"
By Daniel Dunagan, age eleven

Even kids can raise money for missions, especially if we join together with a specific goal! Over the years, I've seen plenty of ways that kids can earn money for missions, and it can be fun.

Sometimes our children's church has put up a "thermometer" poster with a certain missions goal, and when we've gotten to the top, we've celebrated with an ice cream or pizza party. Once our class bought a stove for an overseas family, and another time we bought puppets for missionaries in Japan. For me, it seems to help when there's a picture of what we're working toward, because then I can "see" where my money is going. We raised money to buy stuffed animals for an orphanage, we bought gospel booklets for missionary kids to distribute, and two times our children's class bought bikes to help national ministers in India.

One time when I was at church, I heard about some kids in Africa who were really poor. One story in particular really touched me. I heard about this little kid who had only an old sweatshirt—no shorts, not even any underwear—and the kid was about my age! I heard that anytime a person would come around him, this kid would pull his old sweatshirt down because he was so embarrassed.

The whole next week, I was constantly thinking about this kid. I thought about how horrible it would be to be so poor. I just couldn't get it out of my head.

The Missions Need:
Do you know how the Christian Church
spends every dollar?

96.8 cents
of each dollar
is spent on the 2 billion people
who call themselves Christians.
(Christians spending money on themselves)

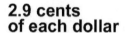

2.9 cents
of each dollar
is spent in those who have
heard and rejected Christ.

only .3 cents
of each dollar
(only one-third of a penny) is spent to
reach the 1.6 billion people throughout the
world who have NEVER heard or had a
chance to respond to Jesus Christ.

Then one night, I thought about it so much, I started crying. I realized that a couple U.S. dollars could buy me some candy or a toy, but for the same amount of money, I could buy a new outfit for that one poor kid.

That night in my room, I decided to do as much as I could. I had some money that I had been saving to open a bank account and to get some things I wanted. But right then, I determined to help as many kids as possible. Only my mom knew about it at the time, but she asked me to share about it so maybe others would be encouraged to give. I do know that the next Sunday, when I slipped my entire savings into the missions offering, all I could think about was how good I felt inside. Altogether our kids' class clothed an entire African village, and I knew that I had had a part!

🎙 TEACHING OPPORTUNITY

Mission-Minded Memory, Oratorical Practice, or Reading Aloud ("My Choice" Poem)

Note: Before reading this simple poem, discuss with your child the blessings of your lives and how we need to surrender all of our blessings to God. This poem was written by a young man named Bill McChesney as he thought about his "rights" and "choices" and then surrendered everything to the Lord. Afterward, he went to Africa and served the Lord for several years as a missionary in the Congo. During a military uprising in that country in 1964, Bill McChesney was tragically killed at the age of only twenty-eight. But this young man had already "given his life" long before that particular day; his choice for all eternity was total obedience to the Lord Jesus Christ.

MY CHOICE

By Bill McChesney

I want my breakfast served at "Eight,"
With ham and eggs upon the plate;
A well-broiled steak I'll eat at "One,"
And dine again when day is done.

I want an ultramodern home,
And in each room a telephone;
Soft carpets, too, upon the floors,
And pretty drapes to grace the doors.

A cozy place of lovely things
Like easy chairs with innersprings.
And then I'll get a small TV—
Of course, "I'm careful what I see."

I want my wardrobe, too, to be,
Of neatest, finest quality,
With latest style in suit and vest,
Why shouldn't Christians have the best?

But then the Master I can hear,
In no uncertain voice, so clear,
"I bid you come and follow Me,
The Lowly Man of Galilee.

Birds of the air have made their nest,
And foxes in their holes find rest;
But I can offer you no bed;
No place have I to lay my head."

In shame I hung my head and cried,
How could I spurn the Crucified?
Could I forget the way He went,
The sleepless nights in prayer He spent?

For forty days without a bite,
Alone He fasted day and night;
Despised, rejected—on He went,
And did not stop 'till veil He rent.

A Man of sorrows and of grief—
"Smitten of God," the prophet said—
Mocked, beaten, bruised,
His blood ran red.

If He be God and died for me,
No sacrifice too great can be
For me, a mortal man, to make;
I'll do it all for Jesus' sake.

Yes, I will tread the path He trod,
No other way will please my God;
So henceforth this my choice shall be,
My choice for all eternity.

TEACHING OPPORTUNITY

Fifteen Ideas to Raise Money for Missions

1. Have your child decorate a special container, perhaps with a photo, and begin saving coins for a specific mission project.

2. For special missions offerings in children's church or a Sunday school class, use attention-grabbing collection plates such as empty coconut shells or African-looking baskets.

3. If raising money for a building project, make a poster of a brick wall and have your child color in bricks (or attach paper bricks) as you advance toward your goal.

4. If raising money for Bibles, make a poster of a stack of Bibles and have your child color in Bibles (or attach paper Bibles) as you advance toward your goal. Decorate with stacks of Bibles.

5. Make a "thermometer" to chart a specific missions goal.

6. Share a fun mission-minded fundraising idea with a leader from your church. One idea is to have a coin-collecting race between your church's youth group and children's department. Both groups could use the same designated coin, or the youth could collect one type of coin (for example, nickels) and the children could collect another type of coin (for example, dimes)—with the idea of seeing which department can raise more money.

7. Help your child collect aluminum cans for recycling, or encourage other families (or children in your church) to canvas their neighborhood and collect cans for a specific mission project.

8. Have your child collect coins and tape them to a long streamer. This idea could also be used in a class, with two groups (perhaps boys vs. girls) competing to see who can reach a predetermined streamer distance first.

9. Your child could find a specific mission project to support, collecting coins from other families as he or she shares this need.

10. Have a family yard sale with all proceeds going for missions, and have your child help with the details.

11. Work with your child to organize a children's bazaar, with handmade arts and crafts, or baked goods, and give all the proceeds to missions.

12. Work with your child to plan a neighborhood missions carnival, with fun booths, popcorn, pop, and candy—with all proceeds going to missions.

13. Your child could offer to do work for family or friends (such as housecleaning, laundry, or yard work) in exchange for people donating toward a specific mission project. A variation of this idea is to have a church "slave auction," where children or youth are auctioned to the highest bidder for a set amount of hours of work, and the proceeds are given to missions.

14. Your family could host a special missions banquet for adults or a formal event for teens and young adults, and donate all the proceeds to missions.

15. Have a "multiply your talents" project. Give your child a certain amount of money with the mission-minded purpose of using this money, along with his or her talents, abilities, and creativity, for a specified length of time (perhaps two weeks or one month) to raise money for a specific mission project. Your child could use the money to buy gas for a lawn mower, to buy lemonade to sell on the corner, or to buy ingredients for a neighborhood bake sale. At the end of the designated time have your child return the original money, along with the surplus he or she raised, and give it toward the mission project.

CHAPTER **10**

World Missions and Your Local Church

"The mission of the church is missions."
—David Livingstone

Is "world missions" *your* church's mission? This was Livingstone's proclamation; yet in far too many of today's congregations, it's too far from true. Take a moment to consider with your child the emphasis on local and foreign missions in your home church:

- How often is God's love for the world emphasized?

- What are the names of the different missionaries your church supports, where do they live, and what is each missionary's particular ministry focus?

- Is your congregation regularly encouraged and challenged to share the gospel?

- Does your church's Sunday school or children's church program emphasize the needs of the world?

Regardless of your current situation, perhaps God has placed you and your child as His mission-minded ambassadors in your local church. Just as Esther stepped forward to help save her people in the foreign land of Persia, you may be called to impact your congregation "for such a time as this." As you encourage your local church to support missions more effectively, you could have a vital role in the gospel reaching many unsaved people.

Q. How can we encourage missions in our local church?

Here are ten practical ideas for you and your child to promote an increased heart for the nations in your local church: help create a mission-minded atmosphere; start a prayer group; support your missionaries; encourage your pastor to go on a missions trip; promote world missions in every department; help your children's department to focus on world needs; purchase mission books; encourage your church to sponsor an adoption project; participate in a church-sponsored missionary outreach.

• Idea #1—Help create a mission-minded atmosphere

When newcomers enter your church building (or your church children's department), can they visually "see" a heart-emphasis toward missions? In some church sanctuaries, international flags reflect a worldwide vision. In some church lobbies, missionary maps and newsletters encourage people to pray. In some church lobbies, maps showing where missionaries are located and newsletters from those missionaries encourage people to pray. In some church hallways, missions souvenirs fill display cases and hint of awaiting adventure.

Years ago I was impacted by my first visit to a wonderful mission-minded church. A giant world map covered the entire lobby wall, a row of clocks displayed current time zones from around the world, and below each clock hung an exciting missionary picture. The preaching (and written literature) was also focused on world missions, but it was the large wall display that left the long-term impression. The mission of that church was obvious, and the atmosphere reinforced it.

🌐 TEACHING OPPORTUNITY

Mission-Minded Church Decorating Ideas

You and your child could help decorate a wall at your church, a Sunday school bulletin board, or a special table with a mission-minded focus. You could also present a particular mission-atmosphere idea to your pastor or children's administrator. One idea would be to ask if your church or children's department would be interested in displaying international flags (either small or large) to represent each country where your church's missionaries serve. You and your child could help to raise the funds for this project.

• Idea #2—Start a mission-minded prayer group (for children or families)

Does your church pray for the world? Some churches set aside regular prayer services for world missions (perhaps weekly or monthly). Other congregations have daily corporate prayer times to intercede for both the needs of the local church and foreign missionaries.

Even a small weekly or monthly home prayer meeting (or a church cell group) with a mission-minded emphasis can make a tremendous impact on your church, your missionaries, and the world. And it doesn't have to be difficult!

TEACHING OPPORTUNITY

Fifteen Steps to a Great Mission-Minded Prayer Meeting

1. Invite people.

2. Make sure your house, or meeting location, is clean.

3. As people arrive, greet them with a smile.

4. Offer something to drink, such as water, juice, coffee, or tea.

5. Gather together and open your meeting with a prayer.

6. Worship God by singing a few songs or reading a psalm.

7. Take turns reading and discussing a few Bible verses about missions and reaching the lost. (See chapter 4 for specific ideas.)

8. Read an encouraging missions motto or short missions quote.

9. Highlight a famous missions hero and/or one current missionary.

10. Present an international news update. Use *Window on the World*, *Operation World*, highlights from the World Prayer Team (www.worldprayerteam.org), recent missionary newsletters, or current international news from a newspaper or an online news source. You could perhaps have the group watch a brief online video news segment on a laptop computer as a focal point for prayer.

11. Spend most of your time praying specifically (and fervently) for international needs and missionary prayer requests.

12. Share any announcements (perhaps about a current mission project).

13. Stand in a circle and close with prayer.

14. End with a time of fellowship, perhaps with a simple international snack.

15. Thank everyone for coming, and say goodbye at the door.

Note: To help facilitate this meeting, assign specific responsibilities to different people—a greeter, a worship leader, a person to share a missions motto and a missionary highlight, a person to read the Bible verses, someone to share an international news update, several prayer leaders, someone to announce upcoming mission projects, and someone to prepare the snacks.

🌐 TEACHING OPPORTUNITY

Fifteen Projects for Your Mission-Minded Prayer Group

1. Have a fundraiser for a specific mission project.
2. Have a car wash for one of your missionaries.
3. Have a multi-family garage sale for missions.
4. Gather items for a missionary care package.
5. Put together a special gift for MKs (missionary kids).
6. Put together gift packets for an orphanage.
7. "Adopt" a child or an unreached people group.
8. Sign a card to give to one of your missionaries.
9. Make a welcome basket for a visiting missionary.
10. Have a birthday party for missionary kids (at any time!).
11. Have a missionary share with your group.
12. Hold an international potluck or try a particular foreign food.
13. Share about Jesus with someone in your neighborhood.
14. Do something nice for a foreign exchange student.
15. Reach out to a local international family.

- **Idea #3—Encourage your church's missionaries**

You would be amazed at what a big difference a little bit of encouragement can make. Missionaries need much more than financial support; they need prayer, they need encouragement, and (like all of us!) they need friends. There are unlimited ways that you and your child can encourage your church's missionaries. Here are a few ideas to get you started.

TEACHING OPPORTUNITY

Fifteen Ways to Encourage Your Church's Missionaries

1. Learn the names of your missionaries and their children.

2. Read the newsletters they send to your church.

3. If they have an e-mail newsletter, sign up to receive them.

4. Pray specifically for their needs.

5. Send an encouraging e-mail to their family.

6. Write an old-fashioned letter or send a fun card.

7. Put together a personal gift package for their family—for Christmas, or for no particular reason.

8. Share their news with other people in your church.

9. Put their family photo on your refrigerator.

10. Greet them and invite them to lunch when they visit.

11. Stay tuned to international news that affects them.

12. Send a quick e-mail just to say "Hi!"

13. Pray specifically for their children.

14. Have your child send encouraging e-mails to a missionary kid.

15. Be their friend.

• Idea #4—Encourage your senior pastor to take a mission trip

Mission-minded pastors will typically schedule regular short-term mission outreaches for themselves and others in the congregation. Even a one to two week trip (possibly only missing one Sunday) to a foreign location can help realign your church's mission priority, refresh your pastor's local and international vision, and renew your pastor's perspective for ministry among the people in your congregation.

At one time our senior pastor needed a time of rest and decided to take a ten-month mission trip/sabbatical to the Philippines. During that season, my husband (a missionary evangelist) served as our church's interim pastor while continuing to lead several short-term mission outreaches. Despite our pastor's absence, or perhaps *because* of our pastor's strong missions emphasis, the congregation did not suffer, but continued to grow.

• Idea #5—Encourage a vision for missions in every department

In a truly mission-minded church, "world missions" is not a separate department but a foundation in every area. You and your child can encourage this focus. Whenever a short-term mission team comes or goes, be available for encouragement, prayer, or financial support. If anyone from your church feels called to mission work, show interest as this person seeks God's will and invest time to nurture what God is doing in his or her heart.

As you are involved in a particular ministry (men's, women's, youth, children, Bible studies, home groups, etc.), allow your missions perspective to "flavor" that ministry. A Bible study could include a discussion about how to more actively fulfill God's Great Commission; a membership class could include information about your church's missions focus; free time at a church retreat could be used to share about an international passion.

If you meet a high school or college student searching for life purpose, present a few adventurous ideas or give a challenge to research a specific mission organization. With a little encouragement, youth can instill an infectious zeal for missions into a congregation. Youth can lead missions fundraisers, have their own prayer services for the nations, or go on short-term outreaches.

TEACHING OPPORTUNITY

Mission-Minded Scholarship Contest

Organize or sponsor an annual "mission-minded scholarship contest" for your church's high school and college-age students. Have students participate by presenting a short speech on a particular missions topic, designing a missions recruiting poster, or performing a special music and/or dramatic presentation. Require an application, several recommendations, and a personal interview to evaluate necessary spiritual maturity. The prize is an all-expense-paid mission trip to visit one of your church's missionaries (to give the church a current report) or to join an outreach with an approved youth organization. This would be something that your child could look forward to as he or she gets older.

•   Idea #6—Encourage a mission-minded children's ministry

World missions can be a major theme in your children's church and/or Sunday school program. Children can support their own missionaries and raise money for their own significant mission projects. (Our church just finished a children's project to clothe one hundred African children in a remote Ugandan village.) You could decorate your classroom walls with maps and missions photos and make an "international post-office box" to collect letters for your church's missionaries.

Children can enjoy listening to stories of famous missionaries from the past and exciting stories about missionaries today. Along with challenges to accept Christ, there can also be prayer times, as the Lord leads, for children to dedicate their lives totally to God's perfect will—whatever that may be. As some of your church families begin to travel overseas (which is quite common among mission-minded churches), encourage children from your congregation to give testimonies from firsthand mission experiences.

•   Idea #7—Purchase missions books for your church

Does your church library (and/or bookstore) include a great collection of mission-minded books? If not, perhaps you could obtain permission to start adding a few new missions books each month.

Include famous missionary biographies, teaching books, practical missionary resources, and motivational missions stories for each major age group. This simple idea could encourage and influence many people in your congregation, both now and for years to come.

- **Idea #8—As your church raises missions funds, raise missions passion**

Most churches have specific times for raising money for missions. As these opportunities arise, use your enthusiasm to talk positively about the opportunity. Even more vital than raising missions funds is raising missions enthusiasm and instilling excitement about expanding God's kingdom.

One of the best ways I have seen for a church to instill a passion for missions is to regularly send lay people from the congregation overseas. In our home church, half of our regular missions commitment supports full-time missionaries and the other half goes into a fund to send members of our own congregation on mission trips.

Before a trip, team members will want to share their vision for missions and their heart for the people who don't yet know Jesus. During the outreach, the congregation will naturally want to pray for them. And following the outreach, these new church-member-missionaries (while still "contagious" with a missionary fever!) will want to share their exciting reports. As a result, others will get inspired about missions, will want to support world missions, and will be encouraged to go on the next mission outreach.

- **Idea #9—Encourage your church to sponsor an "adoption"**

Your church could *adopt an unreached people group* as their own. The congregation could take personal responsibility to learn about this particular people group, pray specifically for them, raise money for projects and missionary translation work geared toward them, and organize short-term mission trips to learn about their needs. Perhaps someone from your congregation will be called to become a long-term missionary to these people.

A local church could *adopt a "sister city" or a "sister church"* across the world. Just after the collapse of the former Soviet Union, a large church I knew of spent an entire year evangelizing the city of St. Petersburg, Russia. This local congregation took personal responsibility to reach the people in "their" sister city. They worked to establish a new sister church in that city, and for an entire year the church sent short-term outreach teams every month.

Perhaps your church could *adopt an overseas children's orphanage.* Families could be encouraged to "adopt" a specific orphan or an orphanage house through prayer and designated support. Your church could have specific projects to send supplies or to build an orphanage building, and ongoing support could help feed and clothe the children and allow them to hear the gospel.

— 👫 FROM OUR CHILDREN'S PERSPECTIVE

"WE'VE GOT FRIENDS AROUND THE WORLD!"
By Mark Dunagan, age ten;
Caela Rose Dunagan, age eight; and Philip Dunagan, age five

It's exciting to have friends from around the world! Kids in our family and many friends from our local children's church are now "kid's-prayer-partners" with boys and girls from our ministry's orphanage in Africa. We pray for each other, we have our friends' pictures hanging by our beds, and we even send special gifts and letters back and forth. Having a heart for missions is great—it's simply having fun with new friends from around the world, and helping other people . . . who are a lot like us!

• Idea #10—Participate in a short-term outreach from your church

Perhaps you (or another member of your congregation) could recruit a team of youth, children, adults, or families to go on a group mission outreach. This team could visit and assist one of your church's missionaries or join together with an established mission organization. Lives (both within your congregation and overseas) will likely be changed forever as individuals see the need for missions firsthand.

Sometimes it is falsely assumed that directing extra missions funds to "inexperienced lay people" will only deplete the church's regular missionary support. In actuality, the opposite usually takes place. God's missions funds are not limited. As new short-term missionaries launch out— with their friends and family members supporting missions and praying for missions like never before—a church's heart for missions will multiply.

🌐 TEACHING OPPORTUNITY

Explore Mission Trip Possibilities

Research mission opportunities with your child. Look up different opportunities for short-term mission outreaches that allow children to participate.

— 👫 FROM OUR CHILDREN'S PERSPECTIVE

"A HEART FOR HELPING ORPHANS"

By Christi Dunagan, age fifteen

Eight-year-old Jennifer huddled in the dark corner of her grandmother's hut. Once again, she was locked in this repulsive room with no food and no hope. Sometimes she was left alone for days while her grandmother wasted what little money they had. Most likely, the old woman would return home—drunk—and beat the girl until she could barely stand.

Jennifer knew nothing of happiness. When she was very young, her parents were victims of Uganda's number one killer: AIDS; and now, she was yet another victim: of poverty, hunger, and abuse.

Hearing footsteps outside her door, Jennifer looked up hopefully. Maybe she would finally be released from this small damp prison she was forced to call home . . . but no. She cringed as the footsteps drew nearer and she recognized them, not as those of her grandmother but as the sound of one of her uncles. Again one was coming. Too often they came to use little Jennifer to satisfy their physical pleasures. When they had enough of her, they left her once again hurt and crying on the mud floor. The latch creaked and Jennifer prepared herself for yet another night of agony and heartache.

She knew she could not last much longer. . . .

* * *

Somehow, the frightened girl escaped and began wandering her village streets. With nowhere to go, Jennifer leaned against the closest building she could find . . . and wept.

A hand touched her shoulder, startling her; but as she looked up, the girl stared into the face of a kind woman. It was Alice, a longtime friend of my family and the local director of an AIDS orphanage that my parents helped establish ten years ago in Mbarara, Uganda.

Along with hundreds of other orphans, this child finally has a home. People are now feeding her, ministering to her hurts, and loving her. Slowly she is learning life is not just pain and horror, and she is discovering joy. Slowly her emotional wounds are healing. Finally Jennifer is becoming the girl she was born to be.

* * *

Recently I had the incredible experience of traveling to Uganda along with my mother and a precious elderly minister. There I met Jennifer and many orphans just like her—and it made an incredible impact on my life. Beginning on that trip, my mom and I have been establishing a brand-new orphanage primarily for AIDS victims. There are many details—organizing orphan photos, recruiting sponsors, doing computer work—but it's worth it. I want to help rescue as many hurting children as I can.

During my journey, I traveled by a rugged dugout canoe to a remote island. There the poverty was so great, and many children were left as orphans due to the trauma of war and AIDS. My mom and I decided we couldn't just sit back. Thousands of children were dying from malnutrition and neglect. We knew we had to do something.

As I walked through the narrow village streets, the air reeked of fish, body odor, and garbage. Little children flocked around me, holding my hands, touching my hair, and gazing deeply into my eyes. As they longed for some sort of love and affection, I wished I could just "wrap them up," hide them in my suitcase, and take them all home.

But obviously that wasn't possible.

Yet since our return home, my mom and I have been working with some Ugandan nationals to build an orphanage on that island for as many children as possible. Our desire is for these orphan children to grow up in an environment where they will be loved and wanted, to provide a happy place where hurting children can receive quality care, nutrition, and education.

Right now our new orphanage is small, but we have a big vision. We started with thirty orphans in a few existing huts and quickly expanded to seventy-five orphans (whom we've just found sponsors for) in eight new orphanage houses; but our goal is to reach many more children. My mom and I know we will never be able to help every orphan in Uganda, but we're doing what we can, and we won't give up.

For these seventy-five children, it is finally an "Oh Sunny Day." No longer will they roam the streets, beg for meals, or sleep "wherever." These little ones will be safe and cared for.

And with smiles on their faces—just like Jennifer now has—these orphans will finally have a chance to become the children they were born to be.

(NOTE: In the first year, Harvest Ministry's orphan ministry grew to support 160 children in 16 homes. By 2020, "Loving Orphans" had expanded to care for over 1200 orphan children in Africa and Asia. See HarvestMinistry.org for current details of this mission outreach.)

**"Pure and undefiled religion before God and the Father
is this: to visit widows and orphans in their troubles,
and to keep oneself unspotted from the world."**

James 1:27

Ugandan Flag

CHAPTER 11

Making Missions Fun— At Home, School, and Church

Sometimes changing those "big things" in our lives—altering our core attitudes and priorities for education and abandoning our rights—can start with a few "little things" in practical areas of our lives. If we want to begin making a change—to give a greater priority to the Lord and His heart for the world—it can help to keep these goals before us: on our walls, on our calendars, and on our lips (what we say and even what we eat!).

Decorate with a Heart for Missions!

Giving your home (or classroom) a missions focus can begin by simply displaying a world map in a prominent place, putting an atlas or an inspiring missions book on your coffee table, or decorating a mission-minded bulletin board.

In our home, we want our family's passion for world missions to be unmistakable to everyone who visits us. An entire wall of our family room is covered by a huge world map (it's actually wallpaper), and our ministry office/guest room is decorated completely African-style: with leopard-style carpet and bedding, our own souvenirs from Uganda, Rwanda, and Congo, and many exciting missionary photos. The emphasis is constantly before our children (and us); and when guests come to visit, these focal points are often conversation starters to help inspire others to increase their heart for world missions.

It's a scriptural principle: If we want God's Word to be established in our children's hearts, we should constantly keep it in front of our children's eyes and ears. As God inspired Moses to exhort His people Israel, "These words which I command you today shall be in your heart. You shall teach them diligently to your children, and shall talk of them when you sit in your house, when you walk by the way, when you lie down, and when you rise up. . . . You shall write them on the doorposts of your house and on your gates" (Deuteronomy 6:6–9).

Sing International Songs

Music is powerful! It can be used to express our praise as we glorify God, or it can be used for evil. Music can tell us so much about a culture. Songs can help us learn a foreign language, and just listening to the variety of styles can give us a "feel" for another land.

Reflecting on my various missionary experiences, I realize how the music of the people is an integral part of my memories. Africa would not be the same without tribal drums and village rhythms, and a visit to Austria is not complete without a taste of classical Mozart. Think about Jewish folk dancing, Jamaican calypso, and Asian clanging and minor chording; music is an essential and often inseparable part of culture.

As you expose your child to music, include music appreciation (including Western classical music and a variety of international music) as well as the practical study of music (including instrumental and voice instruction). Each area is important to the study of music and all can be of benefit to a mission-minded child. Music can be an important tool to help share the Good News; music can be utilized to attract people to a meeting; the message or anointing in music can soften a person's heart to respond to the gospel; and through heartfelt worship, music can draw us closer to the Lord.

# TEACHING OPPORTUNITY

Mission-Minded Music Ideas

The following songs can be used to encourage your child to have a heart for international missions. It can be fun to attempt to sing in a foreign language or to learn a new mission-minded verse to add to a familiar chorus.

- **Jesus Loves Me**

   (English)
   Jesus loves me, this I know
   For the Bible tells me so,
   Little ones to him belong,
   They are weak, but He is strong.
   Chorus:
   Yes, Jesus loves me (3x)
   The Bible tells me so.

   (Missions verse)
   Jesus loves the na-a-tions
   Every tongue and every tribe,
   And He wants to u-use you
   To reach them to be his bride.
   Yes, Jesus loves them (3x)
   The Bible tells me so.

   (Spanish)
   Chorus: Cristo me ama (3x)
   La Biblia dice asi.

(Spanish pronunciation)
Cree-sto may-aa-ma (3x)
La Bee-Blia dee-say aa-see.

(Swahili pronunciations)
Chorus:
Yay-soo ah-nee pen-da (3x)
Bee-blee-ah ah-nee say mah.

(French pronunciations)
Chorus:
Wee, Zhay-zuee meh-mer (3x)
La Bee-bler dee teh-se.

(Arabic pronunciations)
Chorus:
Kahd faa-kah hub-nah (3x)
Ye-hib-bu-nah Yah-so.

(Russian pronunciations)
Chorus:
Lyoo-beet Ee-ee-soos (3x)
E-to tvyer-do snah-yoo yah.

(Japanese pronunciations)
Chorus:
Wah-gah Shoo Yah-soo (3x)
Way-ray oh ah-ee-soo.

- **God Is So Good**

    (English)
    God is so good (3x)
    He's so good to me.

(Spanish)
Dios bueno es (3x)
Bueno es mi Dios.

(Spanish pronunciation)
Dee-oas boo-way-no-ace (3x)
Boo-way-no-ace me Dee-oas.

(Kitumba—Democratic Republic of Congo)
Nzambi ke mbote (3x)
Ke mbotye na mono.

(Kitumba pronunciation)
Na-zam-bee kay mm-bo-tay (3x)
Kay mm-bo-tay nah mo-no.

• **Praise Him**

(English)
Praise Him, Praise Him,
Praise Him in the morning
Praise Him in the noontime.
Praise Him, Praise Him,
Praise Him when the sun goes down.

(Luganda—Uganda)
Tumutende, Tumutende,
Tumutende nga bukende
Tumutende nga mutuntu.
Tumutende, Tumutende,
Tumutende nga buwungela.

(Luganda pronunciation)
Too-moo-ten-day, Too-moo-ten-day,
Too-moo-ten-day n-Gah boo-kan-day
Too-moo-ten-day n-Gah moo-toon-too.
Too-moo-ten-day, Too-moo-ten-day,
Too-moo-ten-day n-Gah boo-woon-gay-lah.

- ## This Is the Day

(English)
This is the day (2x)
That the Lord has made (2x)
I will rejoice (2x)
And be glad in it (2x)
This is the day that the Lord has made,
I will rejoice and be glad in it.
This is the day (2x)
That the Lord has made.

(Indonesian)
Hari ini (2x)
Hari ya Tuhan (2x)
Mari kita (2x)
Pujilah Tuhan (2x)
Hari ini hari ya Tuhan,
Mari kita pujulah Tuhan.
Hari ini (2x)
Hari ya Tuhan.

(Indonesian pronunciation)
He-ree eenie (2x)
He-ree ya too-haan (2x)
Maa-ree kee-ta (2x)
Poo-jee-laa too-haan (2x)

He-ree eenie he-ree ya too-haan,
Maa-ree kee-ta poo-jee-laa too-haan.
He-ree eenie (2x)
He-ree ya too-haan.

• The B-I-B-L-E

The B-I-B-L-E
Yes, that's the book for me!
I stand alone on the Word of God
The B-I-B-L-E.

(Missions verse)
The B-I-B-L-E
It has one story, you see,
To tell all nations of God's love
The B-I-B-L-E.

• How Great Thou Art

(English)
Then sings my soul,
My Savior, God, to thee
How great thou art,
How great thou art (all 2x).

(Hungarian pronunciations)
See-vehm feh-lahd,
Ooy-yohng er-rerm-tah-lay
Meely nady vady Tay,
Meely nady vady Tay (all 2x).

(Missions verse)
Oh, when I think
Of all the many millions
Who do not know
The sound of thy sweet name,
Who do not know
Who never can
Thy great salvation claim.

Then cries my heart,
O teach me, Lord, to care,
Until they know, how great thou art!
Then cries my heart,
O teach me, Lord, to care,
Until they know, how great thou art!

But when they know
That Jesus died to save them,
And when they know
The grace he can impart;
When Jesus shines
His love divine within them,
When he transforms
Their sinful, darkened heart:
Then they shall sing,
My Savior, God, to thee,
How great thou art,
How great thou art!

• ## Till Every Tribe Shall Hear

(To the tune of *The Battle Hymn of the Republic*)
How well we love the story
Of the blessed Son of God,

How he purchased our redemption
When up Calv'ry's hill he trod,
How he told the ones who love him
They must tell his love abroad,
Till ev-ry tribe shall hear.

(Chorus)
Go to ev-ry tribe and nation
With the message of salvation,
Haste the joyful consummation
When ev-ry tribe shall hear.

But there are many millions
Who have never heard his name,
They've no hope of life eternal,
They cannot salvation claim;
For they do not know the message
Jesus told us to proclaim,
Till ev-ry tribe shall hear.

(Repeat chorus)

The Day of God is coming
When the Church of Christ shall stand
Face to face with Christ her Savior
In the blessed glory land;
And we each shall give our answer,
"Did you hasten my command—
That ev-ry tribe should hear?"

(Repeat chorus)

• He Is the King of Kings

(English)
He is the King of kings
He is the Lord of lords
His name is JESUS, JESUS, JESUS, JESUS
O, he is the King!

Following are pronunciations for the name *Jesus* in eight languages other than English. Try simply singing this chorus in English but substituting the other languages' pronunciation of *Jesus*.

(Spanish)
Cristo
Pronunciation: Cree-sto

(Russian)
Iesus
Pronunciation: Ee-ee-soos

(Japanese)
Iesu
Pronunciation: Yah-soo

(Swahili)
Yesu
Pronunciation: Yey-soo

(Hebrew)
Yeshua
Pronunciation: Y'shua

(Arabic)
Yaso'a
Pronunciation: Yah-so

(French)
Jésus
Pronunciation: Zhay-suee

(Hindi)
Pronunciation: Yee-soo

• I Have Decided to Follow Jesus

(English)
I have decided to follow Jesus (3x)
No turning back (2x).

(Hindi pronunciations—India)
Yee-soo kay pee-chay meh chull-nay luh-guh (3x)
Nuh low-doo-gah (2x).

(Eskimo pronunciations—Alaska)
Owl-lah-nik-tuu-nga maleeng-nyah-jee-gah Jesus (3x)
Oo-tee joo-tee joo-mee-nyeyt ngah (2x).

• Our God Is an Awesome God

Our God is an awesome God,
He reigns from heaven above,
With wisdom, power and love,
Our God is an awesome God!

(Missions verse)
Our God is a faithful God,
He keeps his promises,
To reach all nations,
Our God is a faithful God!

• Jesus Loves the Little Children

Jesus loves the little children,
All the children of the world.
Red and yellow, black, and white,
They are precious in His sight.
Jesus loves the little children of the world.

(Missions verse)
Jesus loves the unreached children,
All the unreached children of the world.
Muslims, Buddhists, and Hindus,
Chinese, tribals need him too.
Jesus loves the unreached children of the world.

• Hallelu, Hallelu

(English)
Boys: Hallelu, Hallelu, Hallelu, Hallelujah!
Girls: Praise ye the Lord!
         (Repeat both parts)
Girls: Praise ye the Lord!
Boys: Hallelujah!
         (Repeat both parts 2x)
All: Praise ye the Lord!

(Spanish)
Boys: Hallelu, Hallelu, Hallelu, Hallelujah!
Girls: Gloria a Dios!
         (Repeat)
Girls: Gloria a Dios!
Boys: Hallelujah!
         (Repeat 2x)
All: Gloria a Dios!

(Spanish pronunciation)
Glow-ree-AH ah-Dee-OAS

(Russian pronunciations)
Boys: Hallelu, Hallelu, Hallelu, Hallelujah!
Girls: Ee-ee-sus, gaas-poat!
         (Repeat)
Girls: Ee-ee-sus, gaas-poat!
Boys: Hallelujah!
         (Repeat 2x)
All: Ee-ee-sus, gaas-poat!

(Chinese pronunciations)
Boys: Hallelu, Hallelu, Hallelu, Hallelujah!
Girls: Zchan me choo!
         (Repeat)
Girls: Zchan me choo!
Boys: Hallelujah!
         (Repeat 2x)
All: Zchan me choo!

(Swahili pronunciations)
Boys: Hallelu, Hallelu, Hallelu, Hallelujah!
Girls: Bwanna a see-fee-way!
         (Repeat)
Girls: Bwanna a see-fee-way!
Boys: Hallelujah!
         (Repeat 2x)
All: Bwanna a see-fee-way!

(Luganda pronunciations—Uganda)
Boys: Hallelu, Hallelu, Hallelu, Hallelujah!
Girls: Ye-su ana-kupenda!
         (Repeat)

Girls: Ye-su ana-kupenda!

Boys: Hallelujah!

(Repeat 2x)

All: Ye-su ana-kupenda!

More Mission-Minded Choruses:

- He's Got the Whole World in His Hands

- This Little Light of Mine

- I Will Make You Fishers of Men

- If You're Happy and You Know It
  (Sing: "If you're blessed to be blessing . . .")

- In My Life, Lord, Be Glorified

- I Surrender All

- Hallelujah (sung all around the world)

- Lord, I Ask for the Nations (You Said)

- Shout to the Lord

TEACHING OPPORTUNITY

Taste International Foods

A mission-minded child is not a picky eater! When Jesus sent His followers on a mission outreach, he instructed them to "eat what is set before you" (Luke 10:8 NASB). If we want to train our children to be prepared for world missions, we need to train them to eat international foods. If your child is a picky eater, I encourage you to pray about changing your child-training philosophy in this area. Our children should be able to eat simple and rather bland foods like rice and fish (without complaining) and willing to at least try spicy and unusual foods.

No matter where you live, you can enjoy the fun of discovering delicious international cuisine. Search for foreign foods in your grocery store, try cooking an adventurous new dish, or experiment with an occasional (and perhaps daring) international snack.

Experience world culture at a local restaurant!

Take your family to visit an authentic international restaurant (Chinese, Middle Eastern, Indian, French, Italian, Mexican, Polynesian, etc.), and encourage your child to survey everything about the atmosphere—not only the taste of the food but also the music, decorations, and culture. As you observe, be especially on the lookout for indications of the owner's religion.

You and your child could even go to an international restaurant with a specific plan to share about Jesus. For example, if you are going to eat at a Chinese restaurant, you could bring along the *JESUS* film in a prominent Chinese language (such as Mandarin), a Chinese Bible, or a copy of "The Four Spiritual Laws" in Chinese (printed off the Internet). Most likely you will meet a waiter, hostess, or owner who speaks Chinese. Your gift (combined with a friendly testimony, your family's good manners, a nice tip, and your prayers) could lead to his or her salvation.

International Recipe Ideas:

- Mexico/Latin America:
  Tacos, Nachos, Tortillas, Spanish Rice

- Native America:
  Corn, Popcorn, Cornbread, Fish

- Western Europe:
  Spaghetti, Calzone, Greek Salad, German Sausage

- Eastern Europe:
  Borscht (beet and cabbage soup), Boiled Eggs, Dark Bread

- Middle East:
  Israeli Unleavened Bread, Lamb, Couscous, Pita Bread,
  Falafel (ground chickpeas shaped into balls and fried)

- Africa:
  Bananas, Pineapple, Peanuts, Rice, Boiled Potatoes, Matoke
  (mashed steamed bananas)

- Asia:
  Rice (try eating it with chopsticks!), Egg Rolls, Curried
  Chicken, Sushi, Stir-fry

Funny Missions Stories to Read Aloud to Children

Throughout the years, our family's international travels have led to amusing encounters, humorous misunderstandings, and hilarious adventures. When we have an opportunity to share about world missions, we often enjoy sharing a few of our "funny" missions stories. Although international missions work often means adjusting to curious cuisine and challenging conditions, it can also be extremely fun. Our family has enjoyed Polynesian snorkeling, European museums, African safaris, Middle Eastern camel "excursions," South American professional soccer games, and Australian boat rides. Take our word for it—or better yet, try it yourself—missions is definitely not boring!

— 👫 FROM OUR CHILDREN'S PERSPECTIVE

"GRASSHOPPERS FOR THANKSGIVING?"

By Joshua, at age thirteen

"So, what did *you* eat for Thanksgiving?"

A few days ago, during the week of Thanksgiving, my dad and I were across the world to Uganda, East Africa, holding evangelistic outreaches in remote cities out in the middle of nowhere. It was my second Thanksgiving holiday outside of America. But this time was really different.

In Africa, most people eat the same foods over and over again; at least we sure did. Day after day, meal after meal, we had overcooked rice, matoke (mashed steamed bananas), and a few chunks of tough meat and guts. But for Thanksgiving we had a "special" African treat. Along with our standard food, we were given a plate full of greasy fried *grasshoppers*!! They were about two inches long, with the legs and head still on.

As I stared at these insects, thoughts flashed through my brain. I imagined all the yummy food my brothers and sisters were eating at Grandma's house: turkey and pumpkin pie, mashed potatoes and gravy. I also remembered a time I had eaten big bugs before (at a kid's camp when I was bribed with a bunch of candy). It wasn't so hard to chug down an insect just once or twice on a dare, but this was different. It was Thanksgiving—and I was hungry!

Actually, they didn't taste that bad. As I took my first bite, they reminded me of a cross between popcorn and shrimp—crunchy on the outside and a little gooey on the inside. Soon I was eating one after the other, even throwing them in the air and catching them in my mouth. I must have eaten about sixty of them by the time I was done!

By the way, the ministry went well that night. We preached to thousands of people . . . and I felt just like John the Baptist!

THE SNICKERS BAR AND THE ANTS

By Carol Higgins, missionary to Africa

My husband, Bob, actually found a Snickers bar for me three days ago. I ate half of it and put the other half in the "pass-through" window between the kitchen and dining room—safe from dog and man, right?

The next day I was doing some mending for the children at the orphanage and got so sleepy I could hardly keep my eyes open. I thought about the treasured half Snickers bar and that it would wake me up. I got it, and not that I play with my food, but there is a certain technique I have for eating a Snickers. You know, eat the bottom first, then the caramel, and then the nuts—and, of course, savor every bite.

Well, I noticed a tickling on my fingers. Hmmmm . . . ants.

Then my face was being tickled by the same critters. I looked at my chewed-on candy bar and it was crawling with tiny little ants.

"Oh gross!" I thought as I was in the middle of a savory chew. Spit it out? My precious chocolate? How much ant-covered chocolate had I eaten? Give in to a couple hundred little ants? No way! I knocked the remaining bar on my sewing table; squashed the little buggers off the table, my face, and my hand; inspected it thoroughly; and enjoyed my remaining Snickers as systematically as I had begun: bottom to top.

My Bob thinks I have been in Africa too long. Maybe so!

THE FILIPINO CURE FOR FLEAS

Our family was in a remote Filipino village on one of our first missionary trips, and the national pastor hosting us was very nervous.

"I've never hosted foreigners and don't know what to feed you," he said.

"Oh, we're easy to please," we responded naively. "Just relax; we'll eat whatever you put before us."

A few minutes later the pastor introduced us to the church women who were going to be cooking our food. One of them was eating this very different looking egg. It was black; and as she cracked it open, she started tugging at the insides—pulling out a black embryonic chick!

We found out that *balut* (a fertilized duck egg with a nearly-developed embryo that is boiled and eaten in the shell) was a common Filipino food . . . and we were nervous.

The people gave us an esteemed room in the village—the only room with a rug. Unfortunately, the rug was totally infested with fleas; and within a few days my legs were covered with flea bites.

When the pastor saw the bug bites, he said, "Oh, that is terrible. We must do something about those fleas biting you. Yes, there is only one thing to do."

"What's that?" we asked.

"Well, we must *eat the dog*. I was going to save it for a party, but I think we must eat it now."

A few days later, Jon came into our room. "Guess what we're having for dinner," he said with a raised eyebrow.

Not balut, I hoped. (I didn't know if I was *that* good of a missionary yet.)

I went to visit the church women and to see our menu for myself. These precious ladies were cutting up some strange white-looking meat. When I asked what it was, they talked among themselves in their Filipino language of Tagolog and then went to find someone who could interpret.

A few minutes later one woman came in and distinctly pronounced with wonderful enunciation the new English word she had just learned.

"Dog," she said.

"Dog?" I timidly asked, as my mind whirled with memories of special pets from my childhood.

The woman clarified herself: "Yes. You know—Ruff! Ruff!"

Yes, I knew far too well. But that's what we and our kids had for dinner that night. Our menu actually consisted of nearly-raw dog meat and fried dog intestines.

And we still had fleas!

NEVER SHINE A FLASHLIGHT DOWN THE PIT!

"The Pit" is unlike anything you have likely experienced. It is totally different than a camp porta-potty and has absolutely no resemblance to a typical American bathroom. Not one home decorating magazine is displayed in a basket to read at your leisure, not one pretty towel hangs on a shiny silver bar, and fluffy coordinating bathmats are nowhere to be seen.

The Pit is a cement or mud cubicle with a weathered wooden door, a six-inch square hole in the ground, and an unforgettable "aroma"—all above a very, very deep pit.

One night we were in a remote African village dominated by demonic witchcraft. It was late . . . and dark; and a while after the evening ministry time was over our outreach team got rolling in one of those funny, middle-of-the-night conversations. The topic turned to some very practical missionary advice: "Be sure to *never* shine your flashlight down the Pit!" (Have you ever watched that scene from *Raiders of the Lost Ark* when Indiana Jones throws a torch down into the forbidden tomb and sees what he dreaded the most—the floor alive with snakes?! I think you get the picture. The Pit is often swarming above with flies; and in the unknown depths below, it's alive . . . with no one knows what!)

We all were laughing hysterically, including me . . . until I realized I had to "go," and it just couldn't wait until morning.

I got out my flashlight and went out into the darkness, through the rain—all by myself to the Pit. By this time, nothing seemed funny anymore.

I was very tired and wouldn't have minded those fluffy coordinating bathmats. As I neared the "aroma," I tried to decide my strategy. How could I go about using the Pit without shining the flashlight down?

When I arrived, I quickly threw open the rickety door—and barged in upon the biggest rat I had ever seen in my life! (With its tail it must have been nearly two feet long!) I wish I could say I was your strong, unflinching woman; but I screamed and just stood there, soaking wet, crying in the dark.

My precious husband, Jon, came to my rescue, got rid of the creature, made sure the coast was clear, then stood guard to make sure I was protected.

I bravely reentered the Pit with my flashlight, while my husband reentered his comical, slightly mischievous mood. He told our team to come watch something funny as he rolled a rock toward me under the Pit's door. My reaction did not let them down. I thought the rat was attacking me and I totally freaked out.

Everyone (except me!) thought it was the funniest joke of the evening!

 **FIRE IN THE HOLE!**

My brother participated in an African mission trip and went to use the same Pit where I had seen the giant rat. There were actually two cement stalls with a common hole down below. While he was on one side, one of our African friends wanted to bless our team by trying to clean up the Pit and getting rid of all the bugs. She tied banana leaves together, lit them on fire, and lowered them down the hole in the adjacent stall. But all the gases down below were so strong it caused an explosion, sending fire up both holes!

My brother instantly came bounding out of his stall, pulling up his pants and screaming, "Fire in the hole!"

THE BRIGHT-RED BLAZER

My husband used to have a recurring embarrassing dream. Jon would dream that as he got up to preach he would look down and realize he had nothing on but a red suit jacket!

After years of having this funny bad dream, he was preaching in a village of the Karamajong tribe in northern Uganda—an isolated people group who wear very little clothing. One afternoon a man came to Jon for ministry. He was clothed in nothing but a bright-red polyester blazer, with sleeves so short they came all the way up to his elbows! The man plopped down right in front of everyone with seemingly no realization of how naked (and funny) he looked.

It reminded my husband of his dream, which, fortunately, he never had again.

FUNNY QUESTIONS

Here are a couple of actual questions asked at a village marriage conference in East Africa. The missionaries found it quite hard to keep a straight face. How would you respond if someone asked you these questions?

Q. "Once a month I buy my wife a bar of sweet-smelling soap, but she still smells like a beast. What do I do?"

Q. "Every time my wife is pregnant, she acts like she is demon-possessed. What do I do?"

Another funny question occurred during a Christian teaching seminar in an isolated island village in the Philippines. My friends were the visiting missionaries when a national pastor asked if they could sing the song about the "magic tree."

"I'm sorry," our missionary friend responded, "but I'm afraid I've never heard that one before. Would you mind leading it for us?"

Immediately (and with much gusto) the young pastor began singing their church's very original rendition of Jack Hayford's popular worship chorus, "Majesty":

Magic tree, worship His magic tree,

Uncle Jesus, be all glory, honor and praise!

My missionary friends chuckled, realizing these remote Filipino believers must have thought the chorus referred to God's miraculous power through the cross of our Lord Jesus Christ.

REMOTE VILLAGERS VISIT THE BIG CITY

Over the years, we have had some interesting experiences bringing remote villagers out of the bush for the first time in their lives. It has been interesting to experience our own culture through new eyes. Those who have always lived near the equator often wonder if the world is coming to an end when daylight lasts so long in the summer. Others look totally lost and puzzled as they wander down the dog food aisle at the grocery store.

Reactions to our many food choices are sometimes comical. Most have never imagined so many different foods. Once, at a buffet restaurant, an African villager accidentally loaded his plate with plastic grapes from the display table, along with a helping of jelly beans covered with chicken gravy. Another time, a national pastor (who had never eaten green vegetables) saw my husband fixing a large salad and said, "Oh no, my brother, that is the food of a goat!"

— 👥 FROM OUR CHILDREN'S PERSPECTIVE

"COMPANY'S COMING!"

By Christi Dunagan, at age fourteen

MOM: Christi, we have company over often, including many missionary families, and you are a tremendous help. From your perspective as my teenage daughter, and from a practical point of view, what does "missionary hospitality" mean to you?

CHRISTI: Well, it means I'll have to do more dishes (without complaining), wash my sheets (making sure I've got matching pillowcases), clean my closet (usually two feet deep in clothes), get rid of all my little sister's messes and all my junk in the bathroom . . . and it's all got to be done really *fast* because usually our company's coming any minute!

It means that after a "sit-down, nicer-than-normal" dinner, I'll be in charge of keeping all the little kids quiet while the adults are visiting; and then, when it's time for bed, I'll "get" to sleep on the floor in my little brother's room (with a smile)!

When people from Africa or India come over, they usually think my bedroom is like a royal guesthouse! It reminds me of how much I have to be thankful for and how much I usually take for granted.

Sometimes our visitors have never seen a dishwasher, or a grocery store. One time we all were laughing so hard with our Ugandan friend when he couldn't figure out how a person could fit inside the little talking menu board at the Burger King drive-through! (Our national friend was laughing harder than any of us!) International guests have stood watching in amazement through an entire washing machine cycle—when the lid was up!

It can be interesting, and challenging, to hear exciting stories about how people have helped orphan children or about how missionaries have started Bible schools. It's fun also to have special speakers from church stay at our house (like groups from Teen Mania or Master's Commission). Many times these ministers have really encouraged me to want to do something more for God with my life.

When we welcome others into our home, especially other missionaries, it's not just a lot of work, and an exercise in patience—it's actually missionary training!

— 👫 FROM OUR CHILDREN'S PERSPECTIVE

"MY MOST-MEMORABLE COMMUNITY SERVICE PROJECT"
By Patrick Dunagan, age fifteen

As the last sheets of metal were nailed on, I took a step back to observe the finished product. It was a very simple building: many strong beams holding up a metal roof, and not even any walls. But as I saw the project near completion, I remember the tremendous satisfaction and happiness I felt.

But why be so satisfied over such a simple structure?

To understand how I felt, one must first know where I was. I wasn't in a poor neighborhood of my hometown or even in a big city slum but on the other side of the world, on a remote island in Lake Victoria. During this mission trip to Africa with my dad, I had seen many other island communities, but when we arrived at this particular island I was appalled at the living conditions. All the islands were poor and dirty, but this one left the others far behind. The village was made up of about one thousand people living in cramped, makeshift huts of grass, mud, and old garbage bags. Sewage ran down the narrow paths between the huts. Most children had little or no clothes. The horrible stench made me wonder how anyone could live there.

For them, that small, humble structure was a big event. Now their little island had its first real building, a church and community center for worship, practical health instruction, and teaching.

That night, as I boarded the dugout canoe, I knew God's impact on that little island would be felt for years.

(Note: On this mission outreach, Patrick traveled by a rugged canoe to help establish new churches on four remote Ugandan islands in Lake Victoria.)

— 👫 FROM OUR CHILDREN'S PERSPECTIVE

"EVANGELISM WITH THE *EVANGECUBE***"

By Daniel Dunagan, age twelve

Dozens of Ugandan children were crowded around me as I climbed onto the back of our pickup truck. It was my very first mission trip, and now it was my turn to preach.

As I held up a big *EvangeCube*, I started to share about God's plan of salvation. I talked about Jesus; and phrase by phrase, an interpreter translated the message. Everyone stared intently. They were interested to see how the cube worked, and they were really interested in the message of God's salvation.

The *EvangeCube* is a really cool tool and it's easy to use. It's especially helpful when I'm sharing about how Jesus is the only way to heaven. As I got to the *EvangeCube* picture of "the cross as the bridge" to God, I asked the kids if any of them wanted to receive Jesus Christ as their Lord and Savior. Dozens of hands went up, and it was exciting to lead them in a prayer of salvation. With the *EvangeCube*, evangelism is easy!

*** *EvangeCube* is a tool used to walk people through the Gospel presentation using pictures. The blocks are flipped in different directions to show man's separation from God all the way to his sacrifice and resurrection from the tomb.

TEACHING OPPORTUNITY

Twenty (More) Ideas to Make Missions Fun

1. Put together a world map puzzle.

2. Learn to eat with chopsticks.

3. Check out a library book on origami art and experiment with this fun craft of Japanese paper-folding.

4. Buy (or make) a piñata and have a Mexican-theme party.

5. Have younger children dress up in international costumes, go outdoors, and play "Let's be a missionary!" (For older children, have a party with an international theme and give prizes for the best costumes.)

6. Learn to draw a few Chinese characters.

7. Collect international postage stamps.

8. Look up international time zones for major cities around the world and set several clocks at these times.

9. Make international flag posters. (Have your child decorate international flags and hang them from the ceiling.)

10. Look in the library or on the Internet for fun instructions on how to play a foreign game (like African *mancala*).

11. Send a quick and encouraging e-mail to a missionary. (Better yet, send a handwritten letter or a small care package!)

12. Listen to international music.

13. Watch an inspiring international movie (such as the classic film, *The Inn of the Sixth Happiness*).

14. Visit a local travel agency (or a travel agency on the Internet). Browse through international travel packages.

15. Type a personal letter to a foreign embassy asking for a tourist information packet about their country. (Check out foreign embassy websites on the Internet.)

16. Make a playdough relief map of a foreign country on a piece of cardboard. (Recipe: 1 cup flour, 1 cup salt, water to mix)

17. Look up information about a specific country on the Internet.

18. Sit on the couch and listen to an inspiring missionary biography (such as a story from *Hero Tales* or a Trailblazer book).

19. Visit the children's section of your local library and check out several books about a particular country.

20. Make "missionary passports."

◉ TEACHING OPPORTUNITY

Make a Mission-Minded "Passport"

As your child learns about various areas of the world, a fun idea is to chart this progress on a special "passport."

Instructions:

1. What you need:

a photocopy of the passport pages displayed on the following pages, your child's photo, scissors, glue, colored construction paper, blank white paper, yarn, hole puncher, clear packing tape, and stapler (For fun, add international stickers or stamps.)

2. What to do:

Have your child cut out the passport pages along the dotted lines and glue these pieces to a passport-sized booklet (made from a half-piece of colored construction paper with blank white pages stapled inside). Add your child's photo to the appropriate box, and for strength and durability cover the entire passport with clear packing tape. Punch a hole in the top left corner, and insert a piece of yarn or cording so your child can wear the passport around his or her neck.

3. How to use this passport:

As your child learns about an area of the world, stamp the passport with a culturally appropriate rubber stamp, international flag or globe-oriented sticker, or a foreign postage stamp—all available at most teacher supply stores. This passport can be used to keep track of achievements such as Bible memory or Bible reading progress, or to record a child's personal prayer time as he or she "travels" around the world through intercession.

Cut and paste onto cover of passport (made from a folded piece of construction paper).

PASSPORT

Citizen of God's Kingdom

Cut and paste onto front inside page of passport (on white paper stapled inside).

Mission-Minded Child's Passport Number:

_____

Last Name:

_____

First Name:

_____

Nation of Birth:

_____

Birthday: ____ / ____ / ____   Born Again? (yes/no/unsure) _____

Boy or Girl? _____   Age: _____

Home Address: _____

_____

Phone: _____   E-mail: _____

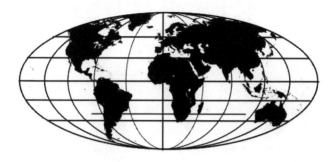

I'm a Mission-Minded Child

_____

SIGNATURE OF BEARER *(Sign your name here)*

 Cut each of these squares and paste onto any page inside of passport (on white paper stapled inside).

Our Great Commision:

*"Go into all the world
and preach the Gospel
to every creature."*

(Words of JESUS CHRIST from Mark 16:15)

THE WHOLE WORLD NEEDS JESUS

By Ann Dunagan

All over the world,
Far away and quite near,
There are millions of people who all need to hear
Of the message of Jesus,
But someone must GO,
And preach the Good News, so the whole world will know!

In God's eyes,
Each person is wonderfully made,
So to witness and share
We should not be afraid.
With the power of His Spirit,
We can be bold!
For the gospel to everyone
Must be told!

Others may have a different color of skin,
Or they may look real strong, or too tall, or too thin.
Their hair may be curly, or wavy, or straight,
But whatever the case, you had better not wait!

The whole world needs Jesus,
Each one needs to hear.
We must all share the news
Till it's reached every ear!

Some folks may be almost a hundred years old,
And they may live in places all icy and cold.
Or they may be real young,

'Bout the same age as you,
And live in the tropics
With seas warm and blue!
They might live in a mansion
Of silver and gold,
Or in a small shack
Made of tin that's real old.

Their words may sound strange,
Speaking French or Chinese,
Or Hebrew, or Russian, or perhaps Japanese!
But no matter what languages others may know,
They may not know Jesus,
So someone must GO!!
And although we're as different
As black is to white,
Each person is precious in Jesus' sight.

Their food may not be what you usually eat:
Some eat raw fish and rice
Or fried chicken feet.
Others eat monkeys,
Or snakes and cooked dogs,
And in some places people are known to eat FROGS!
But it's funny, you know,
'Cause some food that YOU eat
Tastes just awful to them,
Though to you it is sweet.

Your water may come from a faucet turned 'round,
But their water could come from a hole in the ground.
And their bed could be simply a mat on the floor,
While you have a mattress and pillows galore.

Yes, inside every home, some have less,
Some have more,
But people need Jesus behind every door.
Each person is different,
No two are the same;
But God knows everyone all by name.
He created us all from our head to our feet,
And made each person special—completely unique!
But there's one thing that's common and so very sad,
About every child, every mom, every dad.

All over the world,
From the young to the old,
Each person has sinned.
They've not done what God's told.

Some people lie,
Or they steal and they cheat;
Others make golden idols
And bow at their feet.
Some are selfish and greedy
—Not willing to share.
Others say there's no God (and pretend He's not there).

But no matter what terrible things folks have done,
God so loved the world
That He sent down His Son.
Jesus died on the cross for the sins of us all,
And forgives every one if on His name we call.

New life is a wonderful gift for each one.
But some still haven't *once*
Even heard what God's done!

Who will take the Good News
To all those far away?

Who will help?
Who will give?
Who will kneel down and pray?

We all have a part,
So just lend a hand,
Till the message of Jesus
Has reached every land.

The whole world needs Jesus,
Each one needs to hear.
We must all share the news
Till it's reached every ear!

**"So teach us to number our days,
That we may gain a heart of wisdom."**

Psalm 90:12

Looking Back and Looking Ahead

Alone in the car. Hmmm . . . as a busy mother of seven, how often does *that* happen?

As I turned the corner and drove into the familiar campground, it felt significant—like I was supposed to be here to finish this book.

There are some moments in life that lend themselves to "thinking" about things: a child's high school graduation ceremony; a niece's wedding; a special memorial honoring a life well lived. It felt like one of those times.

After sharing hugs and hellos with dear Pastor Allan and Eunice Hanson (what faithful servants!), I lugged armloads of my computer paraphernalia into the red hilltop cabin and then headed out to look around. I reminisced and prayed in the little Victory Chapel, sat in the old Rotunda building, and quietly played "Lord, Have Your Way" on the piano.

Then I headed down that old dirt trail. I wondered if I could find the spot . . . and if I'd be able to recognize it.

And finally, there it was. As if time had stood still, I almost felt like I was a little girl again—as if God and I were meeting together to recall that special moment from my past.

Once again, I sat down on a log and listened to that stream rippling and gurgling beside me. The sun glistened as I looked toward the sky. *Wow,* I wondered, as I gazed up at those majestic pine and birch trees, *how much had those trees grown in thirty years?*

It was definitely "one of those moments."

It was thirty years ago . . . right about this time of the summer . . . right in this very spot . . . that the Lord "called" me to world missions.

I felt so overwhelmingly thankful. So inadequate. So grateful.

The sunbeams looked beautiful and the leaves looked remarkably green. For a long and lingering moment, I simply basked in the Lord's presence.

As a child, this was the place where I had first "heard" His voice and His calling for me to go to the nations, which had now become a reality. Like a whirlwind of memories, jumbled thoughts flooded my mind: the moment I met my husband; the births of our children; smuggling Bibles into China; airplane trips and Filipino jeepney rides; fun birthday parties and big church potlucks; preaching to multitudes; and dancing in an African downpour!

I felt more in love than ever—in love with my handsome husband, in love with our awesome kids, and totally in love with Jesus. I am truly a blessed woman, a happy mommy, and probably the proudest wife in the world (in a good way!). I love sharing how my daring sweetheart had the opportunity to preach the gospel on every continent, including Antarctica, all within this last year! God has been *so* good!

Looking Ahead . . .

A few weeks from now, I'm actually heading overseas to a remote village in Africa for a women's conference. After years of staying home, I'm looking forward to going again. God's plans and purposes have surpassed my childhood dreams. And I know He has more!

For each child we influence and for their generation (and for you!), God has a perfect plan and a destiny. He has purposes as unique as each personality and adventures that may be enjoyable . . . or perhaps very difficult.

He yearns for our children to be rock-solid in faith, bold in witness, and daring enough to live totally for His kingdom! He wants to spare our children the heartaches of disobedience, the regrets of midlife, and the despair of wasted years. Most of all, God sees a lost generation—masses of young people scattered throughout the earth—desperately needing His love!

There's a whole world out there: dirty boys kicking an old ball around a dusty South American field, a little girl lonely for a friend, a middle-school kid drowning in his boredom, an old man dying, and multitudes of precious babies being born.

Who will go to them? And who will raise the spiritual leaders of tomorrow?

> Then the word of the LORD came to me, saying: "Before I formed you in the womb I knew you; before you were born I sanctified you; I ordained you a prophet to the nations."
>
> Then said I: "Ah, Lord God! Behold, I cannot speak, for I am a youth."
>
> But the LORD said to me: "Do not say, 'I am a youth,' for you shall go to all to whom I send you, and whatever I command you, you shall speak. Do not be afraid of their faces, for I am with you to deliver you," says the LORD (Jeremiah 1:4–8).

These words were not just for me. The Lord is calling *your child*! ·

Recommended Resources & Missionary Biographies

- Christian Hall of Fame—www.Christianhof.org: an online resource highlighting many heroes of the Christian faith throughout history.

- *Christian Heroes: Then & Now,* by Janet and Geoff Benge (YWAM Publishing). This best-selling missionary biography series chronicles the exciting, challenging, and deeply touching true stories of ordinary men and women whose trust in God accomplished extraordinary exploits for His kingdom. An accompanying unit study curriculum guide is available.

- *From Jerusalem to Irian Jaya: A Biographical History of Christian Missions,* by Ruth Tucker (Zondervan, 2004). This excellent academic book (written for adults) has been revised and is now available in hardback. It examines the history of Christian missions by emphasizing personal biographies. With details, maps, photos, and charts, it is a helpful resource for home, church, or school.

- *Hero Tales,* by Dave and Neta Jackson (Bethany House). This treasury of true stories from the lives of Christian heroes contains valuable lessons that can be read alone or together for family or classroom devotions. Each of the four volumes consists of forty-five exciting and educational readings drawn from the lives of fifteen key Christian heroes. Geared for ages six to twelve, these books include questions and missionary portraits.

- *Heroes for Young Readers* (YWAM Publishing). Many of the books in this series are mentioned in chapter 6. These illustrated books about famous missionaries are great for younger readers.

- *Heroes of the Faith* (Barbour Publishing). Written by Sam Wellman and other authors, this series covers men and women not traditionally written about in missionary series, like C. S. Lewis, Mother Teresa, and Billy Graham.

- *International Adventures,* by various authors (YWAM Publishing). These exciting classic and new missionary biographies have been collected and repackaged to reach a new generation. Every title emerges as a dramatic episode directed by the hand of God. Current titles include *Torches of Joy, A Cry from the Streets, Adventures in Naked Faith, Living on the Devil's Doorstep, Against All Odds, Tomorrow You Die, Dayuma: Life Under the Waorani Spears, Imprisoned in Iran, The Man with the Bird on His Head, Peace Child,* and *Lords of the Earth.*

- *Is That Really You, God?* by Loren Cunningham (YWAM Publishing, 2001; also available in hardback, by Chosen Books). This practical guide to hearing God's voice shows how an ordinary man who was committed to hearing and obeying God became the founder of the largest interdenominational mission organization in the world. Cunningham's extensive missionary travels have taken him to every country in the world, and his life of faith is an excellent contemporary example for our children. This book is a must-read!

- *Men and Women of Faith Series,* various authors (Bethany House). Written for older readers (seventh grade to adult).

- *Revolution in World Missions,* by K. P. Yohannan (Charisma House, 1995). A challenging book focused on raising and supporting national missionaries.

- The *By Faith Biography Series,* various authors (Ambassador-Emerald International). Designed with younger readers in mind.

- *The Life and Diary of David Brainerd,* by Philip E. Howard, edited by Jonathan Edwards (Baker, 1989).

- *Through Gates of Splendor,* by Elisabeth Elliot (Tyndale, revised edition, 1986), and *The Journals of Jim Elliot,* edited by Elisabeth Elliot (Revell, 2002). Inspiring biographies of Jim Elliot.

- *Trailblazer Series,* by Dave and Neta Jackson (Bethany House). These exciting stories of adventure and faith will entertain your children while teaching them about Christian heroes of the past. This series has won enthusiastic support from families and teachers. Geared for ages eight to thirteen, these missionary biographies are perfect for children to read themselves.

- *Richard Wurmbrand: Voice in the Dark,* by Carine MacKenzie

- Wholesome Words—www.wholesomewords.org: The "Children's Corner" includes many delightful missionary stories for oral reading.

Missions Adventures, Fiction

- *Reel Kids Adventures Series,* by David Gustaveson (YWAM Publishing). Each book in this high-paced international adventure series has a missions theme. The series is written for older children or young adults. Titles include *The Missing Video* (Cuba), *Mystery at Smokey Mountain* (Philippines), *The Mysterious Case* (Colombia), and seven other exciting volumes!

World Missions: Inspiration and Teaching

- *The Passion for Souls,* by Oswald J. Smith (The Chaucer Press, Lakeland Edition, 1983). A powerful missions classic.

- *The Challenge of Missions,* by Oswald J. Smith (Eternal Word Ministries, reprint edition, 2003). An outstanding missions classic.

- *The Missions Addiction: Capturing God's Passion for the World,* by David Shibley (Charisma House, 2001). Inspiring and challenging summary of the need for world missions today.

Other Missions Resources

Dare to Be a Daniel (D2BD): www.daretobeadaniel.com

Extreme Devotion, by The Voice of the Martyrs

3-D Kids Course - Online Training from MissionMindedFamilies.org

Jesus Freaks, Volume 1: Stories of Those Who Took a Stand for Jesus, by
dc Talk and The Voice of the Martyrs (Bethany House, 1999). This
book tells the incredible stories of brave Christians from both long
ago and in recent history who were willing to surrender everything
(even their lives) to follow Jesus. Because of its graphic and vivid
examples, it is not recommended for young children; however,
with adult supervision it is extremely powerful for older children
and especially appropriate for teens and young adults. See also the
sequel: *Jesus Freaks, Volume 2: Stories of Revolutionaries Who
Changed Their World* (Bethany House, 2002).

Operation Christmas Child: www.samaritanspurse.org

MissionMindedWomen.org

Teen Missions: www.teenmissions.org

"The Four Spiritual Laws": www.greatcom.org/laws/languages.html

The JESUS Film Project: www.jesusfilm.org

The Voice of the Martyrs: www.persecution.com

YWAM (Youth With A Mission) King's Kids: www.ywam.org and
www.kkint.net

Wycliffe Bible Translators: www.wycliffe.org

Notes

Opening quotes

Quotes by Hudson Taylor, at age five, and his parents, Mr. and Mrs. James Hudson Taylor: from *Hudson Taylor in Early Years: The Growth of a Soul*, by Dr. and Mrs. Howard Taylor, published by the China Inland Mission, printed in Ann Arbor, MI: Edwards Brothers, Inc., 1943, p. 37.

Chapter 1

Story of Hannah and Samuel from 1 Samuel 1–3.

Chapter 2

"A Passion for Souls"—Herbert G. Tovey, 1888. Words of this hymn are in public domain.

Chapter 3

Missions statistics compiled from the *World Christian Encyclopedia,* edited by David B. Barrett, George T. Kurian, and Todd M. Johnson (Oxford University Press, 2001); *700 Hundred Plans to Evangelize the World,* by David Barrett (New Hope, 1988); *Revolution in World Missions,* by K. P. Yohannan (Gospel for Asia); and a brochure, *The Glaring Injustice of 21ˢᵗ Century Missions* (www.missionindia.org).

"A Hundred Thousand Souls"—Author unknown; poem and quote excerpted from *The Harvest Call,* by T. L. Osborn (Tulsa: The Voice of Faith, Inc., 1953), p. 109. Used by permission of Osborn International.

"The Little Starfish"—Original source unknown; retold by Ann Dunagan.

Chapter 4

Bible chart—Bible verses organized and compiled by Ann Dunagan and Andrew Sloan.

Chapter 6

Missionary biographical information compiled and adapted by Ann Dunagan from various sources, including:

Ann Dunagan, *Teaching with God's Heart for the World, Volume I & II.*

Elmer L. Towns, *The Christian Hall of Fame* (Grand Rapids: Baker, 1971).

Oliver Ransford, *David Livingstone: The Dark Interior* (New York: St. Martin's, 1978), p. 14.

Ruth A. Tucker, *From Jerusalem to Irian Jaya: A Biographical History of Christian Missions* (Grand Rapids: Zondervan, 2004).

Sherwood Eddy, *Pathfinders of the World Missionary Crusade* (New York: Abingdon-Cokesbury, 1945), p. 125.

Will Durant, *The Reformation,* Volume 6 of *The Story of Civilization* (New York: Simon & Schuster, 1957), p. 204.

Current missionary biographies were all checked with each minister's official ministry website, updated 2004–2007.

Missionary statistics checked with online information from the William Carey Library, 2005.

Classic Missionary Excerpts:

"A 'Big Man' Meets a 'Real Man'"—Loren Cunningham, *Winning God's Way* (Seattle: YWAM Publishing, 1988), pp. 46–49. Used by permission of Loren Cunningham and Youth With A Mission.

"The Christian Magna Carta"—Loren Cunningham, excerpted from *Target Earth: The Necessity of Diversity in a Holistic Perspective on World Mission,* by Frank Kaleb Jansen (Kailua-Kona, HA: University of the Nations, and Pasadena, CA: Global Mapping, 1989), p. 86. Used by permission of Loren Cunningham and Youth With A Mission.

"Did Not Your Forefathers Know?"—Mrs. J. H. Worcester Jr., *David Livingstone: First to Cross Africa with the Gospel* (Chicago: Moody Press, 1993), pp. 26–27.

"Dr. Duff's Appeal"—Oswald J. Smith, *The Challenge of Missions* (Waynesboro, GA: Operation Mobilization Literature Ministry, 1959), pp. 37–38. (This book is out of print but was reprinted in 2003 by Eternal Word Ministries.) Used by permission of The People's Church of Toronto, Canada, and the family of Oswald J. Smith.

"The Man in the Clouds"—Paul Eshleman, article excerpted from a JESUS Film Project monthly newsletter, 2003; used by permission of Paul Eshleman and the JESUS Film Project.

"Man of Mission—Man of Prayer"—Dr. and Mrs. Howard Taylor, *Hudson Taylor's Spiritual Secret* (Chicago: Moody Press, 1983), condensed from pp. 234–236.

"Only the Grace of God—Spear-Wielding Killer Now Church Elder"—David Shibley, *The Missions Addiction: Capturing God's Passion for the World* (Lake Mary, FL: Charisma House, 2001), pp. 199–200.

"Our Obligation"—Elmer L. Towns, *The Christian Hall of Fame* (Grand Rapids: Baker, 1971), p. 90. Original quote from William Carey's famous missions book entitled *An Enquiry into the Obligations of Christians to Use Means for the Conversion of the Heathens.*

"The Small Woman"—Alan Burgess, *The Small Woman: The Heroic Story of Gladys Aylward* (New York: E. P. Dutton & Co., Inc., 1957); excerpt from chapter 1.

Chapter 7

Various ideas in this chapter adapted from Jon and Ann Dunagan, *New Life in Jesus* (Hood River, OR: Harvest Ministry, 2000).

Chapter 8

Prayer ideas taken from personal missionary experiences and from the following sources:

Danny Lehman, *Before You Hit the Wall* (Seattle: YWAM Publishing, 1991).

James P. Shaw, senior editor, *Personal Prayer Diary and Daily Planner* (Seattle: YWAM Publishing, 1995), pp. 12–15, 192.

Chapter 9

"My Choice"—Bill McChesney, excerpted from *Winning God's Way,* by Loren Cunningham (Seattle: YWAM Publishing, 1988), pp. 47–49. Used by permission of Loren Cunningham and Youth With A Mission.

"Why We Should Give Money for Missions"—Missions statistics from *The World Christian Encyclopedia,* edited by David B. Barrett, George T. Kurian, and Todd M. Johnson (Oxford University Press, 2001); and *Revolution in World Missions,* by K. P. Yohannan (Altamonte Springs, FL: Charisma House, 1995), p. 129.

Chapter 11

Music and international ideas compiled and adapted from various sources, including:

Bev Gunderson, *Window to India, Window to Japan*, and *Window to Mexico* (Milaca, MN: Monarch Publishing, 1988).

Mary Branson, *Fun Around the World* (Birmingham: New Hope, 1992).

Phyllis Vos Wezeman and Jude Dennis Fournier, *Joy to the World* (Notre Dame, IN: Ave Maria Press, 1992).

Ruth Finley, *The Secret Search* (Mt. Hermon, CA: Crossroads Communications, 1990).

Kerry Lovering, *Missions Idea Notebook: Promoting Missions in the Local Church* (Scarborough, Ontario: SIM International Publications, 1984).

Special thanks to missionary friends Bob and Carol Higgins (of Path Ministries International, www.pathministries.net) for "The Snickers Bar and the Ants," and to John and Katy Ricards (missionaries to the island of Mindanao in the Philippines with Ministries to Christian Nationals) for the "Magic Tree" story.

Illustration Index

Chapter 1

Chapter 4

Chapter 6

David Livingstone	Public domain
Hudson Taylor	The Christian Hall of Fame. Canton Baptist Temple, Canton, OH. Used with permission. All rights reserved (nontransferable).
Amy Carmichael	The Dohnavur Fellowship
John and Betty Stam	Overseas Missionary Fellowship. Used with permission. All rights reserved.
Gladys Aylward	Alan Burgess, *The Small Woman: The Heroic Story of Gladys Aylward* (New York: E. P. Dutton & Co., Inc., 1957).
Cameron Townsend	Wycliffe Bible Translators. Used with permission. All rights reserved.
Oswald J. Smith	People's Church, Toronto, Ontario. Used with permission of the family.
Alexander Duff	Public domain
Bill Bright	Campus Crusade for Christ. Used with permission. All rights reserved.
JESUS Film	Campus Crusade for Christ. JESUS Film. www.jesusfilm.org. All rights reserved.
Loren Cunningham	Youth With A Mission. Used with permission of YWAM and Loren Cunningham. All rights reserved.
Paul Rader	Public domain
Billy Graham	Billy Graham Evangelistic Association. Used with permission. All rights reserved (nontransferable).
Luis Palau	Luis Palau Evangelistic Association. Used with permission. All rights reserved.
Richard Wurmbrand	The Voice of the Martyrs. Used with permission. All rights reserved.
K. P. Yohannan	Gospel for Asia. Used with permission. All rights reserved.

Chapter 9

Chapter 10

The following photo pages are from Harvest Ministry and the Dunagan Family
— in global missions and international travel since 1987 —
collectively sharing the light of Jesus in over 120 nations (and still counting)
and preaching the Gospel on all 7 continents, including Antarctica.

JON & ANN DUNAGAN

ORU ALUMNI OF THE YEAR
DISTINGUISHED SERVICE TO GOD

FREE Video Series on YouTube:
7 Simple Keys for Mission-Minded Families

FREE Video Series for Christian families
with Jon & Ann Dunagan

Designed for churches, families or small groups
Gather a few friends for a 7-week study!

7 videos (20-24 minutes each)
Motivational. Encouraging. Biblical.
FREE workbook pages — for group handouts.

FREE Video Series on YouTube:
7 Simple Keys for Mission-Minded Families

Key #1:
SEE THE CROSS

MISSION QUOTE:

"You don't have to cross the seas to be a missionary;
you just need to see the cross." (author unknown)

BIBLE VERSES:

John 3:3, John 14:6, Luke 22:42, Acts 4:12,
I Peter 3:18, Galatians 2:20

DISCUSSION QUESTIONS:

When did you first understand the power of the Cross of Jesus?
Is it hard thinking about Jesus being the ONLY way of salvation?
How have you taught your kids about Jesus and the Cross?
Do you have a favorite family Bible storybook or resource?
As Christian parents, how are you "making disciples" at home?
Can you think of 7 names for your "7 for Heaven" list?

Key #2:
SEE THE NEED

MISSION QUOTE:

"A little bit of somethin' is better than
a whole lot of nothin'!" (author unknown)

BIBLE VERSES:

Proverbs 31:8-9, Micah 6:8, I John 3:16-17,
James 1:27, Romans 10:14-15

DISCUSSION QUESTIONS:

What local or global need do you care about most?
Has anyone in your family traveled to another country?
What's the difference between a "mission trip" and travel?
If you had a $1000 check to give to any Gospel-ministry,
what specific name would you write on the check?
What's your favorite resource to teach kids about the world?

Key #3:
SEE THE END

MISSION QUOTE:

"There are two days on my calendar:
this day and That Day." — Martin Luther

BIBLE VERSES:

Psalm 39:4-5. Psalm 90:12, Ecclesiastes 12:13-14
Ephesians 2:8-10, Revelation 7:9

DISCUSSION QUESTIONS:

What typical life-goals do many parents strive for?
Have you ever attended a "thought-provoking" funeral?
In the Bible, what's the most important "End" to consider?
How did Jesus "See the End" as He lived His life on earth?
What is one change you could make in your family priorities
to live with more focus on the "End" and eternity?

Key #4:
AIM YOUR ARROWS

MISSION QUOTE:

*"Our children are not a distraction from ministry,
they're our discipleship team." — Jon & Ann Dunagan*

BIBLE VERSES:

Deuteronomy 6:7-9, Psalm 127:3-5, Psalm 144:12,
Proverbs 22:6, Philippians 2:12-13,

DISCUSSION QUESTIONS:

*What are 4 Christian parenting principles we can learn from
the 4 parts of an arrow? — Nock, Shaft, Fletching, Tip
How can we train our BOYS to be men, and men of God?
How can we train our GIRLS to be mission-minded women?
How can we train our kids to develop their unique gifts?*

Key #5:
FIND YOUR PASSION

MISSION QUOTE:

"Don't ask what the world needs; ask what makes you come alive and go do it; because what the world needs is people who have come alive." — Howard Thurman

BIBLE VERSES:

Hebrews 12:2, Galatians 2:20, Ephesians 2:10, I Corinthians 12:4-6, I Corinthians 12:15-18

DISCUSSION QUESTIONS:

What do each of these letters — "P.A.S.S.I.O.N." — stand for?
What is one thing your family is especially passionate about?
What do you enjoy? What is one thing that bothers you?
What example in the video was most inspiring to you?
What unique strengths or "gifts" could your family share?

Key #6:
FAITH NOT FEAR

MISSION QUOTE:

"Fear tricks us into living a boring life."
— Donald Miller

BIBLE VERSES:

Ecclesiastes 12:13, Proverbs 29:25, Proverbs 19:23,
Isaiah 41:10, Philippians 4:6-7

DISCUSSION QUESTIONS:

What particular "FEAR" is a challenge for you or your family?
What's an example of the fear of God or a protective fear?
What's an example of the fear of man or a paralyzing fear?
How can God's Word help us to fight against FEAR?
What's your favorite NO FEAR Bible verse?

Key #7:

SAY "YES!" TO JESUS

MISSION QUOTE:

"Let's live on the YES side of life, not the NO side of legalism." —Jon & Ann Dunagan

BIBLE VERSES:

Galatians 2:20, II Corinthians 1:20, John 10:10, Matthew 16:24-26, Luke 9:23, Luke 18:18-23

DISCUSSION QUESTIONS:

As a follower of Jesus, what "percentage" of our life is His?
What does it mean for your family to say "YES" to Jesus?
What does it mean to be crucified with Christ — yet to LIVE?
How can you become more of a Mission-Minded Family?
Which of the "7 Simple Keys" is your favorite?

Look beyond your children's faces
and see the potential of a new generation—
the *families* they will guide,
the *friends* they will lead to Jesus,
and yes, even the *nations* they will impact.

The
MISSION-MINDED
FAMILY

Releasing Your Family to
God's Destiny

PART 2
Balancing the "How" of World Missions
while prioritizing your own family

Great families and
God's Great Commission
GO together!

Contents

The Mission-Minded
Family Features

/ Hymns and Poems

👫 From My Children's Perspective

🧍 Mini Missionary Biographies

(those marked with an asterisk include a "Mission-Minded Monologue Skit")

📖 Mission Stories

🌐 Teaching Opportunities

What Is a
Mission-Minded Family?

Your family may never be called to become missionaries in a foreign country; yet as followers of Jesus Christ, you are still called to be mission-minded. When Christ gave His Great Commission—"Go into all the world and preach the gospel" (Mark 16:15; see also Matthew 28:18–19)—He wasn't just speaking to special apostles, future missionaries, or a few chosen preachers. Jesus was unveiling His purpose for *all* of us. And His words were not just a "Great Suggestion." As Hudson Taylor once said, "The Great Commission is not an option to consider; it's a command to obey."

Jesus fulfilled God's mission for His life. Yet His ministry continues today—through us. In Acts 1:1, Luke described his "former account" (the Gospel he had previously written) as the testimony "of all that Jesus *began* both to do and teach" (emphasis added). Throughout the world today, the Lord Jesus is *still* saving people and changing their lives; and your family can participate in what He's doing.

Instead of merely asking God to bless *your* kids, meet *your* needs, and fulfill *your* personal goals, seek God for how your family can bless *others*, meet *others'* needs, and help fulfill *God's* goals. Rather than praying, "Lord, please bless *our* plans," find and follow *God's* plans—because God's plans are already blessed!

There are no cookie-cutter shapes or standards for mission-minded families. Such families come in all sizes, nationalities, and social groups, simply sharing a common love for the Lord and the lost.

Our mission is the Great Commission, and this focus affects each family member (as an individual) *and* the entire family (as a unit). Mission-minded families love God, they are focused on expanding God's kingdom, and they are some of the happiest people on earth! Here are ten examples of various kinds of mission-minded families:

- **John and Angelique** sit with their children on the front row of our church every Sunday, intensely focused on worship and always eager to learn from God's Word. John is a professional fishing guide, and Angelique is a homeschooling mom and a preschool teacher. John and Angelique minister to the youth in our church, helping with whatever needs done, and they are passionate about missions. For years their family has sponsored children from several missionary organizations, and they recently adopted a little boy they had taken into their home as a foster child. They give generously to international evangelism, and they earnestly pray for the lost, both overseas and within their own family. A few days ago I heard that Angelique was learning "with" her kids about Gladys Aylward (a missionary to China); and John recently traveled on a short-term mission trip to Africa, an effort that focused on preaching, planting a church, baptizing new believers . . . and teaching people to fish!

- **Delbert and Manja** don't fit the typical missionary mold, but they are two of the most intensely mission-minded people I know. They have a blended family, with "his" and "her" kids from previous marriages; and their eating preference is vegan. Delbert works for Google, and Manja grows organic plants and has a face-painting business (painting children's faces for parties and community events). As God has given them a passion for His mission, it has totally changed how their family thinks, speaks, reads, gives, and obeys. God challenged Delbert's attitude in the area of finances, primarily through Randy Alcorn's book *Money, Possessions, and Eternity*. The couple's focus changed from investing and preparing for retirement to making an eternal difference for

Christ. They dedicated an entire year's profits from their face-painting business to sponsor an overseas orphanage, and Manja and her daughter are currently sewing dresses (each one uniquely designed) for one hundred orphan girls. Their hearts are especially burdened by the needs of the Invisible Children ministry in Africa; and to deepen their compassion for displaced people, their family participated in a gathering of five thousand people who slept overnight in self-made cardboard shelters.

- **Bob and Carol** are godly grandparents. Bob was a contractor and pastor of a small country church, and Carol was a home economics teacher. As they approached their golden years, they decided to surrender their retirement dreams to God and obey whatever He asked them to do. The first direction outside of their comfort zone they received was to visit a local bar several times a week. Although they didn't drink alcohol, they started to establish relationships with non-Christians there and began to share the gospel. A few years later they traveled on a short-term mission trip. And today they are full-time overseas missionaries, training thousands of village pastors, operating a large orphanage they founded, training nationals in construction projects and home economics skills . . . and having the time of their lives! Bob and Carol aren't able to see their grown children and their grandchildren as often as they would like; but when they do, they instill a powerful mission-minded heritage!

- **Brent and Virginia** are newlyweds with a passion for God. Growing up, each felt God's call to missions. Brent led a lunchtime Bible club at his public high school, which grew to reach hundreds of students; he wrote English papers about Christian missionary work; and he participated in many short-term mission trips. Virginia felt led to work with a mission organization and ministered for a while in Asia. After getting married, they were hired by a large church to lead a Master's Commission program. Later they felt called to leave this secure position to become full-time missionaries in Africa. Brent and Virginia are enjoying their early years of marriage in Uganda, where they are helping people come to Christ, caring for orphans and the poor, and building churches.

- **Sonja** is a single mom with a ten-year-old son. Five years ago she was unsaved, addicted to drugs, trapped in an immoral lifestyle, and living on the streets of a large city. A friend prayed for her and invited her to church, and God has totally transformed her life. Today Sonja manages a successful daycare business, and she and her son Austin are part of my family's church and home group. Over the past two years Sonja has organized monthly parents' night out parties, with all proceeds (on a donation basis) going to missions. She has purchased uniforms and educational supplies, along with providing financial support, for several missionaries and national ministers. Sonja has also traveled on several mission trips of her own: to Africa, Europe, and Asia. She led craft projects at an overseas orphanage, she shared about God's grace at a church in Japan, and she helped to distribute thousands of Operation Christmas Child boxes in the Philippines through Samaritan's Purse. Sonja has become a happy person and a good mother. She and Austin are preparing to take a mission trip together. With God, nothing is impossible!

- **Aaron and Carol** are just starting their own business. Carol is a former YWAM (Youth With A Mission) missionary, having ministered for six years in Belize, South America, with a special calling for intercession. As a family with five school-age children, Aaron and Carol teach children about the Lord and encourage others (especially young people and women) to have a greater heart for missions. Their oldest daughter, a young teenager, feels a special drawing to international missionary work. Aaron and Carol are nurturing this calling by taking her to a missions "Perspectives" class and training her to pray for the world.

- **Cassie** is twenty-one years old. Though not yet married, Cassie believes that God has called her to be a mother who has a mission-minded family. She has ministered on mission trips to Haiti, Africa, and India, including a YWAM Discipleship Training School where she trained missionary children from throughout Southeast Asia in intercessory prayer. Cassie has ministered to youth and children for years, and she has been a women's retreat speaker alongside her mother. Cassie envisions herself, in the future, leading short-term family mission trips and encouraging others in missions. In the meantime, she is keeping her heart pure, growing closer to the Lord through worship and studying God's Word, and fervently praying for her future husband.

- **Paul and Eleanor** have been in full-time missionary service for over fifty years. They have lived in many countries and have experienced radical testimonies of God's deliverance and provision (especially during wartime). Even in their eighties their hearts overflow with a passionate zeal for God and missions. All five of their grown children are in full-time ministry (as missionaries, pastors, or youth ministers), and their whole family is mission-minded. This past year I attended one of their grandchildren's weddings (the young couple got engaged in Egypt and were already ministering as worship leaders and youth pastors). The anointing and presence of God were so strong as this godly grandfather prayed over the bride and groom. I'm sure everyone in the sanctuary knew this wasn't just about two beautiful young people; this union was focused toward fulfilling God's purpose for the next generation—and there was hardly a dry eye in the audience!

- **Jayson and Julie** have five children, all attending public schools. Jayson is a road excavator and Julie owns a scrapbook store. Over the years, their family has housed foreign exchange students from Hong Kong, Thailand, China, and Italy. One of these students, from China, has gone on to write several influential books in Chinese and was recently accepted into graduate school at Harvard. Because of their family's influence, this young man (who still calls Jayson "Dad" and Julie "Mom") is no longer a Buddhist. He became a believer and now attends a Christian church. Julie recently went to China to meet and share with this young man's family, while Jayson traveled to Africa to share the gospel and use his road-building expertise to build safe pathways on a remote island!

A Mission-Minded Family

A mission-minded family . . . loves to make God smile!

A mission-minded family . . . learns to be diligent, because there's work to be done and many needs in this world.

A mission-minded family . . . brings a stack of well-worn Bibles to church!

A mission-minded family . . . enjoys presents at Christmastime, but never forgets all the poor little children in Cambodia who have nothing.

A mission-minded family . . . is focused on eternity.

A mission-minded family . . . knows how to look up Afghanistan, Bolivia, Singapore, and Tibet, and imagines more than what they see on a map.

A mission-minded family . . . eats rice!

A mission-minded family . . . learns how to share the "gospel colors" and is excited about the miniature *EvangeCube* that can hook to a kid's backpack.

A mission-minded family . . . dreams of traveling around the world and makes sure each person has an updated passport—just in case!

A mission-minded family . . . thinks about the Irish on St. Patrick's Day—and all the people wearing green who don't have a clue that Patrick was a missionary.

A mission-minded family . . . lives in SUB-mission!

A mission-minded family . . . shakes missionaries' hands after church and invites their family over for dinner.

A mission-minded family . . . knows that when the Lord guides, He also provides.

A mission-minded family . . . keeps the lawn mowed, as a good Christian witness to the neighbors.

A mission-minded family . . . is strategically aimed for God's purpose.

A mission-minded family . . . anticipates the excitement of the teenage years and looks forward to youth group mission trips.

A mission-minded family . . . keeps active and healthy in order to be physically able to do whatever God requires.

A mission-minded family . . . gives generously—even when it hurts!

A mission-minded family . . . enjoys carryon luggage with wheels, final boarding calls, and airline peanuts.

A mission-minded family . . . thinks beyond the box of what's merely expected and hopes to do something big (or something little) for God.

A mission-minded family . . . lives for Jesus!

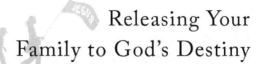

CHAPTER 1

Releasing Your
Family to God's Destiny

God has a destiny for your family. He has an individual plan for each member, as well as a "corporate" purpose for you as a family unit. God will help you, as parents, to train each child toward God's mission for his or her life, and He will help you to focus your family toward making a strong impact for His kingdom—in your community, in your church, in your children's schools, and in the world.

The Bible says in Psalm 127:4, "Like arrows in the hand of a warrior, so are the children of one's youth." This verse recently "hit" me in a new way as I was attending a graduation party. During the evening, a group of church leaders, led by the graduate's father, gathered to pray for this young man. He had been raised to have a fervent heart for God and for world missions, and we prayed for God's purposes to be fulfilled. As I laid my hands on the graduate's mom (my dear friend Karen), I could sympathize with her mixed feelings: happiness and pride combined with a sad realization that this season in their family's life was coming to an end. As we prayed, I "saw" (in my mind's eye) her eighteen-year-old son as a straight arrow in a bow. Afterward, I leaned over and whispered in my friend's ear, "You know, Karen, it's not enough just to aim our arrows; to hit the target we've got to release the string!"

As our children grow, there will be repeated times of releasing each one to God: letting go of a little hand as a baby takes that first wobbly step . . . letting go of total educational control as a child steps onto that school bus or enrolls in that first college course. Or what about that moment when we let go of the car keys and an eager teenager plops into the driver's seat of our car and takes control of the steering wheel?

Sometimes it's very scary.

As I write this chapter, my husband and I have a nearly twenty-year-old son climbing a dangerous mountain and then the following week heading to Oxford, England for a summer-long study-abroad program. Our eighteen-year-old son just graduated from high school and will soon be moving to a university two thousand miles from home. Our nearly sixteen-year-old daughter is just about to get her driver's license.

No matter how many times I have released my children, I continually need to rely on God's fresh grace for today's particular moment. Whether it's dropping off a little one into the arms of a church nursery worker or dropping off a young adult at an international airport, I need to trust God.

Just like Hannah released her little Samuel, I have surrendered each child to the Lord; yet I still have times when God convicts me that I need to rely on Him even more. At a deeper level, I need to *continue* to trust Him. With faith, I need to trust that God will direct each of my kids to fulfill His purposes (without me pushing them to do what I want). I need to trust that God will bring just the right spouse for each of my sons and daughters (without me trying to make something happen). And I need to trust God that He will protect my children as they begin to step out to fulfill His destiny (without me worrying or trying to figure it out).

As I have thought about this need to totally release each of my children to God's purposes, I have tried to imagine—in my own finite way—what our heavenly Father must have experienced when He released *His* Child. God never struggles, but I believe He can relate to my feelings (and yours). He too had to release His Son—His only Son—in order to fulfill His plans for this earth.

Imagine with me:

What if someday God called one of my children . . . let's just say, for an example, to go on a summer mission trip to Calcutta, India?

Would I be able to send him or her with confidence and joy?

If my husband and I prayed about the particular outreach and God gave us His peace about it, I know I would. My husband and I would uphold our child in prayer, and we would trust God's direction. And as a mom, I would rely on Him for grace.

But the sacrifice God made was far greater . . .

What if someday a child of ours decided to *move* to Calcutta, India, for perhaps ten months . . . or ten years . . . or even longer? Could I handle that?

That would be much harder.

Although it would be difficult to live so far apart, I would do my best to support him or her through regular prayer and communication (and I would definitely hope for e-mail access!). If my grown child had a family, I would really miss getting to know my child's spouse and his or her family; and I can hardly imagine how much I would yearn for time with those future grandchildren. Yet, if God was calling my child, I would let my child go . . . and rely on Him for extra grace.

But God's sacrifice was still far greater . . .

So, to take the analogy one step further, what if my husband and I, back in time about twenty years ago, were expecting our first child, and God told us that He wanted us to *surrender* this precious newborn—right from birth? What if God said He had chosen a poor couple in Calcutta, India, to raise *our* baby? What if He said our little one would grow up in some obscure squatter village . . . would live among filth and poverty . . . would spend his life helping people . . . and, in the end, would be rejected, hated, and brutally killed by the very people he was sent to help?

Would I send my son to do that? How could I?

But (perhaps) that is a glimpse of what God did for us.

If we are going to raise a generation of world changers, it is likely that we will need to surrender our children into areas that may make us uncomfortable. He could call our child to pioneer a megachurch in a crowded inner city or to raise a large, God-fearing family in a quiet rural town. He may want our child to impact a corrupt political system or to redirect a greed-motivated business. He could call our precious son to enlist in the military or our pure daughter to have an effect on the media. He could call our child to Cairo, Egypt . . . or to New York City . . . or maybe even to Calcutta, India.

As mission-minded parents, will we "let go" of those arrows and encourage each child to fulfill the Lord's plans? Or will we be God's greatest hindrance?

It's a heart issue, and it's big.

Just as God released His Son for us, we need to totally release each of our children—again and again, every day—for His eternal purposes.

PURSUING GOD'S PURPOSES

An excerpt from *The Missions Addiction*, by David Shibley

We whine, "I just want to know my purpose; I've got to reach my destiny." We race all over the country to attend "destiny conferences," and we devour tapes and books on "reaching your full potential." It would be amusing if it were not so appalling. Even cloaking our self-centeredness in Christian garb and jargon cannot cover the nakedness of this cult of self that has infested much of the church. How can we ever hope to discover our purpose in the earth with little or no interest in His purpose? How will we ever know our destiny when we have so little identification with God's destiny for the nations? It certainly is good to pray, "Lord, what is Your will for my life?" But even this can be a self-absorbed prayer. It is far better to pray, "Lord, what is Your will for my generation? How do You want my life to fit into Your plan for my times?"

Pursuing God's purposes, not our own, is the path to personal fulfillment.

WE'VE A STORY TO TELL TO THE NATIONS

A missions hymn, by H. Ernest Nichol (1862–1928)

We've a story to tell to the nations,
That shall turn their hearts to the right,
A story of truth and mercy,
A story of peace and light,
A story of peace and light.

Chorus:
For the darkness shall turn to dawning,
And the dawning to noonday bright,
And Christ's great kingdom shall come on earth,
The kingdom of love and light.

We've a song to be sung to the nations,
That shall lift their hearts to the Lord,
A song that shall conquer evil,
And shatter the spear and sword,
And shatter the spear and sword.

We've a message to give to the nations,
That the Lord who reigneth above
Hath sent us His Son to save us,
And show us that God is love,
And show us that God is love.

We've a Savior to show to the nations,
Who the path of sorrow hath trod,
That all of the world's great peoples
May come to the truth of God,
May come to the truth of God!

Chorus:
For the darkness shall turn to dawning,
And the dawning to noonday bright,
And Christ's great kingdom shall come on earth,
The kingdom of love and light.

"I have seen the Vision and for self I cannot live;
Life is less than worthless till my all I give."

OSWALD J. SMITH

CHAPTER 2

Three Powerful Dynamics
of a Mission-Minded Family

In a mission-minded family, there's a God-infused energy. There's a focus on God's worldwide purpose. There's a passion for the lost. There's a spiritual depth and hunger that reaches beyond the maintenance mode of cultural Christianity. A mission-minded family emphasizes leadership, calling, and destiny. There's a prevailing attitude of self-sacrifice and an emphasis on total submission to God's will. And there's an unmistakable and contagious joy.

I believe these qualities can be identified and summarized in three powerful dynamics.

Dynamic #1
A Mission-Minded Family Is Focused on Eternity

Mission-minded families have a focused purpose for life. But what is this target? What is our "mission" or our final destination?

In the secular motivational book *The Seven Habits of Highly Effective People*, author Stephen Covey presents a challenge to "begin with the end in mind." He encourages his readers to evaluate their priorities in life by envisioning their own funeral, three years from today:

> As you take a seat and wait for the services to begin, you look at the program in your hand. There are to be four speakers. The first is from your family, immediate and also extended—children, brothers, sisters, nephews, nieces, aunts, uncles, cousins, and grandparents, who have come from all

over the country to attend. The second speaker is one of your friends, someone who can give a sense of what you were as a person. The third speaker is from your work or profession. And the fourth is from your church or some community organization where you've been involved in service.

Now think deeply. What would you like each of these speakers to say about you and your life? What kind of husband, wife, brother, or mother would you like their words to reflect? What kind of son or daughter or cousin? What kind of friend? What kind of working associate?

What character would you like them to have seen in you? What contributions, what achievements would you want them to remember? Look carefully at the people around you. What difference would you like to have made in their lives?

This is an interesting thought. As I've glanced over newspaper obituaries or attended a funeral service, I've often wondered how my life—along with the lives of each member of my family—would someday be summarized. I have heard about a goal-setting project of writing your own obituary, then living your life to fulfill it.

It's good to consider the godly legacy we will leave for the next generation and important to realize that our day-to-day decisions can leave a lasting example, for good or for evil. But as Christians, and as members of mission-minded families, our funeral, or even our godly legacy, is not the end. Our ultimate life evaluation will not be determined by the opinions of those *we leave behind*. Instead, our life will be judged by the One *we go to meet*—our almighty God in heaven.

Because of the death and resurrection of Jesus, and our salvation by grace and through faith in Him, the question of whether our destiny is in heaven or hell is answered. However, the Bible speaks of a time in heaven when God will judge us for our obedience to His purposes and we will be rewarded accordingly (Romans 14:10–12; 2 Corinthians 5:10).

In the Sermon on the Mount, Jesus taught about the importance of laying up "treasures in heaven" (Matthew 6:20). God has rewards in heaven for giving alms (Matthew 6:4), for prayer (Matthew 6:6), for fasting (Matthew 6:18), and even for being "persecuted for righteousness' sake" (Matthew 5:10). The Bible also speaks of special crowns in heaven: an "imperishable crown" for running God's race (1 Corinthians 9:24–27), a "crown of rejoicing" for seeing those we've won to Christ in heaven (1 Thessalonians 2:19–20), a "crown of righteousness" for obedience (2 Timothy 4:7–8), a "crown of glory" for shepherding God's people (1 Peter 5:1–4), and "the crown of life" for Christian martyrdom (Revelation 2:10). And someday, in heaven, there will be a time of casting down crowns as an ultimate act of worship before the throne of God (Revelation 4:9–11).

As we stand before our almighty, holy, and awesome Lord, we will be totally aware of the fact that our self-efforts are nothing but filthy rags (see Isaiah 64:6). Any self-made "crowns" of human efforts in missions or ministry—achieved with wrong motivations, with selfish ambitions, with family or spiritual priorities out of whack, or perhaps accomplished through direct disobedience—will be worth absolutely nothing in God's sight.

I have pictured myself entering heaven with some of these self-made crowns. As I see myself entering the awesome presence of God, all of my own crowns or achievements instantly disintegrate and evaporate into nothing.

God sees our hearts, and He can't be fooled. He sees the big picture, and He wants what's best for the long term. God has a big heart for the whole world; but He also desires a deep and personal relationship with each one of us. God wants our families to reach individuals and to touch nations; but He also wants us to reflect His love and His compassion to the people within our own home.

A mission-minded family keeps God's focus in mind. A powerful dynamic is present when you raise your children to walk daily in the fear of the Lord. It's not about preparing kids to be successful, or to get into a good college, or to make a lot of money to give to missions, or even to do something "famous" for God. Our mission is to love and please God—to live every day in complete obedience.

How this plays out for each mission-minded family will be different. God has unique purposes and callings. But we begin with the end in mind. As we're raising each of our children—from cuddling our babies, to disciplining our toddlers, to teaching and training our school-age children, to encouraging and motivating our teens, to aiming and releasing our young adults to God's call for their lives—we keep the target in focus.

It's all about worshiping God and living our lives for His glory. What we "accomplish" on earth is only a byproduct. As we draw close to God—individually and as a family unit—we will know more of His heart. We will want to follow Him. It's not about works or achievement. It's simply about loving God and doing what He wants. No matter the cost. No matter what.

For us, the "end" that we need to be concerned about is that moment when we enter heaven and appear before the presence of God. Our lives on earth are merely the preparation for our eternal life, which will continue forever. When a family lives with this focus, the dynamic is powerful. You become a family on a mission. And it's not even your own mission; you're on *God's* mission.

Dynamic #2
A Mission-Minded Family Lives in SUB-mission

A mission-minded family is submitted. There's a total submission to God and to His purposes. In archery, the arrow doesn't choose its destination; it simply rests in the archer's hand to be aimed toward his chosen target. When the archer is ready, the arrow will be released; and as long as the arrow is properly aligned and unhindered by outside forces, it will soar forward (on a straight path) toward its appointed destiny.

How SUB-mission Relates to Missions

The only difference between *submission* and *mission* is that little prefix *sub*—which means "under, beneath, or below." As mission-minded families, our daily submission to God, and our yielding to His under-the-surface guidance and His pruning in our lives, will directly affect our overall mission fulfillment and fruitfulness. It may sound more important to board an overseas-bound 747 or to have the opportunity to influence a huge crowd of people, but these activities may not be God's best plan for this particular moment (or season) in our lives.

We're all called, as believers, to be a part of God's worldwide plan; but His expectations for us, as individuals and as a family, may be much smaller, yet possibly even more challenging to obey. Today's mission-for-the-moment simply may be to open our Bible and read a few chapters or to take a minute to pray for a friend. Maybe right now all God wants is for us to snuggle up on the couch with a little one and read a fun storybook. Or perhaps God's perfect will is merely for us to quit procrastinating, turn off the computer, and go finish those loads of laundry!

When I think about the word *submission*, I like to imagine a submarine advancing silently underwater. Without sonar detection, others may not even know it's there, because it's so far beneath the surface; yet steadily and powerfully that vessel is still moving toward its goal.

Or when I think about my need to submit to God, I sometimes picture a late-winter scene with newly pruned fruit trees. Our family lives in a beautiful area of Oregon, known for its pear and apple harvests. After years of driving through the orchards, I've come to appreciate how God's fruitfulness comes in seasons. Even when the branches look barren, I know that the tree roots are growing deeper. And if I see the local farmers doing some heavy-duty pruning, I know it's only because they want an increase in their summertime harvest!

In the same way, as we establish godly and submissive hearts, we can keep advancing forward (like that underwater submarine) and growing deeper and firmer roots (like those fruit trees) to fulfill God's purposes for our lives. Even if no one notices the little things we do or the little attitudes we change, God knows it all. He knows exactly where we are right now and exactly where He's planted us. And He has not forgotten about us, or our dreams.

Submission to God involves every area of our lives: our personal maturity (spiritually, mentally, physically, and financially), our attitude toward our marriage, our family priorities, our disciplines in home management—along with our ministry callings. As we allow God to refine those *sub* areas in our lives, we can trust that He will fulfill all of His mission promises to us . . . in His timing.

SUB-mission and the Joyful Family

When God created the family, He decided upon a family structure that He knew would work best. His plan is:

- God is the leader of the family, and God's Word is the ultimate, final word.

- Dad submits to God and leads the family according to God's direction, not necessarily because he is most qualified or deserving, but because he is God's choice. Dad loves Mom with a self-sacrificing love like Christ loved the church.

- Mom submits to God and has a willing heart of submission toward her husband. Mom supports and loves Dad with a heart attitude of admiration, respect, esteem, and encouragement.

- Together, Dad and Mom seek God and God's will for their family. They diligently train each child to follow them—as they follow God.

- Each child submits completely to God and to Dad and Mom with a heart of obedience, honor, and respect. Older children are a godly example and an encouragement to younger children.

- God's purpose for this family (and for each family member) is fulfilled. The whole family loves God, and the family lives in joy.

We can't always change the actions or attitudes of others in our family, and it's not our responsibility to make sure that the people in authority over us are doing everything right. We just need to submit and obey what God is telling us.

SMUGGLING BIBLES INTO CHINA

My Personal Story of SUB-mission

Jon and I were overseas on one of our first mission trips. I was a young and adventurous twenty-two-year-old, recently graduated from college, pretty much still a newlywed, and a fairly new mommy (with a toddler in hand and baby number two on the way). Both Jon and I felt "full of faith," and we were ready to do anything for God. We had been preaching throughout remote Filipino villages and sharing in Hong Kong church services for several weeks. And on this particular morning we were preparing to smuggle Bibles (for the second time) into Communist China.

Only one week earlier, we had loaded our suitcases with Bibles and fearlessly transported God's Word through the Chinese customs department. On that first attempt our blond-haired toddler totally distracted the security guards, and no one even checked our bags! It was like we were living our very own missionary adventure; and just like the stories of Brother Andrew smuggling Bibles behind the Iron Curtain, God was once again "blinding the eyes" of foreign officials. Although we were directly disobeying a man-made law, we were totally confident in our radical obedience to God's higher law. We knew that God was blessing our actions, and we were excited to deliver His Word to believers who so desperately needed it.

However, on the morning before our second Bible-smuggling mission, my husband woke up with a feeling of apprehension in his spirit. It wasn't that Jon was fearful of what we planned to do; but he just didn't feel a peace about me going. Although he didn't know why, Jon simply felt I was not to participate in that day's outreach. Instead, he felt I was supposed to stay back and pray.

But, to put it mildly, my strong-willed, goal-oriented nature didn't quite agree with my husband's simple idea.

"You have got to be kidding!" I protested. "Do you really think I'm going to just sit here in this little room all day while you're off on our mission? I know you think I'm pushing myself too hard, but I am not too tired, and just because I'm pregnant doesn't mean I shouldn't go! I'm just fine, and I'm not going to miss out! You know, God didn't tell just *you* to 'Go into all the world and preach the gospel'; and I'm not going to sit here doing nothing! No matter what you say, I am going!"

Just like before, I felt justified in my radical obedience to God. Despite my seemingly defiant attitude, I felt totally submitted to God and His Word. (Wasn't I?) And I was steadfastly determined to fulfill God's mission.

I still had a lot to learn.

Later that morning, at our predelivery meeting place, I crammed my bags totally full of Bibles—completely assured that God would once again "blind the eyes" of anyone who would oppose us. Jon and I were assigned to cross the border at the same time as two other American pastors. As we all advanced toward the border, we hooked our little "blond-haired distraction device" into the baby-pack on Jon's back.

As the five of us came to the customs area, the two pastors decided to go through first . . . and just as we had prayed, there was no problem. Next, Jon and our son went through their line . . . and once again, there was no problem. It was as if the bags were completely invisible.

So with total assurance, I stepped forward and approached the customs desk. But suddenly a guard grabbed my heavy bag and began to unzip it. He pointed to my stacks of Bibles and began yelling in Chinese. A flashing red light began spinning above my aisle as more guards came toward me. Security guards halted Jon at the exit door, and then they ushered us into a stark room with brick walls and mean-looking officials. I tried to hold my composure and appear brave, as an English-speaking guard was called in to interpret; but as they began to yell, my wall of confidence began to crumble.

Because of our citizenship (and current international relations), the officials merely threatened us and confiscated all of our Bibles. Afterward, we were released to enter the country . . . with our empty bags. At this point, we were scheduled to go to a secret underground meeting room, where our Bibles could be sorted and organized for distribution. But now, what were we supposed to do? Together, Jon and I walked in silence for several blocks, as we tried to distance ourselves from the two pastors.

I felt so miserable, there was no need for an "I told you so." I realized that I had not just gone against my husband; I defied God and I rejected God's authority and covering over my life. Because of my stubbornness, God's protection had been removed. Instead of just doing something "little" (staying back and interceding for the group), I stubbornly pushed for my own big plan—hindering the entire mission and endangering our family.

We finally sat down, and I openly repented to Jon and the Lord. We decided to browse through an open market and eventually purchased a Chinese vase for our living room. For twenty years this vase has reminded me of how I felt that day and how deeply I want to follow God's way rather than my own.

"It is better to obey God rather than men."

BROTHER ANDREW

WHO IS BROTHER ANDREW?

Brother Andrew is known as "God's Smuggler" for his Bible distribution through a ministry called Open Doors. For years, this mission outreach has focused on areas where open propagation of Christianity is forbidden— often defying government laws and authorities to fulfill God's Great Commission. As Andrew explains, "It is better to obey God rather than men." Smuggling Bibles into "closed" countries is only one facet of Open Doors' ministry, though it's the most widely known (especially as a result of Brother Andrew's impacting book, *God's Smuggler*). This type of "illegal" ministry has stirred both controversy and tremendous support. Yet despite opposition, millions of people have received God's Word, and multitudes of people have come to know Jesus Christ as their Lord and Savior.

Dynamic #3
A Mission-Minded Family Is Strategically Aimed

Each person in your family has specific gifts and callings, and you also have a destiny as a family. God has placed you together as a powerful mission-minded unit, so it is important to seek the Lord for His purpose for you as a team.

- Is your family called to hospitality?

- Is your family called to active leadership within your local church?

- Is your family called to specifically impact your neighborhood?

- Taking into account your family's specific gifts, abilities, and resources, what are ways you can participate in God's Great Commission?

With an inward determination, the archer reaches across his shoulder and selects a favorite arrow. He checks the alignment, then places it in his bow. With his eye focused on the target's center, he gently pulls back, feeling the string tighten and the tension increase.

Our children are God's reward and our heritage. Our descendants have the potential to take God's mission into future generations—and to a higher and more effective level. They're our arrows, our most strategic weapons to aim toward the future.

Our goal is not to raise kids to be popular, famous, or wealthy. The goal is not to somehow get our teenagers to "survive" their youth without tasting a drop of alcohol, puffing on a cigarette, or experimenting with illegal drugs. It's not enough to "hope" that each child will turn out OK or "trust" that they won't be "too bad." As we influence tomorrow's world changers, our vision must be infinitely higher.

Can you imagine an archer distracted by his surroundings and pledging, "OK, in today's competition I'll try not to hit that tree, and I won't shoot any arrows into the river; I'll work at aiming higher than the grass and try not to skewer my opponent"?

This contestant will likely miss even the outer rings of his target!

Instead of focusing on the "NO" side of human legalism (emphasizing our never-ending rules), it's much more fulfilling and productive to challenge young people to live on the "YES" side of God's life (emphasizing His eternal plans).

For example, if a daughter keeps focused on her desire to have a happy family with a godly, mission-minded husband, she will be self-motivated to make pure and wholesome relationship decisions throughout her childhood and young adult years.

If a son is attentive to a specific calling on his life toward a particular ministry, he will realize the importance of developing his personal prayer life, he will want to faithfully study the Bible, and, in God's timing, he will begin to step out in areas of Christian leadership.

As we keep each of our children focused on God's long-term goals, today's short-term decisions will make sense. And today's temptations, by God's grace, will be easier to withstand. Why would our kids want to smoke or take drugs? They'll want to set nations "on fire" for God! Why would our teens seek satisfaction in ungodly relationships? Their hearts will be burning with the fear of God and will be focused on His passion for the lost! (And if that attitude is not a reality in our kids' lives today, let's pray for it—in faith!)

Proverbs 22:6 tells us, according to *The Amplified Bible*, "Train up a child in the way he should go [and in keeping with his individual gift or bent], and when he is old he will not depart from it." This instruction goes beyond training a child merely to "believe" in God. Our responsibility as mission-minded parents is to train each child to "know" Jesus personally, to hear His voice, and to follow God's direction for his or her life.

As you consider each family member, and your family as a unit, several questions can help you "aim" toward God's mission-minded purpose:

- What is each family member's unique talent, gift, or personality strength?

- What does each family member love to do?

- What is each family member passionate about? (Conversely, what causes him or her to get extremely frustrated?)

- What could be one of God's purposes for each person?

- As a family, how can we make the best use of the childhood and teenage years for the kingdom of God—both for the present and for the future?

With his eye focused on the target, the archer pauses a moment. He relaxes ever so slightly . . . then prepares his arrow. He points it toward the bull's-eye and makes certain the aim is correct. Then, at last, he releases the string.

As our children grow, increasingly we will need to challenge them to step out and try new things (in a good way). If a child is trained and disciplined properly during the younger years, the older years will not be a time for our gripping harder, but for relaxing our "hold" to begin letting go. The teen years are a time to practice aiming our arrows. Especially during the middle school and high school years, it is important to encourage our children to take godly risks, to discover God's desires, and to work with them to develop every area of life:

- **Spiritual Development**—The core of our mission-minded foundation is each family member's personal relationship with Jesus. If this goal is not in place, nothing will line up. Each child can be challenged to read through the Bible, to pray for the nations, and to step out in leadership. Perhaps a child could assist with a children's Bible study or become a prayer leader. Perhaps a teenager could help lead a youth worship team or go on an adventurous mission trip.

- **Mental Development**—Educationally, think about God's purpose for your family and for each of your children. Will God's calling require a university degree, advanced mathematics or science, writing skills, or knowledge of computer technology? How should that affect your family's attitude toward education? Is your family gifted in music or art? That talent should be developed and focused toward God's kingdom. If future finances for college will be a challenge, begin researching scholarships (and encourage your kids in areas these scholarships evaluate, such as GPA, test scores, community service hours, and leadership).

- **Physical Development**—A mission-minded family is active and physically fit. The childhood years are important for developing a wholesome lifestyle, and an adventurous attitude can be encouraged. God's life purpose may require strong physical abilities or a daring mindset. Perhaps your family should invest time in athletic training, competing on a local sports team, simply working on losing excess weight, or changing unhealthy eating habits. Physical fitness is not merely for appearance and the thrill of competition; it's vital for health, self-discipline, and becoming more goal oriented.

As mission-minded families, we can seek God's direction and then begin to serve as God's facilitators and motivators. If we can encourage our children to discover God's plans and to *want to* develop specific God-given abilities, it will totally change everything. Instead of dealing with surface issues, we begin to train our children's hearts and to focus on staying aimed toward God's purpose. A change at this root level alters everything, from grades in school and success in activities to confidence in leadership and a spiritual desire to develop God-glorifying friendships.

— 👫 FROM MY CHILDREN'S PERSPECTIVE —

MISSION-MINDED LEADERSHIP

By Christi Dunagan, age seventeen

As I've grown up in leadership and as I've grown into increased responsibilities, I've learned that leadership from God's standpoint is not a part-time activity. Leadership requires living a continuous and "real" lifestyle that others can follow, whether "leading" a specific activity or not.

A godly leader can't just *talk* about how to do things; instead, he or she needs to *walk* it out. That means setting a positive example and "guarding the gates" of life—the eye gate (including what movies I watch and what I read), the ear gate (including what music I listen to and who I talk to), and the mouth gate (what I say). I realize it is very important to stand firm in my beliefs, moral standards, and convictions, even when it's tough, because I never want to cause anyone to stumble or fall.

One thing my family has taught me about mission-minded leadership is that a "big" aspect of leadership is being "small" enough to be a servant. As a leader, it's not that we're "more important"; we're simply willing to sacrifice our time, energy, and emotions to concern ourselves with others. We must look beyond our own needs to help make a difference in the lives of others. We need to put other people's needs ahead of our own and keep the best interests of others in mind. As a leader, it's not that we're "above" other people; but we need to live "above the norm," with a higher standard—which often simply means working harder, being willing to be different, and not being afraid to walk alone.

So how do you reach God's destiny for your family? Practically speaking, it's as simple as the sport of archery. Point A is the tip of the arrow (where you are today). Point B is the center of the bull's-eye (where God wants you to go and what He wants you to do). God is the Archer, and our part is simply to allow Him to aim us—on a straight line—toward His purpose.

As individuals, and as a family unit, we allow God to use the gifts He has given us to fulfill His plans for our lives. We realize that each child is God's special arrow; therefore, as parents we help to keep each one polished, aligned, and aimed toward his or her destiny. As mission-minded families, we train and prepare "on target" with God's plans.

Walking to the target, the archer gives a faint smile. He pauses to admire how fine his arrow looks in the center of that red circle. Finally, he gives a slight tug, polishes his arrow, and then places it back in his quiver. Today's shot was only practice; but someday, when it's time for a real battle, he knows this arrow will hit its mark.

THE CALL FOR REAPERS

A missions hymn, by John O. Thompson (1782–1818)

Far and near the fields are teeming
With the waves of ripened grain;
Far and near their gold is gleaming
O'er the sunny slope and plain.

Send them forth with morn's first beaming;
Send them in the noontide's glare;
When the sun's last rays are gleaming,
Bid them gather ev'rywhere.

O thou, whom thy Lord is sending,
Gather now the sheaves of gold;
Heav'nward then at evening wending,
Thou shalt come with joy untold.

Chorus:
Lord of harvest, send for reapers!
Hear us, Lord, to Thee we cry;
Send them now the sheaves to gather,
Ere the harvesttime pass by.

"The supreme task of the church is the
evangelization of the world."

"Untold millions are still untold."

"You have one business on earth—to save souls."

JOHN WESLEY

**Do we have to choose between
"raising our kids" and "reaching the lost"
or is it possible to do both?**

CHAPTER 3

Divine Tension for Our Family Bow

Jesus asks us, "What will it profit a man if he gains the whole world, and loses his own soul?" (Mark 8:36). I also wonder what it will profit a mission-minded family to lead multitudes of unreached people to Christ . . . and lose even one of its own kids.

We need to balance our outward calling to others with our inward calling to love God and our own family. We need to balance our desire to "do" something for God with His calling for us simply to "know" Him. Yes, we need to love and reach the world; but we also need to love those God has placed in our closest circle of influence.

THE PRAYING MOMMAS AND THE SCREAMING BABIES

About five thousand women gathered for a week of ministry, teaching, and worship. The accommodations for our African village conference were humble. Bamboo awnings covered with tarps provided shade from the hot sun, and most of the women simply brought straw mats for sleeping. Many women also brought little children and nursing babies, whom they cared for as they listened to the sessions. One morning I got up and took an early morning prayer-walk, and I was blessed (and challenged) to see hundreds of women gathered for a time of fervent prayer.

As I walked quietly behind the group, I noticed a few women who were praying very hard and loud, but then I noticed that these women were totally oblivious to the needs of their little babies—sitting with bare bottoms in wet little puddles in the dirt, screaming at the top of their lungs. As I watched for a few moments, I wondered what God thought about their fervent prayers. One by one I picked up the babies and tried to help them stop crying, handing each one to his or her momma.

Later that day I shared with the women about the importance of balancing our ministry with our family priorities. Yet I was also challenged on a personal level. How many times does God see my own out-of-balance efforts, like when I'm at work on the computer or busy with a mission project—and my little kids are plopped down in front of one-too-many videos? I want God to hear my prayers, and I want my efforts to be actions of obedience. I need to keep balanced.

God wants Christian marriages to be reflections of Christ's love, and He wants each parent-child relationship to be a reflection of the heavenly Father's care. There will be times of sacrifice, of course, but our families shouldn't be neglected because of our mission-minded commitment.

Coming to Terms with Our Missionary Heritage

The other day I received a thought-provoking e-mail from a new college graduate who recently became acquainted with our family. "I have always had an issue with the family/missions life." This young man explained, "I could never fix those two together in my head. But now I know there is plenty of hope to have the large family I've always wanted (Bless my wife!) and being in full-time missions."

The more I've thought about this comment, the more I've realized how hard it is to find solid examples of world-impacting missionaries who also had strong family priorities. We can't deny that complete obedience to God's call requires sacrifice. There may be occasions of separation, financial challenge, or even death. It's possible that a family member could step out in perfect obedience—and contract some tropical illness, or be martyred, or die in an accident. In fact, instead of just "blowing off" those missionaries who didn't keep their priorities in order, we need to realize that many great men and women of God earnestly sought God for answers. International travel was very difficult in days past, and missionary work was dangerous. But if the missionary pioneers wouldn't have made these sacrifices, who knows where the worldwide church would be today?

One example is Jonathan (1859–1936) and Rosalind (1864–1942) Goforth and their eleven children. This tremendous Canadian missionary family brought the gospel to China in the early years of the twentieth century. Their passion for the lost resulted in multitudes coming to Christ, often through creative ways of evangelism. One year their family invited over twenty-five thousand people (all curious to learn how foreigners lived) to tour their house; as small groups came through their home, Jonathan preached the gospel (up to eight hours a day) while Rosalind and the children served tea and visited with the women. They traveled as a family to many villages throughout China, staying in an area until a national evangelist and a new church could be established. But it wasn't always easy. Five children died in childhood, and there were excruciating times of family separation. The following excerpt is especially thought provoking.

THE DIFFICULT DILEMMA OF JONATHAN GOFORTH

An excerpt from Goforth of China, *by Rosalind Goforth*

While Rosalind fully supported her husband's dedication to the Lord, she was naturally concerned at times about his dedication to her and the children. Of course God's will was paramount, but must it be at odds with what was in the best interest of the family? As a wife, she never doubted his love, but she did on occasion feel less than fully secure in her position. Before she and the children returned to Canada alone in 1908, she probed him concerning his commitment to her: "Suppose I were stricken with an incurable disease in the homeland and had but a few months to live. If we cabled you to come, would you come?"

Goforth obviously did not want to answer the question. An outright "no" would have been too harsh, but Rosalind persisted until he gave his answer—in the form of a question to her: "Suppose our country were at war with another nation and I, a British officer in command of an important unit. Much depended upon me as commander as to whether it was to be victory or defeat. Would I, in that event, be permitted to forsake my post in response to a call from my family in the homeland, even if it were what you suggest?" What could she say? She had no choice but to sadly reply, "No."

When my husband and I dedicated our lives to full-time missions over twenty years ago, we committed ourselves to a ministry characterized by a strong marriage. In our view, raising and training our seven children is not a distraction to our mission calling; it is our primary ministry! And today, as our children grow and pursue God's call on their lives, our family's mission-minded impact is multiplying!

There will be times of laying down our lives and taking up our cross, but we need to live in the power of the resurrection. One of my favorite quotes comes from George MacDonald: "We die daily. Happy those who daily come to life as well." That theme is similar to Paul's words, "I have been crucified with Christ; it is no longer I who live, but Christ lives in me" (Galatians 2:20). God has called us to live and to share His abundant life! Our marriages, and our families, and each of our children should benefit from our walk with God—in a way that non-Christians would envy.

As mission-minded families, how can we balance our passion for missions with our heart for our home? Is it possible to make a significant world impact while maintaining God's peace and joy in our own families? Do we have to choose between "raising our kids" and "reaching the lost"—or is it possible to do both?

I believe that God always has a perfect balance for these two pursuits; yet His guidance for one family is not necessarily the same as His guidance for another. Even within our individual lives, God's direction for today may be different from His direction for tomorrow. The important thing is that each of us, as parents and as servants of Jesus Christ, must come to God day by day and simply obey what He tells us to do!

Every Family Needs This Balance!

This godly tug of war—between our passions for our family and for missions—doesn't just affect full-time missionaries. Perhaps a little one tugs at a mother's legs as she's in the middle of a desperate phone call from a friend who needs prayer. Perhaps a dad feels overloaded with responsibilities at church, but God urges his heart to take time to nurture his own marriage. What about times when you're so busy reaching out for God that you don't take time for God to reach out to you?

If you're passionate about missions *and* passionate about your family, there will be times when this godly tug of war will seem intense, with both sides pulling hard. Have you ever sat in a mission-focused worship service and listened to a compelling message about the plight of the lost or the urgent need for world evangelization . . . and then looked at those precious children sitting next to you and prayed, *Lord, how can I possibly respond to this urgency I'm feeling in my spirit? I desperately want Your heart for the lost and for the nations, but I also know that You've called me to raise and train my kids! What am I supposed to do?*

As the preacher finishes his heart-wrenching sermon, have you ever tried to balance your inward dreams with your current reality? Have you ever longed to do something BIG for God, while knowing that He does see (and smile at) every little thing you do? Have you ever felt an inward tug of war in which your heart desperately longs to do more for missions, yet you want to be obedient by maintaining a deep and real contentment by doing less (especially if nothing you are doing at the moment feels very "significant" for God's kingdom)?

I know I sure have!

But I believe these two pulls can be a godly struggle. We need to keep pressing in toward God to get more of His heart and His love for the world; and at the same time we need to keep moving forward, little by little, to help raise up a new generation for Jesus. By keeping these two callings in balance, our families (and our ministries, and even our children's future ministries, in God's timing) will powerfully radiate His love!

It is true that being a godly parent is a mission in and of itself, yet we cannot forget that Jesus died for more people than the few precious individuals who sit around our dining table! God's love reaches beyond our homes, beyond our churches, and beyond our local areas. God sees from a different dimension than we do. His perspective is from eternity, and His vantage point is from heaven. As He views every decision we make, He sees His entire universe! So if we want our decisions to line up with His will, we need to seek the truth from God's unchanging Word, be willing to see the needs of this world, and seek God's perfect wisdom through prayer!

God's heart is for His kingdom and for the world . . . and He needs our families to be strong. As mission-minded families, living with these two seemingly opposing passions can sometimes seem like a delicate balance. But perhaps, if we keep this bowstring tight, with both sides pulling intensely and in balance, our family's arrows will shoot farther and more accurately than ever.

 DIVINE ORDER FOR EACH DAY

An excerpt from *Extravagant Worship*, by Darlene Zschech

For years, I tried to juggle all the elements of life. I knew there was a God call on my life to be in ministry, and yet I also knew that it could never be at the expense of my family. When I tried to juggle all the boxes,

I learned the hard way that it is difficult to keep them all from crashing down. So I no longer have boxes for marriage, ministry, and motherhood. Instead, God has shown me that there is a divine order for my life.

Instead of trying to make sure that everything is balanced (there is no prescribed formula of balance), God showed me that I am to break out of the box mentality and instead seek Him for divine order for my life. Each day differs from the day before. The dynamics change, but the call on my life doesn't. Marriage, motherhood, and ministry are all cohesively part of that call. God anoints us for our entire call.

WHO IS DARLENE ZSCHECH?

Darlene Zschech is a worship leader and a world-impacting minister from Sydney, Australia. Her passion is leading people into the presence of God and seeing them realize their full potential in Him. Darlene has written over seventy worship songs, including "Shout to the Lord," a beautiful chorus sung by millions of churchgoers. Many of her songs emphasize the importance of reaching the lost: "You Are My World," "Call Upon His Name," "Touching Heaven, Changing Earth," and "Change Your World."

Darlene and her husband, Mark, serve as a vital part of the leadership team of their church; and Darlene leads worship most weeks for a television program, which reaches over 180 countries around the globe. She also ministers through teaching, writing, supporting her husband, and being a loving mother to their three children.

Finding the Divine Tension

Two strong pulls are required for powerful divine tension in a mission-minded family. First, there needs to be a fervent heart for the family (inwardly founded on a personal relationship *with* Jesus); and second, there needs to be a fire to fulfill God's purpose (outwardly focused on reaching others *for* Jesus).

Such a family is like a mighty bow with a string securely fastened on both ends. It doesn't just have a flippantly tied strand that is "well-balanced," but it has a heavy-duty line with a divine tension that is strong, tight, and powerful!

 FAREWELL TO THE BALANCED LIFE

An excerpt from *The Missions Addiction*, by David Shibley

The normal Christian life is anything but balanced, as popularly defined. . . . The normal Christian life is high risk and high joy. The normal Christian life releases the temporal to embrace the eternal. It is a life lived in the love of God.

It is normal for us to be passionate about what God is passionate about! . . . This is not a call to discard balance, but rather to redefine it. Yes, there is a rhythm of life, and long-term effectiveness mandates that, like our Lord, we have seasons when we "come aside . . . and rest a while" (Mark 6:31). It's OK to stop and smell the roses. But the flip side of that coin is there is also a time to "spend and be spent" for the gospel.

God is not calling us to win the world and, in the process, lose our families. But I have known those who so enshrined family life and were so protective of "quality time" that the children never saw in their parents the kind of consuming love that made their *parents'* faith attractive to them. Some have lost their children, not because they weren't at their soccer games or didn't take family vacations, but because they never transmitted a loyalty to Jesus that went deep enough to interrupt personal preferences.

Mission-Minded Families

I want my family to have that kind of consuming love, with high risk and high joy. I want to live out my faith in a way that is not only attractive but also compelling and irresistible! I want to be moved by the passions of God's heart—and for my kids to take these godly passions to a deeper level. I want to hand off the baton to my descendants and have them run faster and farther than I ever did. I want my kids to impact their generation with a greater boldness, wisdom, and effectiveness than I ever have. Why? Because God's Word tells us, "Of the increase of His government and peace, there will be no end" (Isaiah 9:7). As Christians, we should always be moving in the right direction. Or as the famous missionary evangelist David Livingstone once said, he was willing "to go anywhere, provided it be forward."

May each of our arrows be aimed with exact precision, with just the right "divine tension" on our family's bowstring, so that every arrow released will pierce God's intended bull's-eye. May each of our arrows do damage to the enemy's cause and make a strategic difference for the kingdom of God.

**As a family, who are your HEROES
and your role-models?**

**Who do your kids look up to?
As parents, who do you esteem?**

Chapter 4

Missionary Heroes and Their Families

Many missionaries have accomplished great things for God. Some have been courageous single men (such as Patrick, Francis Xavier, and "Bruchko" Olson) or daring single women (such as Amy Carmichael, Lottie Moon, and Rachel Saint). But many missionary heroes have had families, with spouses to care for and children to train.

It is interesting to consider the families of renowned missionaries, looking at how they balanced the dual responsibilities of their ministries to others and their duties at home. Unfortunately, it doesn't take long to realize that many missionary heroes *with* families were not heroes *of* the family. A few of the "biggest" names in missions history (such as William Carey, David Livingstone, and C. T. Studd) had severe family problems; yet others (such as William and Catherine Booth, Hudson and Maria Taylor, and George and Mary Müller) found a powerful and harmonious ministry-family balance.

When God commissions a person for a ministry assignment, He sees the whole picture. Yes, God wants His mission accomplished; but He also wants that person to remain steadfast in relationship with Him and to leave a godly and lasting legacy. With a divinely ordered life, a person's family *and* ministry can be fruitful and full of joy. If these two "pulls" are balanced, a person's ministry can be *more* effective; and when that individual's life is over, his or her descendants can continue (with similar passions and convictions) to expand God's kingdom into the next generation.

◉ TEACHING OPPORTUNITY

Mini Mission Biographies and
Mission-Minded Monologue Skits

This chapter includes mini-biographies of many prominent missionary heroes, with an emphasis on couples and families. These brief summaries can serve as a quick missionary reference guide. Included are recommendations for great family-friendly resources (to help introduce you and your children to the lives of these men and women of God), classic missions excerpts, and seven informative "mission-minded monologue skits" for a member of your family, or someone else, to perform.

An Old Testament Missionary Hero: FATHER ABRAHAM

The calling of a patriarch and his family

Family-Friendly Resources:

*   The biblical account in Genesis 12–18

*   Read the story of God's covenant with Abraham from several Bible storybooks, and compare the vision for reaching the nations with the Genesis account.

In many missions-training programs, God's covenant with Abraham is emphasized, showing God's heart for all people and how Abraham and his family were blessed (God's "top-line" blessing) to be a blessing to the nations (God's "bottom-line" blessing): "In you all the families of the earth shall be blessed" (Genesis 12:3). Abraham left his father's land to go to an unknown land; he interceded for two wicked cities; and he was chosen because God knew that he would train his children.

The Lord said, "Shall I hide from Abraham what I am doing, since Abraham shall surely become a great and mighty nation, and all the nations of the earth shall be blessed in him? For I have known him, in order that he may command his children and his household after him, that they keep the way of the Lord, to do righteousness and justice, that the Lord may bring to Abraham what He has spoken to him." (Genesis 18:17–19)

A New Testament Missionary Hero: PHILIP THE EVANGELIST

A faithful servant, with a mission-minded family

Family-Friendly Resources:

*   The biblical accounts in Acts 6, 8, and 21

*   Mission-Minded Monologue Skit (below)

Mission-Minded Monologue Skit #1

Costume: *Have Philip wear a Bible-time robe*

Setting: *Inside Philip's home; include a few simple props, such as a mat, table, or basin*

PHILIP: Welcome to my home! I am the only one here now, since my wife is gone and our four daughters are with some of our Christian friends who live near the synagogue. And *Who am I?* you might ask. My name is Philip, and I am an evangelist. I live here . . . in the city of Caesarea . . . on the coast of the Mediterranean Sea, although I have traveled to many different places to share the Good News of my Lord Jesus Christ.

My ministry actually began quite humbly, since the apostles in Jerusalem needed some help to care for the widows. These church leaders were looking for "men of good reputation, full of the Holy Spirit and wisdom"; and I was one of the seven brothers chosen. I know how important it is to have a servant's heart, so I was willing to do whatever needed to be done. Then the seven of us rejoiced as the word of God spread and the number of disciples multiplied greatly.

Some time later our church in Jerusalem began to suffer persecution, so I went to Samaria. There I had the opportunity to preach the gospel, and multitudes came to Christ—with mighty miracles, deliverances, and healings. But then, right in the middle of all that citywide excitement, an angel of God spoke to me with a word of direction. The Lord wanted me to leave and go to a specific road out in the middle of a desert! It didn't make sense, but I obeyed.

As I was alone in that wilderness . . . I waited for a while . . . and wondered why God had called me to that barren place.

But then I noticed a chariot in the distance, and the Holy Spirit spoke to me and told me to go up to this chariot. Immediately I ran and caught up with the chariot, and I met a high-ranking governmental official from Ethiopia. This important African man was sitting in his chariot reading from the Book of Isaiah, but he couldn't understand what the Scripture passage meant. God helped me as I began with the passage in Isaiah and told the man about Jesus.

It was a powerful time of sharing the gospel. The official gave his life to Christ and immediately wanted to be baptized—in some water alongside of the road! Then, before I could even begin any "salvation follow-up procedures," something miraculous happened. God instantly transported me—or "zapped" me—to the city of Azotus, where I began preaching the gospel in city after city.

I love to go to different places to preach, but I also enjoy being home. Did you know that when the apostle Paul and his ministry team needed a place to stay, my family and I housed them right here in our home for many days? Hospitality is important to me. And I consider it an honor to raise my children for the Lord. I have four unmarried daughters who are known for their purity of heart and as young women who prophesy, or speak forth God's word, by the power of the Holy Spirit.

My children deeply love God and are sensitive to the Spirit's leading. Together, as we follow our Lord Jesus Christ, we have a family ministry. We want to obey whatever God tells us to do (whether big or small), and our home life is in order. People call me "Philip the evangelist"; but I see myself as God's humble servant . . . with a family that simply loves Jesus.

An Early Church Martyr: PERPETUA

A single mother who put God first

Family-Friendly Resources:

* The Voice of the Martyrs website (www.persecution.com), which has many excellent resources for children and families pertaining to persecuted believers.

* Mission-Minded Monologue Skit (below)

Mission-Minded Monologue Skit #2

Costume: *A middle-aged woman richly dressed in an elegant gown*

Setting: *A wealthy home during the third century; for effect, add a white pillar, a stone bench, plants in stonelike pottery, or a trellis*

PERPETUA'S MOTHER: It has been over two hundred years since that Jewish teacher Jesus was crucified. Yet His life still affects the whole Roman Empire. Here, in the city of Carthage, in North Africa, my husband is a respected and wealthy nobleman. I want to tell you about our twenty-two-year-old daughter, Perpetua. Our leaders were persecuting followers of this Jesus; yet, despite this risk, our daughter decided to join them.

Perpetua hadn't been married long when she lost her husband. So she was responsible, as a single mother, for her little baby, my grandson. And she was also following that dangerous group of Jesus followers, called "Christians."

My husband and I were so worried for Perpetua, and then our greatest fears were realized as she was thrown into prison because of her beliefs. My husband even went to visit her in that terrible cell in an attempt to convince her to reject her newfound faith. He begged our daughter to put family considerations above her creed, but Perpetua refused to turn from her faith in Jesus. She was genuinely grieved about the pain she caused her father and me, especially as she entrusted her little son into the care of her brother and me. As she handed me her baby, I knew that she deeply loved her child; yet it was evident that she was even more concerned about her loyalty to Christ.

What happened next was horrifying. My daughter was sent into the arena with a wild cow, where she was tortured so brutally the crowd began to yell, "Enough!" But afterward, I heard how she comforted her Christian friends by saying, "Give out the Word to the brothers and sisters; stand fast in the faith, love one another, and don't let our suffering become a stumbling block to you." My daughter was finally beheaded by a gladiator.

Perpetua chose her Christian faith over her family's pleas that she renounce her faith to save her life—but because of her steadfastness, I now know that my daughter's faith was real.

NARRATOR: After Perpetua's death there was relative peace for nearly fifty years, and the Christian church grew. [1]

Colonial Missionaries:
JOHN AND HANNA ELIOT

"Apostle to the Indians" (1604–1690)

Family-Friendly Resource:

• Mission-Minded Monologue Skit (below)

Mission-Minded Monologue Skit #3

Costume: *Traditional "Pilgrim" or early American style dress, with knee-length dark pants, white socks, dark shoes, dark jacket, and white shirt, with a ribbon tied at the neck*

Setting: *The early colonial years in America; John Eliot is sitting outside, perhaps on a log, holding a small Bible opened to the Book of Psalms*

JOHN ELIOT: My name is John Eliot. People often refer to me as the "Apostle to the Indians." I was born in England and educated at the famous university at Cambridge. After graduating, I met a Puritan pastor and saw in his family the life-giving power of godliness. This family led me to know Jesus Christ in a personal way. I was so moved by the experience that, in 1631, I set sail for the new land of America to become a minister myself.

A year after my arrival, my lovely fiancée, Hanna Mumford, joined me; and in October of 1632, we were married (which was the first recorded wedding in our town). For eleven years we ministered in a colonial church, but Hanna and I began to see the need to focus on reaching the Indians.* When I turned forty, I began studying a tribal language and traveling with a young interpreter.

As I led meetings for these native people, I often ministered to children and families, and many times I distributed treats following the services. I liked to drill the children in recitation of the catechism—the foundational truths of Christianity—and the parents would learn as they listened. At times, when I preached on the Ten Commandments and on Christ's love, some of the people would respond with tears and weeping. There were questions that followed—but the most difficult question to answer was "Why has no white man ever told us these things before?"

The new believers were often rejected by their families, so my wife and I set up towns of "Christian Indians." By 1671 we had gathered 1,100 believers into fourteen "praying towns." Desiring their spiritual growth, I worked hard to translate the Bible into their native language, although I was often criticized for "wasting time" with a tribal tongue when I could have been teaching them English.

Hanna and I were blessed with six children, although several died in infancy. Despite hardships, I have always believed in being positive. I love God's Word, and many consider it interesting that I published the very first book in America: a Christian book about the Psalms. [2]

now known as Native American or First Nations people

THE GREAT REMORSE OF COUNT ZINZENDORF

Count Nicolaus Ludwig von Zinzendorf (1700–1760) founded the Moravian Church, which emphasized single-mindedness, identification with the cross, and world evangelization. In 1727, the Moravians began a prayer vigil that continued, uninterrupted, twenty-four hours a day, seven days a week, for over a hundred years. As a result of this prayer movement—combined with Moravian missionary evangelism—a tremendous revival began. The Moravians helped spread Christianity throughout the world.

Yet the success of this great movement came at great expense to family life. The Moravians emphasized that the needs of the ministry took priority over the needs of the family. Youth were challenged to accept the call of lifelong singleness; and when permitted to marry, they often had their spouse selected for them (or chosen by lot). Everything was abandoned for the sake of the cross. Wives and children were frequently left behind, since God's "mission work" took absolute priority.

The Moravians' founder, Count Zinzendorf, was a prime example of this ambitious missionary focus. His wife, Erdmuth, was a proficient assistant in regard to missionary office work; but she and the Zinzendorf children were usually left behind (once for more than ten years) as Nicolaus ministered abroad. During the last fifteen years of their marriage, the couple's affection toward each other became cold and lifeless. Yet it was not until after Erdmuth's death that Nicolaus finally realized his errors, with repentance and regret. Count Zinzendorf deeply grieved his loss—not only for the loss of his wife but also for the life together they never had.

In *Count Zinzendorf,* biographer John R. Weinlick writes, "The count's sorrow was aggravated by remorse. He had not been fair to Erdmuth. Cynics to the contrary, he had not been unfaithful during their long periods of separation; but he had been extremely thoughtless. He had forgotten that she was a woman, a wife, and a mother." [3]

WILLIAM AND DOROTHY CAREY

The "Father of Modern Missions" . . . and his sad family

William Carey is known as the "Father of Modern Missions." His motto, "Expect great things from God; attempt great things for

God!" has challenged believers for generations. He led great translation works and encouraged many Christians to become actively involved in world missions. Yet despite these achievements, a mere glance at William Carey's family life presents a sobering message. God's work should not be done at the expense of everything else. God used Carey in a mighty way; but important lessons can be learned from this famous missionary's mistakes, as well as from his victories.

William Carey had long been interested in the needs of world missions; yet when he finally decided to go to India himself, the response he received was terrible. His church was distressed about losing its pastor, and his father thought he was fanatical. Yet these oppositions were nothing compared with the outrage of Carey's wife. At the time, William and Dorothy Carey had three young children, and Mrs. Carey was pregnant with their fourth child. The proposed five-month voyage to India was extremely perilous, and Dorothy had no desire to live, and to raise their children, in that dangerous tropical land. The current political situation made the decision even more treacherous, since France had just declared war on England.

As Ruth A. Tucker explains in *From Jerusalem to Irian Jaya*, "Other women had willingly made such sacrifices and thousands more would in the future, but Dorothy was different. If there is a 'Mother of Modern Missions,' it is certainly not she. She defiantly refused to go. . . . Carey, though distressed by her decision, was determined to go, even if it meant going without her." [4]

Because of an unexpected turn of events, Carey's missionary venture was delayed; and by that time Mrs. Carey had delivered their baby (just a few weeks earlier). With much urging, and despite her grumbling, Dorothy and the children were persuaded to join the group right before the team's departure. However, the decision proved to be a disaster.

Physically, Dorothy's health was weak; emotionally, she continually complained; and mentally, she was quite disturbed. When one of their children (a five-year-old son named Peter) tragically died, all of these problems intensified; and from this point, it seems that Dorothy Carey had a complete mental breakdown. Coworkers began to refer to Mrs. Carey as "wholly deranged" and even "insane."

In John Marshman's biography of Carey, he describes the great missionary focused on his translation work, "while an insane wife, frequently wrought up to a state of most distressing excitement, was in the next room." [5]

Dorothy Carey died when she was fifty-one years old (in 1807); yet it seems as if William Carey felt more *relieved* than *grieved* by the loss. For years, she had contributed nothing to the mission work except problems and complaints.

William Carey seemed to also ignore his parenting responsibilities. Similar to the neglectful fathering of the biblical high priest Eli (who grieved over his disobedient sons but would not restrain them; see 1 Samuel 2:22 and 3:13), Carey knew that his sons were having problems, but he was unwilling to confront them.

Again, Ruth A. Tucker explains, "As busy as he was, Carey was unable to give his children the fathering they so desperately needed. Even when he was with them his easy-going nature stood in the way of firm discipline, a lack that was plainly exhibited in the boys' behavior." [6]

When a fellow missionary, Hannah Marshman, mother of Carey's biographer John Marshman, first met the Carey family in 1800, she was shocked by the way in which William Carey looked after his four sons—noting that they were undisciplined, unmannered, and even uneducated. Carey hadn't spoiled them but had simply ignored them. Hannah wrote, "The good man saw and lamented the evil but was too mild to apply an effectual remedy." [7]

Even though Carey is remembered as the "Father of Modern Missions," he was severely deficient in his commitment to "father" his own family.

American Pioneer Missionaries: MARCUS AND NARCISSA WHITMAN

Missionaries in the Oregon Territory; martyred in 1847

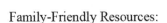

Family-Friendly Resources:

- *Attack in the Rye Grass: Marcus and Narcissa Whitman* (Trailblazer Books), by Dave and Neta Jackson, Bethany House, 1994

- Mission-Minded Monologue Skit (below)

Mission-Minded Monologue Skit #4

Costume: Prairie-style dress and bonnet

Setting: A rugged outdoor area

NARCISSA WHITMAN: Oh, isn't this area beautiful? With its towering evergreen trees, majestic waterfalls, and gorgeous mountains, this land in the northwest region of America is truly breathtaking. My name is Narcissa Whitman; and my husband, Marcus Whitman, and I are Christian missionaries here in the vast and rugged Oregon Territory.

Back when I was Narcissa Prentiss, before I was married, I heard a passionate plea made by a missionary named Samuel Parker. As he shared about the need for taking the gospel of Jesus Christ to the unreached Indians* of the West, I wanted to go—and I wanted to go alone—but the mission board would not accept me as a single woman.

Later, Marcus Whitman approached me with his own missionary ambitions, for that same missionary had influenced him. Mr. Whitman presented me with the idea of marriage, primarily as a business or ministry proposition. But naturally I had to think about it for a while.

He went ahead and traveled on a mission outreach by himself but returned home within only a few months to ask again for my hand in marriage. I decided to accept his invitation, and the day after our wedding we left for Missouri to join our missionary expedition to Oregon. A year later, when Marcus and I found out that God was blessing us with a baby, I finally realized . . . that I was in love!

Although the journey was difficult, I loved the wilderness and was overwhelmed by the beauty of God's creation. In Oregon, we settled in an area called Waiilatpu, and we began to minister to a tribe of people called the Cayuse.

Our missionary group was entirely on our own, so we became very busy building shelters and planting crops. We began to minister—trying to learn the native language, helping with medical needs, and sharing the gospel. Other missionaries came to join us, but this new "help" was actually nothing but trouble. Usually I was so busy caring for visitors and seven precious children whose parents had died on the journey that I had little time for anything else.

Just recently, the people we have been trying to reach have faced a terrible plague. Marcus and I, and our coworkers, have attempted to help them, yet the tribe thinks that our "white man's medicine" contained poison. Right now, the situation is intense. I don't know what will happen. Yet I know that God brought us here, and I believe that the message of the gospel will continue to go forward . . . no matter what.

now known as Native American or First Nations people

NARRATOR: In 1847, five Cayuse Indians (whom the Whitmans knew well) came to the Oregon mission and massacred Marcus, Narcissa, and twelve other men. Years later, missionaries witnessed a great movement of God as hundreds of native people were converted to Christ and baptized.

The Father of American Missions: ADONIRAM JUDSON

A sad missionary family "saga"

Family-Friendly Resources:

- Wholesome Words website: "Adoniram Judson: American Baptist Missionary to Burma" (http://www. wholesomewords.org/biography/ biorpjudson.html); "Ann H. Judson: The First Lady of American Foreign Missions" (http://www.wholesomewords. org/biography/biorpannjudson.html); Children's Corner, Missionary Heroes: "The Three Mrs. Judsons" (http://www. wholesomewords.org/children/heroes/hmrsjud.html)

- "Adoniram and Ann Judson: America's First Foreign Missionaries," in *Hero Tales*, Vol. 1, by Dave and Neta Jackson, Bethany House, 2005

- *Imprisoned in the Golden City: Adoniram and Ann Judson* (Trailblazer Books), by Dave and Neta Jackson, Bethany House, 1993

Adoniram Judson (1788–1850) is known as the "Father of American Missions." He married three times during his lifetime, since twice he suffered the death of a beloved wife. Adoniram's family was often separated for extended periods, and seven of his thirteen children died. As a missionary, he made a significant impact for God; yet the Judson "saga" (as it is often called) presents an example of the personal suffering many missionary families endure.

Adoniram was born in Massachusetts, the son of a minister. He was well educated as a young adult, graduating as valedictorian of Brown University in only three years. For a short time he rejected his Christian upbringing. But after attending a new seminary with which his father was involved, Adoniram made a "solemn dedication" of himself to God. After reading an inspiring British mission message, he vowed to be the first American missionary sent from a mission society.

As a young woman, Ann ("Nancy") Hasseltine (1789–1826) had a life-changing spiritual conversion and, as a result, a great burden for the unevangelized. Only three days after Adoniram and Nancy's wedding, the young newlyweds set sail for India. Nancy said she was not going because of "an attachment to an earthly object [i.e., Adoniram]" but because of an "obligation to God," with "full conviction of its being a call." Her life is a testimony of faithfulness as a wife and of total surrender to God's call.

Adoniram and Nancy began their ministry in India, yet they were soon forced to leave that country and go to Burma—which was actually their original first choice. The young couple decided to live among the Burmese people instead of in a secluded mission house. Nancy spoke daily with the women and quickly learned the Burmese language. They built a traditional, Burmese-style *zayat* (an open shelter) where many came to hear the gospel in a relaxed and culturally acceptable atmosphere. And from the start the Judsons actively included the Burmese believers in their work.

The Judsons faced many hardships over the years. While traveling to Asia, Nancy experienced a stillbirth and had to be carried off the ship. In Burma, she gave birth to a son, Roger; and at six months old, he died of a fever. Adoniram was accused of being a spy (during a war between Burma and Britain) and was confined to prison for a year and a half. Nancy pleaded almost daily with the guards for his release. During this time, she gave birth to their third child, Maria. Not long after Adoniram's release from prison, Nancy and then Maria died of a fever.

At this point, Adoniram went into deep mourning for several years. To overcome his grief, he immersed himself in his work. Fourteen years after Nancy's death, he finally completed his Burmese Bible translation.

Eight years after Nancy's death, Judson married a missionary widow named Sarah, and within ten years they had eight children (two died in infancy). Sarah died a year after giving birth to her last child.

During a furlough in America, Judson met a young (half his age) secular-fiction writer named Emily. Judson believed Emily's writing talents could be better utilized for God's purposes and persuaded her to write Sarah's biography. Just a month after meeting, the two became engaged. And only five months later, they were married—which was quite controversial. At the time, different families were raising several of the Judson children, and the separation was causing hardship. In the end, Emily went to Burma with Adoniram, where she assisted him for three years. They also had two children, one of them stillborn.

Adoniram Judson died of an illness on a sea voyage, having served as a missionary for thirty-three years. Despite challenges and opposition, Judson's life made a significant impact for Jesus Christ; and two of the Judson children (by Sarah) became ministers.

Note: Although Adoniram Judson is referred to as "The Father of American Missions," in actuality a former slave named George Liele was America's first foreign missionary. Liele went to Jamaica thirty-three years before the Judsons left for Burma.

ROBERT AND MARY MOFFAT

Patriarch of South African Missions

Family-Friendly Resource:

- Wholesome Words website: "Robert Moffat: Pioneer Scottish Missionary to South Africa"

(http://www.wholesomewords.org/biography/biorpmoffat.
html); Children's Corner, Missionary Heroes: "Robert Moffat:
Missionary to South Africa" (http://www.wholesomewords.
org/children/heroes/hmoffat.html)

Robert Moffat (1795–1883), known as the "Patriarch of South Africa Missions," was born in Scotland. His parents imparted to him a strong missionary zeal as a child. Robert's mother would often read aloud stories of mission heroes, which led to his decision to become a missionary. Robert served the Lord for over fifty years in Africa—with only one furlough—ministering as an evangelist, Bible translator, educator, explorer, and diplomat.

In 1819, while sharing about his mission work in Cape Town, Robert met and eventually married Mary Smith (1795–1871), who had recently come from England. Their marriage was a "happy union"—not only at the start but also throughout their fifty-three years together. Mary adapted well to missionary life as she assisted her husband in the work. Their home was described as "a homey atmosphere with children always at play." Robert and Mary had ten children, although three died in childhood. Of the seven who survived, five Moffat children became actively involved in missionary work in Africa.

Despite their own missionary work, Robert and Mary Moffat are primarily remembered as the in-laws of David Livingstone, the great missionary explorer. Originally Robert encouraged Livingstone to go to the unreached areas of Africa. "On a clear morning," he challenged, "the smoke of a thousand villages could be seen where the name of Christ had never been heard." Yet after Livingstone married their daughter (also named Mary) and pursued that challenge, Robert and Mary often disagreed with Livingstone's method of fulfilling that call. From the Moffat's perspective, Livingstone's famous exploratory work often came at the expense of his family.

After fifty-three years of successful ministry in Africa, Robert and Mary Moffat returned to England. But within a few months Mary died. For the thirteen remaining years of his life, Robert ministered as a dynamic missionary spokesman.

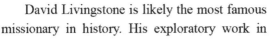

"On a clear morning, the smoke of a thousand villages could be seen where the name of Christ had never been heard."

ROBERT MOFFAT (TO DAVID LIVINGSTONE)

The Great Explorers: DAVID AND MARY LIVINGSTONE

The famous explorer . . . and his neglected family

David Livingstone is likely the most famous missionary in history. His exploratory work in Africa was heralded by Christian and secular leaders. He wrote many missionary slogans that continue to be influential today, and his name is nearly synonymous with *missionary*. Yet his famous life was not flawless. It was very difficult for Livingstone to balance his consuming passion for reaching the unreached with the love he had for his family. His wife, Mary, had been raised in Africa and was willing to follow him anywhere; but as their family grew, and especially as they faced pressure from Mary's parents, none of their options seemed to work. It was difficult to travel together, and it was difficult to be separated. In the end, Livingstone chose to concentrate on his missionary calling—a choice that came with a great expense. Livingstone's neglect of his wife and children became a permanent scar on his celebrated missionary biography.

One sad occasion occurred when David Livingstone's nineteen-year-old son, Oswell Livingstone, accompanied a search mission for his father led by Commander Dawson. When their team met up with the returning Henry Stanley (the New York reporter whose search party had found Livingstone), Dawson's search was aborted. Less than a year later, David Livingstone died in Africa . . . and Oswell never saw his father again. Perhaps the young man had not been searching for his famous father, but for his own identity and purpose. Unfortunately, it seems that he found neither.

Excerpts about David Livingstone's Family Life

David Livingstone passionately explained why he had decided to take his pregnant wife and young children with him on a difficult missionary expedition: "It is a venture to take wife and children into a country where fever—African fever—prevails. But who that believes in Jesus would refuse to make a venture for such a Captain?" [8]

Later, Livingstone received a harsh letter from his mother-in-law:

Mary had told me all along that should she be pregnant you would not take her, but let her come out here after you were fairly off . . . but to my dismay I now get a letter—in which she writes, "I must again wend my weary way to the far Interior, perhaps to be confined in the field." O Livingstone, what do you mean—was it not enough that you lost one lovely babe, and scarcely saved the others, while the mother came home threatened with Paralysis? And still you again expose her and them on an exploring expedition? All the world will condemn the cruelty of the thing, to say nothing of the indecorousness of it. A pregnant woman with three little children trailing about with a company of the other sex—through the wilds of Africa among savage men and beasts! Had you found a place to which you wished to go and commence missionary operations the case would be altered. Not one word would I say were it to the mountains of the moon—but to go with an exploring party, the thing is preposterous.

I remain yours in great perturbation,

M. Moffat. [9]

Additional Quotes Regarding Livingstone's Family Priorities:

"Nothing but a strong conviction that the step will tend to the Glory of Christ would make me orphanize my children." Livingstone [10]

Livingstone genuinely loved his children, and in later years regretted he had not spent more time with them. [11]

While Livingstone was on his exciting, exploratory adventures, Mary and the children were "homeless and friendless" and "often living on the edge of poverty in cheap lodgings." It was even rumored among the missionaries that Mary had "lapsed into spiritual darkness and was drowning her misery in alcohol." [12]

In England, Livingstone was given a state funeral at Westminster Abbey, attended by dignitaries from all over the country. It was a day of mourning for his children, who came to say goodbye to the father they had never really known. [13]

GEORGE MÜLLER (1805–1898) AND HIS FAMILY

A family of faith: caring for orphans and reaching the world

Family-Friendly Resources:

- Wholesome Words website: "George Müller: English Evangelist and Philanthropist" (http://www.wholesomewords.org/biography/biorpmueller.html)

- *The Bandit of Ashley Downs: George Müller* (Trailblazer Books), by Dave and Neta Jackson, Bethany House, 1993

- "George Müller: Man of Faith," in *Hero Tales*, Vol. 1, by Dave and Neta Jackson, Bethany House, 2005

- Mission-Minded Monologue Skit (below)

Mission-Minded Monologue Skit #5

Costume: George Müller is wearing a suit and tie, covered by a large overcoat.

Setting: Müller is praying by the grave of his first wife, Mary. For a simple prop, place a cross in the ground and have Müller hold some flowers.

(As he puts the flowers on Mary's grave, Müller begins to pray.) MÜLLER: Oh Father, I thank Thee for Thy many blessings on my life. I thank Thee for all the joys Thou hast given me . . . and Thy wonderful provision . . .

(Müller notices the audience.) Oh, hello there! How are you? My name is George Müller. I am a Christian evangelist and a coordinator of orphanages here in Bristol, England. In fact, I have had the privilege of caring for over 120,000 precious orphan children.

For forty years my beloved wife, Mary, worked alongside me. And were we happy? Verily we were! Did you know that just three weeks after our wedding, Mary and I decided to depend on God alone—and not on the small salary I received as a preacher? Ever since that day, God's provision has never ceased to amaze me.

Our orphanage vision started when we received a letter complaining about the nuisance of all the orphans. And hmmm . . . let me see . . . I was forty years old back then in 1845, and after thirty-six days of prayer God gave us just enough money to get started on our building project!

Oh, and I remember one morning when all the plates and cups and bowls on the table were empty. There was no food in the larder and no money to buy food. The children were standing, waiting for their morning meal, when I said, "Children, you know we must be in time for school." Then lifting up my hand, I prayed, "Dear Father, we thank Thee for what Thou art going to give us to eat."

There was a knock on the door. The baker stood there, and said, "Mr. Müller, I couldn't sleep last night. Somehow I felt you didn't have bread for breakfast, and the Lord wanted me to send you some. So I got up at 2 a.m. and baked some fresh bread, and have brought it."

I thanked the baker, and no sooner had he left, there was a second knock at the door. It was the milkman. He announced that his milk cart had broken down right in front of the orphanage, and he would like to give the children his cans of fresh milk so he could empty his wagon and repair it. [14]

During the last seventeen years, my dear second wife, Susannah, and I have been doing missionary work throughout the world: preaching in the United States, India, Australia, Japan, China, and in forty-two other countries. In fact, we've traveled over 200,000 miles, which is quite extensive for this day and age in which we travel by ship.

People call me "the man who gets things from God." And I can tell you, God has been so very faithful to meet all of our needs.

And He can meet yours too!

George Müller spoke the following words at his wife Mary's funeral. His comments represent a good example of the joy God gives when ministry and family priorities are balanced:

> Were we happy? Verily we were. With every year our happiness increased more and more. I never saw my beloved wife at any time, when I met her unexpectedly anywhere in Bristol, England, without being delighted so to do. I never met her even in the Orphan Houses, without my heart being delighted so to do. Day by day, as we met in our dressing room, at the Orphan Houses, to wash our hands before dinner and tea, I was delighted to meet her, and she was equally pleased to see me. Thousands of times I told her, "My darling, I never saw you at any time, since you became my wife, without my being delighted to see you." [15]

"Unless you intend your wife to be a true missionary, not merely a wife, home-maker, and friend, do not join us."

HUDSON TAYLOR
(TO POTENTIAL MISSIONARY RECRUITS)

Did You Know?

As a testimony to Hudson Taylor's spiritual legacy, several of his children became involved in Christian ministry and missionary work. Even today, his descendants (including Rev. James Hudson Taylor III and his son, Rev. James Hudson Taylor IV) continue in full-time Christian ministry work in Hong Kong and Taiwan.

WILLIAM AND CATHERINE BOOTH

Founders of the Salvation Army—and faithful to their family

Family-Friendly Resources:

- "William and Catherine Booth: Founders of the Salvation Army," in *Hero Tales,* Vol. 1, by Dave and Neta Jackson, Bethany House, 2005

- *Kidnapped by River Rats: William and Catherine Booth* (Trailblazer Books), by Dave and Neta Jackson, Bethany House, 1991

- Mission-Minded Monologue Skit (below)

"General" William (1829–1912) and Catherine (1829–1890) Booth found a powerful mission-minded balance. They had both a fervent passion for unbelievers and a sincere dedication to their family. They founded the Salvation Army and considered their family an asset and a priority in their lives.

> "Go straight for souls, and go for the worst."
>
> WILLIAM BOOTH

"There is an old adage, that
'They who rock the cradle rule the world,'
and they certainly do; but I am afraid that the world has
been very badly ruled, just because those who rock the
cradle have not known how to train the child."

CATHERINE BOOTH

Mission-Minded Monologue Skit #6

Costume: Red winter coat, winter hat, scarf, gloves, and a bell next to a hanging red bucket, to look like a Christmastime Salvation Army bell ringer

Setting: A contemporary Salvation Army worker presents this monologue. This person should have a red bucket and a bell. Have him or her begin by ringing the bell and greeting imaginary shoppers.

SALVATION ARMY BELL RINGER (speaking to imaginary shoppers): Merry Christmas, sir! . . . And how are you, ma'am?

(The bell ringer rubs his or her hands together, as if cold, and says quietly, "Hmmm, it's kind of cold today." Then he or she speaks again to imaginary shoppers.) And merry Christmas to you, too! . . . Oh, thank you for your gift! . . . God bless you, sir!

(The bell ringer then turns to speak to the audience.) Oh, hello there! I'm a volunteer for the Salvation Army. You've probably seen folks like me at stores at Christmastime—with our bells and our buckets, raising money to help the poor. But do you know why we're called the "Salvation Army"? Well, let me tell you.

Over a hundred years ago our founder, William Booth, lived in England. General Booth (as we call him) and his wife, Catherine, had a passionate desire to reach the needy and the social outcasts with the Good News of Jesus Christ. In 1865, they began their ministry of street preaching and helping the poor. On ministry banners they wrote the motto "Blood and Fire"—a reference to the blood of Christ and the fire of the Holy Spirit.

Over the years, millions of people, like me, have come to know Jesus through this ministry. And many of us still refer to Mrs. Catherine Booth as the "Mother of the Salvation Army." That amazing woman preached alongside her husband and wrote books and mission pamphlets. On top of all that, the Booths raised eight mighty children who were all workers in the kingdom of God—taking the gospel to many nations, including India, France, Switzerland, and the United States.

One day General Booth had a vision in which he saw a huge ocean filled with drowning people. Some of these people were rescued and put on a rock (which represented people being saved and coming to Jesus). But nearly all the people on the rock were distracted by something, such as making and saving money, amusing themselves with their favorite pastimes, or dressing up in different styles in order to be admired by others. They didn't even care about the other people who were drowning.

William Booth was impacted by the vision, so he wrote down what he saw. I've read it, and it's pretty powerful. It's one of those things that makes a person think. And it really made me realize how much people need Jesus.

Well, I'd better get back to my job here, and I'll let you get back to all you have to do. I do wish you a merry Christmas. And like General William Booth always said, "Go straight for souls, and go for the worst"!

Denny Kenaston reflects upon William and Catherine Booth's exemplary home life:

> William Booth's home was a godly home at its best.
> . . . They had a beautiful balance of two major commands
> in the Word of God. They were to win souls, and to raise

your children. God's kingdom is built in these two ways. We are commanded to train up a generation of children who love God with all their heart, mind, and soul. We are also commanded to preach the Gospel and to make disciples in the world around us and in all the world. These two commands can easily get out of balance. History is full of examples of men who won the world and lost their children. On the other hand there are innumerable cases where parents focused on the children, and did nothing to win a lost world around them. This type of parent tends to raise a generation of separatists who quickly become ingrown, legalistic, and unconcerned for their neighbors' lost condition. William and Catherine Booth had a beautiful, balanced vision of both of these commandments. [16]

FANNY CROSBY AND HER FAMILY

A mission-minded vision

Family-Friendly Resources:

*   *Fanny Crosby: The Hymn Writer* (Heroes of the Faith Series), by Bernard Ruffin, Barbour Publishing, 1995

*   "Rescue the Perishing," a missions hymn by Fanny Crosby (below)

*   Mission-Minded Monologue Skit (below)

> "When I get to heaven,
> the first face that shall ever gladden my sight
> will be that of my Savior!"
>
> FANNY CROSBY
> (A MISSION-MINDED HYMN WRITER,
> WHO WAS BLIND)

Mission-Minded Monologue Skit #7

Costume: *Fanny is dressed in a long Victorian-style dress with a high-necked collar; her hair is up in a bun; and she is wearing dark, round glasses.*

Setting: *Fanny is seated in a rocking chair, holding a hymnal or pages of sheet music.*

FANNY CROSBY: When I was born, my parents gave me the name Frances Jane Crosby, but they always called me "Fanny."

When I was only six weeks old, I became blind; and when I was just a baby, my father died. But my mother and grandmother, who raised me, believed that God had a special purpose for my life. As a little girl, I was encouraged to be happy, delightful, and confident. I learned to dress myself and fix my own hair; and I loved to ride horses, explore nature, and climb trees. But most of all, I was raised to love Jesus. My grandmother would often read long passages of the Bible to me; and by the time I was ten years old, she had helped me memorize nearly all of the New Testament and at least five books of the Old Testament.

I have always lived in complete darkness. But when I received God's salvation, it was like a "floodtide of celestial light" came into my life. I often volunteer at local ministries; and whenever anyone asks me a question, I enjoy witnessing one to one, as I share the "light" of Jesus.

One time a preacher told me, "I think it is a great pity that the Master did not give you sight when He showered so many other gifts upon you." But I didn't want him to feel sorry for me. Without bitterness, I happily replied, "When I get to heaven, the first face that shall ever gladden my sight will be that of my Savior!"

Although I cannot see, God has shown me His vision and purpose for my life. I have always loved music and poetry; and over the years He helped me compose over eight thousand hymns and hundreds of poems, including many that convey the need for missions. To share a little more of my heart, I would like to read one of these hymns, which is about sharing the gospel with the lost. This hymn is called "Rescue the Perishing." As you listen, remember that God has a special purpose for your life too!

RESCUE THE PERISHING

A missions hymn, by Fanny Crosby (1820–1915)

Rescue the perishing,
Care for the dying,
Snatch them in pity from sin and the grave;
Weep o'er the erring one,
Lift up the fallen,
Tell them of Jesus, the mighty to save.

Rescue the perishing,
Care for the dying;
Jesus is merciful,
Jesus will save.

Rescue the perishing,
Duty demands it;
Strength for thy labor the Lord will provide;
Back to the narrow way
Patiently win them;
Tell the poor wand'rer a Savior has died.

Rescue the perishing,
Care for the dying;
Jesus is merciful,
Jesus will save.[17]

C. T. AND PRISCILLA STUDD

Recruited hundreds of new missionaries

Family-Friendly Resources:

* Wholesome Words, Children's Corner: "C. T. Studd: Cricketer and Pioneer" (http://www.wholesomewords.org/children/biostuddcc.html)

* *C. T. Studd: No Retreat* (Christian Heroes: Then & Now Series), by Janet and Geoff Benge, YWAM Publishing, 2005

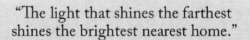

"The light that shines the farthest
shines the brightest nearest home."

C. T. STUDD (AN IRONIC QUOTE)

Charles Thomas (C. T.) Studd (1860–1931) was fervent about world missions and reaching the lost for Jesus Christ. He wrote, "We do need to be intense, and our intensity must ever increase." Yet his ever-increasing and unbalanced intensity eventually led to his downfall.

C. T. was led to the Lord by his father, who dramatically exchanged a life of horse racing for preaching the gospel. C. T. committed his life to Christ and to missionary service. During the Student Volunteer Movement, he and six friends—known as the Cambridge Seven—left England to become missionaries to China.

In China, he met Priscilla Stewart, a missionary with the Salvation Army. The two were soon married, and within ten years they had four daughters. During the early years their individual ministries in China began to grow, as C. T. helped opium addicts and Priscilla reached out to women. Once, upon receiving a large inheritance, he gave it away. Studd explained, "If Jesus Christ be God and died for me, no sacrifice can be too great for me to make for Him."

In 1900, after six years of successfully preaching about missions throughout Europe and the United States, Studd moved his family to India, where their focus shifted (very unhappily) from evangelism to ministry to English-speaking believers.

At age fifty-three, Studd felt God calling him to the "heart of Africa." Priscilla strongly objected and was overwhelmed by the decision. Physically, she was unable to go; yet he strongly felt that the work of the ministry had to come before the needs of the family. From 1910 until the time of Priscilla's death, in 1929, the two were together for less than two years. Only once during his eighteen years in Africa did C. T. return home to England (where she had remained). Even when he learned that his wife had suffered serious heart complications, he refused to turn back.

Studd's ministry was known for being radical, but his views became excessive. He believed in total commitment, which meant "no diversions, no days off, no recreation." He believed laziness was a sin (which could lead to damnation) and often worked relentless eighteen-hour days. He lived with Spartan simplicity and expected everyone around him to make extreme sacrifices. In the end, Studd began to take morphine to counterbalance the strain caused from overworking; and his own mission organization had to dismiss him. It was a great shame, and within a few weeks he died.

Though his personal life and family were sacrificed, C. T. Studd left a lasting impact on missions. He recruited hundreds of committed volunteers, and his son-in-law (who honored him, yet acknowledged his errors) continued WEC International: Worldwide Evangelization Crusade. This ministry has remained strong in pioneer missions, Bible translation, church planting, and evangelizing unreached people. They also produce *Operation World*, a much-used, country-by-country, world-mission prayer guide.

"Some wish to live within the sound of church or chapel bell. I want to run a rescue shop within a yard of hell!"

C. T. STUDD

📖 C. T. STUDD SPEAKS TO HIS DAUGHTER FROM HIS DEATHBED

As he was dying, C. T. Studd conveyed to his daughter his sincere heart for Jesus. While bidding farewell, the old man said, "Pauline, I would like to give you something before you go." He looked about him as if to find a suitable parting gift. His table held some gadgets; and he had a few boxes on poles (to keep them from the termites), containing some clothes and a few small possessions. From the roof hung a banjo for leading the singing and some pots for cooking. Then he quietly said, "But really, I have nothing to give you because I gave it all to Jesus long ago."

T. L. AND DAISY OSBORN

Mission-minded mass evangelist

Family-Friendly Resource:

*   *Soulwinning: A Classic on Biblical
    Christianity*, by T. L. Osborn
    (Harrison House, 1994)

They never received a "call" to ministry, but for over fifty years T. L. and Daisy Osborn have ministered through open-air mass evangelism to millions of people. (Daisy passed away in 1995.) Their ministry films and videos have been translated into nearly eighty languages, and their literature has been published in 132 languages and dialects—influencing multitudes to believe the gospel of Jesus Christ. T. L. and Daisy Osborn have written many books and inspiring articles concerning evangelism and world missions, including *Soulwinning*.

 ## GOD'S HIDDEN INHERITANCE

An excerpt from T. L. Osborn's 1964 book, *Frontier Evangelism*

The treasure of one thousand million heathen souls lies hidden in the remote fields of the earth today and within the reach of the present generation of the church. This priceless treasure is lying as an unclaimed inheritance. It is waiting to be possessed by men [and women] of vision, of faith and of courage who will "sell all" and dedicate themselves to buy this field. . . . The responsibility to invade these enormous frontiers and possess this treasure demands unselfish and sacrificial devotion to the cause for which Jesus died—the evangelization of the world. Paul's life was constantly in peril as he advanced to possess the heathen treasure of his generation. Today, rugged men [and women] of courageous faith must arise to the challenge of this generation. They must possess this inheritance regardless of peril, regardless of sacrifice, regardless of resistance.

Where are the rugged pioneers of faith today who will respond to this challenge?

Where are the men of vision who are no longer content to rest in the security of an established congregation and salary?

Where are those who look with keen anticipation to the unprecedented possibilities of pioneering heathen frontiers for Christ?

Where are the fearless preacher's wives who will stand by the side of their husbands while they blaze new trails to reach the lost?

Where are the brave men who are tired of the monotony of religious competition?

Where are those who yearn to proclaim Christ in a field that has not been burnt over by the hordes of religious opportunities and gospel commercializers?

Where are the courageous mothers who will forsake the established conveniences of a modern civilization to take their children in an advance to stake unclaimed treasures among the souls of the heathen?[18]

"One Way—Jesus; One Job—Evangelism"

T. L. AND DAISY OSBORN'S MOTTO

REINHARD AND ANNI BONNKE

German founder of Christ for All Nations

Family-Friendly Resource:

* *Evangelism by Fire: Igniting Your Passion for the Lost*, by Reinhard Bonnke
  (1940 - 2019)

Reinhard Bonnke grew up in Germany as a pastor's son. He gave his life to the Lord when he was nine years old; and before becoming a teenager Reinhard felt called to the mission fields of Africa. In 1969, he and his young wife, Anni, and their baby son went to Maseru, Lesotho. For seven long years Reinhard and Anni ministered as traditional missionaries, but seeing "little fruit" for their efforts frustrated them.

Reinhard kept having visions of a "blood-washed Africa" and mass-evangelism outreaches. But as he shared what he believed to be God's calling, others criticized him and claimed he was full of pride. Bonnke submitted his ideas to God in prayer; and he believed the Lord responded by saying, "If you don't do it, I'll just have to find someone else." From that time on, Reinhard began holding mass-evangelism meetings, initially in a tent accommodating eight hundred people.

Prior to his death in 2019, Reinhard Bonnke led open-air outreaches across the world (especially Africa), and drew crowds of more than half a million people in a single meeting! Many churches join together to support these citywide events, since salvation through the sacrifice of Christ is emphasized. Bonnke's Christ for All Nations has offices in Africa, Germany, the United Kingdom, Canada, Singapore, and the

United States. He has written several missions books, including one of my favorites: *Evangelism by Fire.*

> "Cool, casual Christianity will accomplish nothing. Our . . . most urgent need is the flaming message of the cross—now and not at our leisure."
>
> REINHARD BONNKE

DON AND CAROL RICHARDSON

Missionaries to New Guinea

Family-Friendly Resources:

- *Peace Child* (YWAM Publishing, 2003) and *Eternity in Their Hearts* (Regal Books; revised edition, 1984), by Don Richardson

- *Peace Child*, the film (Gospel Communications, 1974). This powerful movie, available on DVD, shares the amazing testimony of Don and Carol Richardson. There is brief nudity, in the native fashion. A missions classic.

In 1955, a young couple responded to a specific missionary call to reach the Sawi people, a cannibalistic tribe of headhunters in New Guinea. Don and Carol Richardson and their baby arrived in the remote village in a simple dugout canoe. They didn't know what to expect, but they knew they were obeying God's direction for their lives.

After learning the people's language, Don and Carol shared about God's love. Yet their noble attempts seemed completely futile. The savage tribe honored treachery, so when the people heard the story of Christ, they believed Judas—not Jesus—was the true hero. It was not until the Richardsons discovered an important aspect of Sawi culture, called "the peace child," that they were able to share the gospel effectively. The Sawi people believed that if an enemy tribe offered to give them one of their own babies, as a sign of peace, then that enemy tribe could genuinely be trusted. Don used this analogy to share about the birth of Jesus, and finally the Sawi people understood God's Good News.

The Richardsons lived for fifteen years among this primitive tribe in Irian Jaya, and more than half of the Sawi people accepted Jesus Christ as their Savior and Lord. As a nurse, Carol ministered to the physical needs of the people—at times treating nearly 2,500 patients each month. Together, Don and Carol worked on a Bible translation project and completed a Sawi translation of the New Testament. Using traditional building techniques, their ministry built a huge "Sawidome" church (seating over one thousand people) to be used for Christian work.

In Don Richardson's book *Peace Child*, he shares this moving story; and in *Eternity in Their Hearts,* he encourages missionaries to look for "redemptive cultural analogies." Richardson has also studied and written about the needs of the Muslim world, and he is a prominent spokesman for world missions.

More Examples of Mission-Minded Legacies

Around the world today, there are many powerful examples of mission-minded families with generational legacies that are impacting the world.

- As featured in the movie *End of the Spear*, **Steve Saint** (the son of Nate Saint, a famous missionary martyred while attempting to reach an isolated tribe in Ecuador) is seeing tremendous ministry results among this remote people.

As the founder of I-TEC, Indigenous People's Technology and Education Center, Steve and his family continue in his missionary heritage through his ministry, writing, and speaking.

- **Walter and Valerie Shepard**, along with their children, live and minister in the Democratic Republic of the Congo. For Walt, this is a return to the country of his youth, where his parents served as missionaries. For Valerie, the daughter of well-known missionaries Jim and Elisabeth Elliot, this is a continuation of a lifelong missions call, fulfilled both as a stay-at-home mother and as a missionary.

- **Dave and Neta Jackson** are mission-minded authors, motivating multitudes of children and young people through their family-friendly missionary books, such as the *Hero Tales* books and the Trailblazer series.

- **Rick and Kay Warren**, using the principles of Rick's book *The Purpose-Driven Life*, impact many people throughout the world for Jesus. They donate 90 percent of their book proceeds to local and international mission projects, especially focusing on the AIDS epidemic in Rwanda.

- **Ken Ham** was inspired by his father's deep love for the Bible and his own convictions about creation. His family sent him as a missionary from Australia to America, where he founded Answers in Genesis, emphasizing the authority of God's Word.

- **Loren and Darlene Cunningham** were both raised in strong mission-minded families. They founded Youth With A Mission (YWAM), one of the world's largest missionary organizations.

- **Leo and Phyllis Kaylor** responded to General MacArthur's plea for missionaries following World War II. For fifty-five years they have served as missionaries in Japan—planting churches, training Christian workers, and raising and homeschooling their six children (all of whom learned to speak Japanese fluently and have a fervent mission-minded heart). Today, Leo and Phyllis Kaylor's children, grandchildren, and great-grandchildren are grateful for their strong Christian heritage, and several are involved in the Kaylors' mission work in Japan.

Month by month, international holidays can give our families an insight into our world's need for Jesus.

CHAPTER 5

Enjoying Missions
throughout the Year

International Holiday Ideas

Throughout the year, acknowledging international holidays can give our families an insight into our world's need for Jesus. These vibrant festivities are filled with colorful expression, yet often these traditions are rooted in false religion and fear.

As your family looks at current traditions around the world each month, you can utilize these specific days to target different people groups for prayer and to increase your family's mission-minded vision. You may even want to commemorate some of these days. However, I am *not* encouraging your family to celebrate evil or pagan holidays. This international holiday list is simply to help your family learn about world cultures and to regularly remind you about the need for specific mission-minded prayer.

🌐 TEACHING OPPORTUNITY

Make a Mission-Minded Family Calendar

Get out your family calendar, and take a moment to write down the names of these holidays on their respective dates. Throughout the

year, you can then come back to this section of *The Mission-Minded Family* to read about each holiday and pray accordingly.

JANUARY

1 • New Year's Day, International—Around much of the world, this day is celebrated as a time of new beginnings. Many people make New Year's "resolutions," or promises, for the coming year.

As mission-minded believers, pray for and seek God's direction for the new year and take time to evaluate and realign your priorities.

6 • Epiphany, International—In many countries throughout the world, this day is celebrated to remember the wise men who came to bring gifts of gold, frankincense, and myrrh to the Christ child, Jesus. In Spain, children receive gifts on this day instead of on Christmas. Children put hay in their shoes and find the hay replaced with treats the next morning.

Pray for the people of Spain to recognize Jesus Christ as Savior and Messiah, just as the wise men did.

14 • Pongal, India—In southern India, this day marks the beginning of a four-day harvest festival. The people gather to watch a pot of newly harvested rice boil. If it boils quickly, the people believe it is a sign of a prosperous new year.

Pray for a mighty *spiritual* harvest in India.

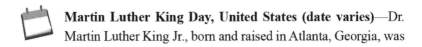

Martin Luther King Day, United States (date varies)—Dr. Martin Luther King Jr., born and raised in Atlanta, Georgia, was a Christian minister and a civil rights leader. King was active in seeing segregation laws in the South abolished, and in 1964 he received the Nobel Peace Prize. He was assassinated in 1968. The third Monday of January is set aside as a national holiday to remember King's leadership and the importance of civil rights.

Pray for harmony and love between different races and nationalities and for God to give you love and compassion for other people groups.

JANUARY/FEBRUARY

Chinese New Year (date varies)—In China, families clean their homes to prepare for the new year and to rid their lives of any misfortunes or bad luck from the previous year. People wear new shoes and clothing and often decorate with red candles, symbolizing good luck. Processions are held, often led by a huge dragon, also symbolizing good luck. Firecrackers are set off (sometimes to rid the area of evil spirits), and families participate in gift giving and meals.

Pray for an outpouring of God's Holy Spirit and revival in China. Pray that the Chinese people would not trust in superstitions and luck, but in the newness of life found only in Jesus Christ.

Eid-al-Fitr, Islamic countries (date varies)—In the Islamic month of Ramadan, devout Muslims fast from both food and water during the daylight hours (fasting during Ramadan is one of the five pillars of Islam). At sunset on the last day of the month, the people celebrate the breaking of the fast (Eid-al-Fitr) with celebrations, food, and gifts.

Pray for Muslim people around the world to recognize Jesus as God's Son and accept Him as their personal Savior.

FEBRUARY

14 • Valentine's Day—This holiday, also known as St. Valentine's Day, was named after two early Christian martyrs named Valentine and is observed by Western and Western-influenced cultures. In the United States and some other countries, cards and gifts are given to friends, sweethearts, and family members to express love.

Pray for contemporary Christians who are being persecuted for their faith in Jesus Christ. See www.persecution.com for updated reports from Voice of the Martyrs, or read a selection from the powerful book *Jesus Freaks*, by dc Talk.

STARTLING MISSION-MINDED FACT

From Neal Pirolo's 1991 book, *Serving as Senders*

On just one day, February 14, Americans spend over 700 million dollars to say "I love you" with Valentine's Day cards. Less than that is spent in the whole month of February (and in each of the other months) to tell a lost and dying world that God loves them!

FEBRUARY/MARCH

Holi, India (date varies)—Children from India celebrate the coming of spring by showering each other with brightly colored water and paint powders. Huge bonfires are lit to "burn away" the old season.

Pray for people bound in Hinduism all throughout India to find new life and forgiveness from their sins through Jesus Christ.

MARCH

17 • St. Patrick's Day, Ireland—Patrick was the first Christian missionary to Ireland (see the mini-biography below). In the United States, celebrations include city parades, Irish cultural celebrations, and the wearing of green.

Pray for peace in Ireland, especially between Protestants and Catholics. Pray for the true message of salvation to spread throughout Ireland and for missionaries who are sharing the gospel in Ireland today.

WHO WAS ST. PATRICK?

Born in Britain, "Saint" Patrick (c. AD 389–461) is widely known as the first Christian missionary to the Irish people. Patrick actually went to Ireland twice—first as a slave and later as a missionary. When he was sixteen, he was captured and taken to Ireland, where he remained until he escaped and returned to his homeland. While in Ireland, young Patrick repented of his sinful, backslidden condition. Sometime later, back in Britain, he received a vision from God calling him to return to the Irish people to proclaim the gospel of Christ. Patrick obeyed God's call and went back.

For the remainder of his life, Patrick ministered among the heathen tribes of Ireland—confronting idolatry and sorcery, converting many to Jesus Christ, and baptizing thousands of people. Tradition says he used the three-leaf clover to teach the unity of the Father, Son, and Holy Spirit.

Patrick is known today as the patron saint of Ireland, and throughout the world people celebrate "St. Patrick's Day" during the month of March.

MARCH/APRIL

Passover, Israel (date varies)—This Jewish celebration remembers how God delivered the ancient Hebrews from slavery in Egypt as the death angel "passed over" their homes. A special dinner, called the Seder, includes unleavened bread (matzo), lamb, and bitter herbs. Jesus celebrated the Passover every year; and through His death on the cross, He fulfilled it. God has provided freedom from the bitterness of sin and eternal death, for "Christ, our Passover Lamb, has been sacrificed for us" (1 Corinthians 5:7 NLT).

Pray for Jews around the world to recognize Jesus Christ (Yeshua) as their promised Messiah.

Holy Week, International (date varies)—Christians around the world celebrate the death and resurrection of Jesus Christ during Holy Week. In many Latin American countries there are huge processions in which large statues of Jesus and other religious relics are carried through the streets. There is little or no mention of the resurrection in many of these settings. In other places, such as in the Philippines, men actually allow themselves to be nailed to a cross— done as "penance" (a religious self-effort to pay part of the punishment for their sins).

Pray for people around the world, especially for those in Latin America, to hear of the resurrection and to receive God's salvation through faith in Jesus Christ—not by their own works.

APRIL/MAY

📅 **Hana Matsuri, Buddha's Birthday (date varies)**—Throughout Asia, Buddhists celebrate the birthday of the founder of their religion. In Japan, people celebrate Hana Matsuri on April 8 by bringing flowers to shrines and holding parades. In Southeast Asia, the date for this holiday (known as Vesak) varies. People decorate buildings with lights and paper lanterns and hold rocket festivals.

Pray for the salvation of Buddhists around the world. Intercede for their spiritual eyes to be opened and for the light of the gospel to reach them so that they can turn to the living Savior, Jesus Christ.

MAY

📅 **1 • May Day, International**—Many different holidays are celebrated around the world on the first day of May, including ancient pagan celebrations and the more recent International Workers' Day. A tradition in America is to secretly deliver flowers to friends and neighbors. You may want to help your children bless your neighbors with flowers and homemade cards that share the love of Jesus Christ. Some who practice Roman Catholicism give special veneration and honor to the Virgin Mary on this day.

Pray for the salvation of your neighbors and for those who hope and trust in Mary for their salvation—that their faith would be in Jesus alone.

📅 **1 • Lei Day, Hawaii**—Throughout Hawaii, people make and wear leis (flower necklaces) with tropical flowers and perform traditional dances. The first Lei Day was held on May 1, 1928; and later the phrase "May Day is Lei Day" was coined.

Pray for Christians throughout Hawaii to share the love of Jesus on this day and to glorify the Lord through traditional Hawaiian dances.

5 • Children's Day, Japan—Kites in the shape of fish are flown to signify strength and courage. Children throughout the country participate in religious ceremonies where they are blessed by their parents. (Many other nations celebrate International Children's Day on June 1.)

Pray for the children of Japan to turn from false religions and ancestral worship to find faith in Jesus Christ. Pray for these children to know how much Jesus loves them.

Mother's Day, International (date varies)—A day for honoring mothers is celebrated on various dates throughout the world. Mother's Day is celebrated on the second Sunday of May in many countries. People often take their moms out to lunch and give them cards, flowers, and gifts.

Thank God for your mother, especially if she is a godly influence in your life.

Pray today for orphan children throughout the world who do not have a mother, that God would care for them and lead them to a family that can help them or adopt them. Pray also for any mothers and grandmothers you know who are not believers (for example, in your extended family or neighborhood).

25 • African Liberation Day, Africa—African countries that are members of the Organization of African Unity celebrate their independence on this day through traditional dances, celebrations, sports, and rallies.

Pray for peace throughout the continent of Africa and for revival to spread to those who have yet to hear of God's gift of freedom in Christ.

JUNE

Father's Day, International (date varies)—A day for commemorating fatherhood and honoring fathers is celebrated on various dates throughout the world. Father's Day is celebrated on the third Sunday of June in many countries. People give their dads gifts and do fun things with them.

Thank the Lord for your father, especially if he is a godly example in your life.

Pray today for the lost, especially in your nation, that they would come to know their heavenly Father.

JULY

1 • Canada Day, Canada—On this day, Canadians celebrate the birthday of their country with parades, fireworks, and barbecues.

Pray for the people of Canada to recognize their need for God and for Christians throughout this country to reach the lost.

4 • Independence Day, United States—Americans commemorate the signing of the Declaration of Independence on July 4, 1776, by celebrating with parades, fireworks, and picnics.

Pray for the citizens and leaders of the United States to live out their Christian roots and to be mission-minded people.

14 • Bastille Day, France—On July 14, 1789, the French Revolution began with the storming of the Bastille (a royal prison). This was the beginning of freedom from oppression by the monarchy. The French people celebrate with parades, fireworks, and dancing in the streets.

Pray that those in France who aren't believers would recognize the devil's oppression and desire God's true freedom, found only in Jesus Christ.

JUNE/JULY/AUGUST

Sun Dance, Native Americans—Across the US and Canadian plains, Native Americans (or First Nation people) perform an ancient Sun Dance ceremony honoring the buffalo.

Pray for Native American people to recognize the living God who created everything. Pray that they don't view Christianity as only a "white man's religion," but as God's salvation for them.

SEPTEMBER

11 • Enkutatash, Ethiopia—After the rainy season has ended each year, the people of Ethiopia celebrate their new year on September 11, which is the first day of the Ethiopian month of Meskerem. Children gather flowers and go from house to house, singing songs and giving flowers. In return, the children receive coins or candy.

Read in Acts 8 how Philip shared the gospel with an Ethiopian official. Pray for peace, evangelism, and spiritual revival throughout modern-day Ethiopia.

16 • Independence Day, Mexico—On September 16, 1810, Father Miguel Hidalgo first sounded a call for Mexican independence from Spain. The revolution ended in 1821, with Mexico becoming a free country. On the evening of September 15, Mexicans gather in public squares to hear a call for independence at eleven o'clock, which is followed by fireworks and dancing.

Pray for the people of Mexico to hear God calling them to Himself. Pray for missionaries and national ministers throughout Mexico to preach God's freedom through Jesus Christ.

SEPTEMBER/OCTOBER

Rosh Hashanah, Israel (date varies)—At the beginning of the Jewish New Year a ram's horn, or shofar, is blown in the synagogues. This is a festive time of special food and family celebrations as the Jewish people reflect on the new year.

Pray for Jews throughout the world to recognize Jesus (Yeshua) as their Messiah.

Tet Trung Thu, Vietnam (date varies)—This celebration of the moon comes at the time of the harvest moon. Mooncakes are eaten, and children make lanterns in the shapes of animals and other objects. At night, the children carry their lanterns in processions.

Pray for God's light to shine throughout Vietnam and for many to come to know Jesus Christ, through whom God created the sun, moon, and stars.

OCTOBER

9 • Hangul Nal, Korea—On October 9, South Koreans celebrate the creation of the Korean alphabet in the fifteenth century. North Koreans celebrate Hangul Day on January 15.

Children take part in calligraphy contests instead of their regular school classes.

This is a good day to have a handwriting contest with a special missions verse. Pray for the Lord to pour out His Holy Spirit on children in both South Korea (where the Christian church is strong and mission oriented) and North Korea (where there is great spiritual need).

31 • Halloween, Western countries—Halloween was originally a pagan festival observed by the Celts of Ireland and Britain. It was later transformed to the "Hallowed Eve" of All Saints' Day (November 1), a holiday in which Roman Catholics and some Protestants remember believers who have died. In the United States, children carve pumpkins on Halloween, dress in costumes (sometimes as witches, ghosts, devils, or other evil characters), and go "trick-or-treating" throughout neighborhoods to receive candy.

Satanic rituals reportedly take place on Halloween, and people attempt to make contact with the dead. Pray for wisdom as a Christian family, school, or church to discern good from evil. Realize Satan is real and not something to have "fun" with or to make light of. Many churches utilize this day to have a "harvest party" or dramatic outreach. Pray for eyes to be opened to the reality of evil and for many to come to Christ.

OCTOBER/NOVEMBER

Diwali, India (date varies)—Throughout India, people celebrate this "Festival of Lights" by placing lamps in their homes and windows and on roofs and roads. They believe that these beautiful lamps welcome Lakshmi, the goddess of good luck. People clean their homes and make designs with colored powder on their floors.

Pray for the people of India to turn from this false religion and to recognize Jesus as the true Light of the World.

NOVEMBER

Loy Krathong, Thailand (date varies)—For hundreds of years, the people of Thailand have celebrated this festival of floating leaf cups. On the night of the full moon in November, people make little boats out of banana leaves and flowers and place a candle inside. They take their decorative rafts to a river, light the candle, make a wish, and then put the leaf boat in the water. If the candle stays lit until the boat disappears from sight, they believe that the wish will come true.

Pray for the people of Thailand to put their hope and faith in Jesus, the light of the world.

Thanksgiving, United States (date varies)—The Pilgrim settlers of Plymouth Colony in Massachusetts established a holiday of feasting and praising God after their first harvest in 1621. They were especially thankful for Squanto, the Native American who taught them how to catch fish and grow corn. Many US presidents proclaimed a national day of thanksgiving to God. In 1939, President Franklin Roosevelt set the date for the holiday on the fourth Thursday of November. Canada observes a similar national Thanksgiving holiday on the second Monday in October.

Be thankful for God's blessings in your life. Pray for revival in North America, especially among Native Americans (or First Nations people).

NOVEMBER/DECEMBER

Hanukkah (or Chanukah) (date varies)—About two hundred years before the birth of Jesus, Syrian Greek rulers disgraced the Jewish temple and then ordered the Jews to worship Greek gods. For three years the people of Israel fought for freedom and finally defeated their enemies. The Jews cleansed their temple and then lit a special candelabra called a menorah. They had enough oil to last only one day, but the menorah stayed lit, supernaturally, for eight days. Throughout the world, Jews celebrate the "Festival of Lights" by lighting candles each night for eight nights. Celebrations also include giving gifts, eating traditional foods, and playing games.

Whenever you see a menorah, pray for peace in Israel and for Jewish families to come to know Jesus as their Savior and Messiah.

DECEMBER

13 • St. Lucia Day, Sweden—In Sweden (and other Scandinavian countries), there is a legend of St. Lucia, a Sicilian girl who gave away her dowry to feed the poor. She is known as the Queen of Light. Coming at the time when the nights are long in Scandinavia, this holiday also celebrates the ability of light to overcome darkness. Every year, the oldest girl in each family plays the part of St. Lucia. In the morning, she puts on a white dress with a ring of candles on her head and brings coffee and special rolls to her parents.

Pray for the people of Sweden to come to know Christ as the Light of the World. Pray for missionaries and ministers in this country to bring the light of Jesus to those who are spiritually poor.

16–24 • Las Posadas, Latin America—Throughout Mexico and Latin America, families celebrate Christmas by acting out the story of Mary and Joseph searching for lodging. This scene is reenacted each evening from December 16 to 24. In some areas children carry nativity figures of Mary and Joseph, while in other areas a man and woman wear costumes to look like them. As they go from house to house, asking for a place to stay, a procession forms behind them. Finally, "Mary and Joseph" arrive at a house, are allowed in, and are placed by a manger. Everyone then joins in a celebration, complete with a piñata for the children.

Pray that the gospel spreads throughout Latin America as people open the door of their hearts to accept Jesus Christ as their Lord and Savior.

25 • Christmas, International—The celebration of Jesus' birth is an important time for us as Christian believers. It is a time to remember Christ's love and sacrifice in coming to this earth, a time to thank God for His salvation, and a great time to share God's love with others.

Throughout the Christmas season, use evergreen trees to remind your children of God's gift of everlasting life through the cross of Calvary. As you see Christmas lights and candles, remember that Jesus is the Light of the World and that we are to be lights for Him. As you receive presents, remember the gifts of the wise men—and the greatest gift of God's salvation. Discuss how the birth of Jesus declared His coming for all people: rich and poor, Jew and Gentile, those near and those far away.

Thank the Lord Jesus for coming to earth to be our Savior!

MISSION-MINDED CHRISTMAS CAROLS

- "Joy to the World"
- "Hark! The Herald Angels Sing"
- "Go Tell It on the Mountain"
- "Silent Night"

"For God so loved the world, that he gave his only begotten Son, that whosoever believeth in him should not perish, but have everlasting life."

JOHN 3:16 (KJV)

LOTTIE MOON: SHE GAVE EVERYTHING ...ON CHRISTMAS

Missionary to China (1840–1912)

Does your family know about Lottie Moon? In Southern Baptist churches, her testimony of missionary service and sacrifice is something of a legend. She is the namesake of a yearly international Christmas missions offering; and her beautiful yet sad story of sacrificial giving has been retold each year, inspiring many (especially during the Christmas season) to a deeper commitment to missions.

Charlotte "Lottie" Moon grew up in Virginia as a wealthy, cultivated Southern girl, well educated by private tutors. She was the third of seven children. When she was thirteen, her father was killed in a riverboat accident. Although petite in body, she was strong in mind and spirit. Lottie became a missionary to China, and for thirty-nine years she ministered faithfully. She wore traditional Chinese clothing, adopted the language and customs of the people, and did all she could to share the gospel of Jesus Christ. She also wrote influential letters back home about the world's great need to support missions and established a new Christmas missions offering.

In 1912, during a time of war and famine in China, Lottie gave and gave, not counting the personal cost. She urgently wrote home for help, but to no avail; the mission board was heavily in debt and unable to send anything. Lottie's sharing of her personal finances and food with anyone in need severely damaged her physical and mental health. Fellow missionaries became alarmed and arranged for her to be sent home. However, as her ship docked in Japan, Lottie died . . . on Christmas Eve.

"I Gave Myself"

It was Christmas, and the Liberian Christians had been asked this year, instead of receiving gifts, to help carry the gospel to others. As in many mission fields, they brought, not money, but produce. Presently, the great plates were piled high with offerings of rice, cocoa, bananas, palm nuts, pineapple, and cassava.

There was a moment's pause . . .

Slowly a twelve-year-old boy walked forward and solemnly placed his feet in one of the plates.

Afterward, when the missionary questioned him, the boy said, "We are very poor. I did not have anything else to give . . . so I gave myself."

I'll Be Home for Christmas?

It was only a few days before Christmas as Bernie May, a pilot for Wycliffe Bible Translators, successfully delivered emergency medical supplies to the isolated Amazon village. Now he eagerly anticipated being back with his wife and children in their South American home-away-from-home. Yet as the evening grew dark, he knew he would not be able to fly out until the morning.

With his pontoon plane waiting on the river, Bernie arranged for temporary protection for the night. But then . . . it began to rain.

The rain continued, even up until Christmas Eve, as the missionary felt increasingly depressed by his misfortune. His wife, Nancy, and their boys were six hours away; and by this time, they would have received his radio message: he would not be home for Christmas.

As a family, they had prepared their hearts to be separated from their loved ones and friends, but it was Christmas Eve . . . and they were now separated from even each other.

Back in Pennsylvania, everyone would be coming home from church—to the sound of caroling, the smell of roasting turkey, and the sight of falling snow.

But where was God's missionary? Here he was . . . stuck in a remote jungle . . . in a makeshift shelter . . . in the pouring rain . . . alone.

In Ruth Tucker's book *From Jerusalem to Irian Jaya*, Bernie May tells of his experience:

> "Oh God," I moaned, "I'm in the wrong place." . . . But that night, under my mosquito net, I had a visitation from God—something like those shepherds must have had on the hills of Bethlehem. There were no angels, and no bright lights. But as I lay there in my hammock, desperately homesick, I felt I heard God say, "My son, this is what Christmas is all about. Jesus left heaven and on Christmas morning He woke up in the 'wrong place'—a stable in Bethlehem. Christmas means leaving home, not going home. My only begotten Son did not come home for Christmas—He left home to be with you."

CHAPTER 6

Becoming Prayer Champions

We all know, at least in our heads, that prayer is important. Yet how many of us honestly believe that *our* prayers, the simple prayers of *our* far-from-perfect family, can really make a difference? If we could comprehend, deep down in our spirits, the true power of prayer, we would *all* pray more—and the difference would radically impact our lives and the lives of everyone around us.

This chapter focuses on becoming a spiritually effective family through *intercessory prayer*, helping God's purposes to be released and fulfilled on the earth. To learn about encouraging children in *personal prayer* and helping them establish their own special quiet time with God, please see the chapter on prayer in *The Mission-Minded Child*.

Q. What is the difference between "personal prayer" and "intercessory prayer"?

Personal prayer is a vital part of our daily Christian walk. The primary purpose of our personal prayer life is to know our wonderful Lord and to grow closer to Him. This discipline (and this daily time of delight) flows from a constantly growing and ever-changing relationship with the never-changing God. Our time of personal prayer and communion with God is a vital expression of our love and worship.

Intercessory prayer is praying on behalf of someone else. The primary purposes are to spiritually support and defend God's purposes here on earth and to help "stand in the gap" for His will to be accomplished. In Ezekiel 22:30, the Lord says, "I sought for a man among them who would make a wall, and stand in the gap before Me on behalf of the land, that I should not destroy it; but I found no one."

God is all-powerful; yet He has established a self-imposed requirement that human beings pray in order for His will on earth to be accomplished. Our prayers can make a difference, and there is tremendous strength in the power of agreement in prayer as a family. Our children are people too. (Isn't that a revelation?) Just think what that could mean! I believe that even a child's prayer—especially when that child has been trained in the truth of God's Word—can fulfill God's requirement just as strategically as an adult's prayer. And perhaps, because of a child's simple faith and absolute trust, God might even see his or her prayers as *more* effective than ours.

There is great strength when a husband and wife agree together in prayer; and when an entire family unites in corporate prayer and intercession, it's *really* powerful! As a praying, mission-minded family, we can "work with God" to help see His purposes come to pass—in individuals, in situations, and even in the nations of the world.

What an enormous privilege and responsibility.

"Give me the love that leads the way,
The faith that nothing can dismay,
The hope no disappointments fire,
The passion that will burn like fire!"

AMY CARMICHAEL

Intercession Keys

Three keys of intercession that can help our families to become prayer champions for God are found in James 5:16: "The effective, fervent prayer of a righteous man avails much."

- Key 1—God is looking for "righteous" people to pray.

- Key 2—Our prayers must be effective.

- Key 3—Our prayers must be fervent.

Q. What does it mean to stand "righteous" before God?

As a family, we're very aware of our differences and our faults. We've all sinned, and we need to acknowledge that no one on earth can stand blameless before our perfect, holy, and awesome God. No matter how good we try to be, our own works are nothing but filthy rags in His sight (see Isaiah 64:6). To pray effectively as a family, we need to grasp the importance of the "fear of the Lord." We don't need to be "afraid" of God in a fearful sense of the word, but we need to realize how powerful and mighty He is. In Revelation 1:17–18, the apostle John recounted, "And when I saw Him, I fell at His feet as dead. But He laid His right hand on me, saying to me, 'Do not be afraid; I am the First and the Last. I am He who lives, and was dead, and behold, I am alive forevermore. Amen.'"

🌐 TEACHING OPPORTUNITY

Mission-Minded Object Lesson: Filthy Rags

In Isaiah 64:6 the Bible says, "All our righteous acts are like filthy rags" (NIV). The next time you come across an extremely dirty rag in your house, use it as an opportunity to share an important lesson with your child. We may think our own self-efforts help us earn "Brownie points" with God. But, to Him, our human works are as worthless as stinky rags. If we try to *earn* favor with God—instead of trusting in Jesus—it's like collecting yucky rags. The more they pile up, the more they stink and mildew.

Only by the cleansing sacrifice of Jesus Christ on the cross have we become "righteous" or in "right standing" before God (Romans 5:19; 2 Corinthians 5:21). It is only because of Christ's forgiveness and His righteousness that we can come before God with boldness and authority to intercede on behalf of others. Along with making us righteous, God also commands us to "put on" righteousness as a part of our spiritual armor (Ephesians 6:14). In prayer, each of us must come to God in an attitude of total surrender and humility, keeping our hearts clean and open before Him.

Even a child can pray as a "righteous man" (James 5:16). Continue to remind your child that his or her spirit can be strong and mature, no matter how young he or she may be! When God spoke to young Samuel, He didn't treat Samuel like a little kid, telling him some cute message just to keep him happy. No, God treated Samuel as a "man of God" and revealed to him a hard-hitting message about the high priest of all Israel (1 Samuel 3:10–14).

Q. How can our family pray more effectively?

In order to make an impact for God's kingdom, our prayers need to be effective and accurate. Broad requests, such as "God bless the missionaries" or "Please help poor people to have enough food," are not examples of effective prayer. Instead, our prayers should be specific, knowledgeable, and on target.

 TEACHING OPPORTUNITY

Mission-Minded Object Lesson: Bull's-eye Target

Using a target as an illustration, share with your family how God has a plan for our prayers. He doesn't want us just to say any random thing that comes to our mind or to mindlessly ramble (like shooting an arrow any which way). Rather, God wants us to "hit the bull's-eye" in prayer. By finding out more about a situation and by learning from God's Word, we can aim or focus our prayers toward His perfect will.

When you and your child know more about a situation, you can pray more effectively. Through increased understanding, your prayers will be more heartfelt, and you can intercede with more authority and boldness. Learn as much information as you can about the people or situations you are praying for. If you are praying for a missionary family, read their newsletters or research current world events affecting them. If you are praying for a particular nation, look for information in *Operation World*, at the library, or on the Internet. If you are interceding for a group of people, look on the Internet (for example, www.joshuaproject.net) for specific details about their beliefs, and pray against specific strongholds keeping these people in bondage.

Effective prayer is also biblically accurate. We need to search the Scriptures for God's will and seek His direction on how to pray. How can we know the difference between God's will and our own desires? Hebrews 4:12 tells us, "The word of God is living and powerful, and sharper than any two-edged sword, piercing even to the division of soul and spirit, and of joints and marrow, and is a discerner of the thoughts and intents of the heart." And as we learn more about God's heart and His desires, we'll find that our thoughts and prayers will increasingly line up with His will.

Q. How can we pray with more fervency?

God desires our prayers to be fervent and intense. One definition of *fervent* includes the phrase "hot and boiling over"!

Mission-Minded Object Lesson: Boiling Water

The next time your child is in the kitchen while you're boiling water, talk about how God wants our prayers to be fervent, or "boiling hot," for Him. As you watch the water boil, explain how our prayers can become more effective as they grow in fervency. Sometimes a prayer can become "hot" immediately, but other times it takes a while for a prayer to become intense and effective.

Our prayers need to be hot for God! We need to pray with all of our heart, soul, mind, and strength. If you pray for the lost, pray as if these individuals are depending on your prayers and you are the only one praying for them. It could be that their souls *do* depend on your prayers, and it *may be* that you are the only one interceding on their behalf.

Fervent Prayer in Africa

On my first mission trip to Africa, I was amazed at the fervent prayers of the Ugandan believers on our ministry team. Everyone usually prayed aloud at the same time, as different individuals led along different themes. Some were kneeling or sitting, others were standing, and a few were even lying on the ground. There was a combination of loud prayer and praise as we interceded for a mighty harvest.

Fervent Prayer in South Korea

In Seoul, South Korea, I had the exciting opportunity to attend a Sunday service at the world's largest church, which is led by Pastor Yonggi Cho. I was surprised how much of the service was devoted exclusively to prayer. The huge building practically shook as thousands of Korean believers prayed intently for their nation and the world. Everyone shouted and prayed so fervently that the leader had to ring a bell to get everyone to stop. It was awesome!

Fervent Prayer Is Intense (Not Just Loud!)

Praying with fervency doesn't necessarily mean just praying with a loud volume. In 1 Kings 18, Elijah and the prophets of Baal both prayed for fire to consume a sacrifice. The prophets of Baal cried loudly for hours. Their prayers were noisy and fleshly, yet worthless. Elijah, however, prayed a simple prayer to God with intensity and authority. If we want our prayers to avail much (James 5:16), we must pray with true Spirit-led fervency.

 **TEACHING OPPORTUNITY**

A Mission-Minded Prayer List

Create a prayer list that your family can use together. Through intercession we can "stand in the gap" for:

- Individuals

Family members	Friends
Unsaved loved ones	Church leaders
Government leaders	Unreached people

- Ministries/Organizations

Our church	Ministries
Schools	Missionary outreaches

- Geographic areas

Our city	Our state, province, or region
Our nation	Other nations

♟ TEACHING OPPORTUNITY

Two Strategies of Intercession: Offensive and Defensive

In most sports it is important to have an offensive and a defensive strategy, and this principle is true for effective intercession. Encourage your family to think about a sport (such as soccer, football, or basketball) that requires both an offense and a defense. Refer to the sports positions (such as forwards, defenders, or goalie), and discuss how these relate to interceding effectively—both offensively and defensively—for God's will to be done.

- **Defensive Intercession:** When there is an emergency—a financial crisis, sickness, or some other trouble—we come against our "opponent" and pray defensively. Yet it's important to remember that we can't win with only a defensive plan!

- **Offensive Intercession:** We shouldn't just wait around to focus our prayers on major problems in our lives or church. Instead, we need to pray offensively. We can follow the Lord's leading and focus on whatever the Holy Spirit wants us to pray about!

Intercession includes a twofold strategy. First, there must be a defensive plan: to come against—or bind—the opponent and his works. Second, there must be an offensive plan: to pray for the power of God to flow—to be loosed—in God's opposite work (see Matthew 18:18). For instance, if you pray for a geographical area where there has been hatred and war, ask God to bind the hatred and loose His love and forgiveness. As your child prays, encourage his or her focus to be on God, not on the devil.

Mission-Minded Object Lesson: Ropes

Write the words "God's Plan" and "Devil's Plan" on two pieces of paper, and tape each paper to the front of two people. Wrap a rope around the person with the "God's Plan" paper. Demonstrate how our prayers of intercession can have two purposes. We "bind" the plans of our enemy. (Take a rope and wrap it around the person with the "Devil's Plan" paper, illustrating how prayer can help to stop bad things.) We also "loose" the plans of God. (Remove the rope around the person with the "God's Plan" paper so that he or she is free, illustrating how prayer can help release good things to happen.)

Our prayers should exalt Jesus Christ and His plans and purposes. Through our fervent intercession, God will show us His mission strategies. Pray for laborers to be thrust into the harvest fields (Luke 10:2)! Pray for open doors to preach the gospel! Pray for boldness in witnessing, and seek God for your part in His global plan.

Recognizing Opposites— Praying against Evil and for God's Purposes

When teaching your family about prayer and intercession, it is important to recognize the works of the enemy and to know how to pray for God's will in that circumstance. When there is sin, we bind the enemy's works and then ask God to release His opposite works. The following are examples of these opposing works:

When there is sin, we can bind the enemy's works of:	We can pray for God to release His "opposite" work of:
Anger	Gentleness
Confusion	Peace, wisdom
Cursing	God's blessing
Death, murder, suicide	God's life
Despair	God's hope
Discouragement	Encouragement
Division	Unity in Christ
Fear	Faith
Hatred	Love, reconciliation
Independence	Dependence on God
Lust, impurity, bad thoughts	God's love, purity
Poverty	Provision
Prejudice	Unconditional love
Pride	Humility
Religious bondage	Spiritual freedom
Selfishness	Generosity
Self-righteousness	Righteousness in Christ
Sickness, disease	Health, God's healing
Spiritual rebellion	Submission to God

Prayer Stops the Plans of Terrorists

In Kampala, Uganda, a group of African widows live in the meeting place of a church with which we often work. These women live very simply, with only a small mat on the dirt floor. Their sole purpose in life is to intercede. They pray for many hours every day, and during a special mission outreach they often intercede around the clock.

During one outreach, these women "knew" (in prayer) that we were in danger and began to fast and fervently pray for our protection. As they interceded, one of the women saw in a vision our entire ministry team encircled by angels. These prayer partners were able to get a message of warning through to us. That day in the Tanzanian city where we were preaching, local police caught four Islamic terrorists attempting to plant a bomb on the ministry outreach grounds. Our lives had been spared through intercession and a word of warning from our partners.

Q. Are all Christians called to intercession?

All Christians—including children—are called to pray. We are also called to intercede, as the Lord leads, for regular intercession commitments, as a personal intercessor (or prayer partner), in an emergency, or for a geographical area.

"Regular" Intercession

 **TEACHING OPPORTUNITY**

Weekly Prayer List—
Pray for a Major Area of Society Each Day

You may want to make a list of regular, or ongoing, prayer commitments, which can include family members, your church, missionaries you support, school leaders, government leaders, and other people you are specifically praying for. In YWAM's daily prayer diary, regular responsibilities include prayer for the following seven areas of society, one area each day.

Weekly Prayer List

- Sunday: church and religion
- Monday: family and the home
- Tuesday: the media
- Wednesday: government

- Thursday: education
- Friday: business and commerce
- Saturday: arts and entertainment

Visual Prayer Reminders

Kids often relate better to pictures than to a prayer list. One idea is to have your child make a photo prayer-collage on a bulletin board, on poster board, or in a mini-album. My boys, Mark and Philip (ages ten and six), simply use pushpins to tack photos of all kinds of prayer needs around their beds. These pictures remind them as they drift off to sleep to pray for children in an African village, specific missionaries, and special friends. Encourage your children to be flexible and sensitive to the Holy Spirit as they pray. It is good to have a regular prayer plan, but it's even better to be open to *God's* plans.

"Prayer Partner" Intercession

God raises up people to be prayer partners for individuals, churches, or ministries. Through the years, my husband and I have been grateful for the people—including the children—God has called to faithfully intercede for our ministry and our family.

A Young Prayer Partner's Creative Idea

We heard about a little boy who made a wristband with our family's name on it in order to remind him to pray for us and the mission work we do. We were humbled and blessed by his prayer partnership with us.

Encouragement from a Prayer Partner

One precious friend has been a personal intercessor for our ministry for over sixteen years. This woman has called at times to share a word of encouragement, which has always been timely.

Once, when I was discouraged and unsure about going on a particular mission trip to Jamaica, she felt led to call and encourage me to go. As we spoke on the phone, she shared two words that she felt the Lord had given her in prayer for me. The two words were "No resistance!"

Because of her encouragement, I decided to go—and the outreach was a total success! Throughout the trip, our family met *no resistance* to our ministry. We were encouraged, and God opened many doors! We preached on streets and in churches and even shared the gospel in public schools across the country. Not one principal turned us down for an assembly, and over five thousand people surrendered their lives to Jesus Christ!

"Emergency" Intercession

As you grow in intercessory prayer, you (or even your child) may wake up in the night with an urge to pray for someone. Or you may be about your daily routine when you suddenly think of a particular person or need. When this happens, be aware that God may be using you to intercede for a crisis.

1. *Be on call for prayer.* We may never know the impact of our prayers, but we should always be "on call" for emergencies. And as one person in our family is feeling this need to pray, we can all agree together.

2. *Be instant in prayer.* When God gives a "strong thought" about someone or a sudden burden to pray, we need to pray! When this feeling of urgency comes, pray as soon as possible and continue praying until the heaviness leaves.

3. *Be obedient in prayer.* Pray hard, as if your prayers will make a difference between life and death—because, at times, it *is* this important!

Emergency Intercession for Our Lost Son

Years ago, when our children were young, my husband and his parents were fishing at a nearby river with two of our boys when they suddenly realized that our five-year-old son, Patrick, was missing.

Desperately, Jon ran up and down the river, looking for Patrick. The river turned into fierce rapids not far downstream, and he feared Patrick could have fallen into the water.

During his search along the riverbank, Jon met several young fishermen who were relaxing and enjoying their day. "Please," Jon yelled, "have you seen a little blond-haired boy? He's lost and may have fallen into the river!"

Not one of these men seemed to care. It wasn't their problem. They didn't want to be bothered—and they just kept fishing.

Jon continued to search, and eventually several police officers joined in to help. A helicopter patrol scanned the river; but even after hours of frantic searching, no one could find our son . . .

That afternoon, across the country, a longtime friend of mine and her three children were sitting on the floor, folding laundry. I had not seen this woman since college, and I hadn't even spoken with her for several years. Yet she suddenly felt a tremendous burden to pray. As she started to pray, the Lord directed her prayers toward our son, Patrick! In the midst of little kids and unfolded clothes, she interceded for him fervently. She felt that he was lost, so she began to intercede specifically for Jon to find him. She prayed for me to have peace and for God to lead us to Patrick . . .

Back at the river, a man on a mountain bike came to Jon and said, "I haven't seen your kid, but I think I know where he is."

A while later, this man returned with little Patrick on his shoulders! The man told us that the night before he dreamed of finding a little blond boy on a certain mountain trail. When the man heard about the search, he immediately went to that trail. Sure enough, there was our son (alone, yet unhurt, other than some scrapes and scratches). Patrick had wandered up a steep cliff and had strayed over a mile away.

That day, we experienced firsthand the power of God—released through emergency intercession.

We also learned a vital lesson about how it feels to be a parent urgently searching for a lost child. How our heavenly Father's heart must break for the lost! He sees His children in sin! He knows the situation is urgent! He knows it's a matter of eternal life and death. Yet how many of us sit back in complacency, not wanting to be bothered? How often do we respond like those selfish fishermen by the river? May we have His heart of compassion!

Protected through Emergency Intercession

One of my first experiences of God's protection through others' prayers happened when I was sixteen years old. One afternoon a girlfriend and I were walking on a back street of a major US city. Suddenly a rough-looking street gang approached us, and we felt helpless as these young men surrounded us and began to harass and slap us. We were all alone with no one near.

At the very same time, however, my parents were hosting a prayer meeting at our house with several family friends. They had committed the entire day to prayer and fasting. Suddenly a woman in the group felt a tremendous burden to pray for the protection of their children. In unity, the entire group prayed earnestly for God to surround each of their children with angels and supernatural protection . . .

Also at the same time, a close teenage friend of mine (a missionary's daughter, by the way!) suddenly thought about me. She started praying, and in her mind she began to "see" a picture of me walking down a street. Then suddenly, in her vision, a circle of darkness surrounded me. My friend continued praying fervently until she "saw" a bright light shine in the center of the circle; then suddenly the darkness left.

From my perspective, this street gang—for no apparent reason— suddenly turned and ran away. My friend and I immediately ran to her house and, together with her parents, called the police to report the incident.

A few months later, I had to testify in court against these men. We learned that this street gang had been arrested for attacking and raping several girls. When the judge asked them why they ran away from my friend and me so suddenly, they had no answer; they just felt they had to "get out of there fast"!

I knew that God intervened because people were praying.

Fleeing Rwanda

Many of our prayer partners felt a heavy burden to pray as my husband was ministering in Rwanda in 1994, shortly after the terrible Rwandan genocide.

Early one morning, on the day of a planned outreach in the city of Gitarama, Jon had a dream of Joseph and Mary escaping to Egypt with baby Jesus (which he said was as clear as if he were watching a Bible video). He then "saw" in his dream the outreach grounds where they planned to preach that evening. In his dream, he saw the crowd attacked in a massive slaughter; and he, along with six other team members, felt God's direction to *Get out of the country—now!*

The team packed and left immediately, escaping across the border just before it was closed. Within hours after their departure, war broke out in that very city of Gitarama, and over seven thousand people were killed.

We were so thankful for God's protection through prayer!

"Area" Intercession

Sometimes God wants us to intercede for a specific geographical area, such as a city, nation, or region of the world. In Genesis 18, Abraham interceded for Sodom and Gomorrah, and in Psalm 122:6 we are encouraged to "pray for the peace of Jerusalem." Ephesians 6:12 states that "we do not wrestle against flesh and blood, but against principalities, against powers, against the rulers of the darkness of this age, against spiritual hosts of wickedness in the heavenly places."

Four Examples of Area Intercession

- *A prayer journey to Bhutan*: Some friends of mine traveled to Bhutan (as tourists) for a "prayer journey." Their purpose was to intercede at specific key locations throughout this central Asian country. I wondered, at first, if this was a waste of ministry resources. But only a few months later, political laws changed to allow foreign missionaries to enter the country!

- *Praying corporately for peace in an African city*: My husband and several other ministers with Harvest Ministry traveled to Kitgum, Uganda, on the border of Sudan—a remote city filled with refugees. For nearly thirty years this area has been devastated by war and paralyzed by the fear of rebel soldiers. Approximately forty thousand people gathered each night of the outreach to hear the Good News of Jesus; and this massive crowd prayed, corporately and fervently, for peace. One evening, many people had a strong sense that something "broke" in the spiritual dimension. One week later the news reported an official cease-fire in the war in Southern Sudan. Some may think it was just a "coincidence," but we choose to believe it was one of those "God-incidences" that happen when believers pray!

- *Praying in Washington DC*: When I spent a few days in Washington DC, I took time to pray for the United States. I visited the National Cathedral and spent time prayer-walking around the grounds and throughout this beautiful place that was built to honor Jesus Christ. I prayed for God's grace over this country. As an American citizen, I repented on behalf of my nation and asked God to forgive the sins of my country. As I visited the US Supreme Court Building, I prayed for the judicial courts of this land and interceded for evil laws, such as legalized abortion, to be changed. Throughout my tours I prayed for God to have mercy (God's favor that we don't deserve) on our land, despite our great faults. My location may not have made a difference to God, but being in those places definitely helped me to pray with increased fervency and passion.

- *Prayer-walking a neighborhood*: In a nearby city, a local church organized a summer of prayer-walking its community. The pastor told us how encouraged and surprised he has been by the positive response and cooperation from the congregation. At least once a week, one to three individuals walk and pray through every street of their city, including the business district, praying for blessing, for a softening of people's hearts, and for wisdom in evangelism. The leader of this outreach walked through her neighborhood and noticed many unkempt yards and overgrown weeds. She asked, *Lord, is there a spirit of oppression over this neighborhood?* Then she specifically prayed against it. The following week, many of these same yards were mowed and cleaned up. She felt the Lord say to her, *See how prayer is making a difference? And you can't even see all that's happening in the spiritual dimension!*

Daniel 10:10–13 gives us a glimpse into the effect of prayer over particular areas. In this passage, an angel is sent because of Daniel's prayers, yet for twenty-one days the evil prince of the kingdom of Persia withstands him in the heavenly realm. As Daniel continues to pray, another angel, the chief prince Michael, is sent to help, and finally the victory is won.

Throughout the earth, a spiritual battle is taking place; and it is not a game! For God's will to be achieved, we need to pray and intercede with accuracy and fervency. We need to emphasize to our children that the battle is not in the flesh but in the spirit. Second Corinthians 10:4 tells us, "The weapons of our warfare are not carnal but mighty in God for pulling down strongholds."

God has defeated the devil through the cross of Calvary and the resurrection of Jesus Christ. At the same time, a quick glance at our world's current situation definitely reveals that the devil still has quite a bit of authority and power. In Ephesians 2:2 the enemy is called "the prince of the power of the air." His strongholds can be through belief systems (such as Hinduism or atheism) or through major sins of a particular area (such as a people group bound by witchcraft or immorality). The devil can also have strongholds in individual lives through fear, depression, anger, hatred, or addictions. As Christians, we must realize that God has delegated His authority to us—as people in His kingdom who are living on this earth and made righteous through Christ—to "pull down" these strongholds through prayer.

A PRAYER ROOM IN INDIA

By Cassie Diacogiannis

Our "prayer room" was set up with cushions on the floor, pictures and maps on the walls, and soft music playing in the background. Every area of the room was focused on praying for different nations, people groups, or mission needs. Crayons and markers lined the edge of the floor so that children could write their prayers on the paper-covered wall.

"All right, kids, when we go into our prayer room, remember that we're not playing around but praying and being serious."

I knew these seventy-five kids understood what I was saying, but I wasn't sure how they would respond. This mission outreach in India had been full of surprises, but I couldn't have prepared myself for what happened next.

The children and I were part of the Western India YWAM Family Conference in the city of Lonavala, India; and I was responsible for teaching all the "YWAMer" kids while their parents were having intense times of networking and conference sessions. When our YWAM base leader gave me permission to bring all the children into the prayer room during the sessions, I jumped at the opportunity. I knew it would be powerful to see missionary kids from around the globe praying for the world. And I couldn't have been more blessed by what I witnessed.

As the kids entered the room, they took off their shoes and lined them up in rows. As they quietly entered this place of worship, the older children helped the younger ones remember why we were there. A moment later, as I walked into the room, it's hard to explain what I saw. The room was filled with seventy-five praying children, all of them under twelve years old. The children were praying for the United States, Pakistan, Iraq, many other nations, and YWAM bases around the world. Some prayed loudly, some prayed silently, and others were worshiping with their hands lifted high to Jesus. A few were sitting quietly on the red cushions and simply watching. But all were very seriously focused on the Lord.

As I walked over to the "wailing wall," the area set aside for specific prayer requests, I saw that a little boy had written the word *Antarctica* in his best penmanship. He had his hand near the word and was praying softly in a strange language. As I came near, he explained that he was praying for the scientists there to see the beauty of God's creation so that they would know Him. A few moments later, a seven-year-old girl named Samaya asked if we could pray for a little boy who was missing his mamma. Before I had barely said, "All right, . . ." Samaya had gathered many children to pray for this little boy who had been crying and had not wanted to stay in class. These children put their little hands on the sad boy and started praying in English, Hindi, and other languages.

Whether it was praying for the nations or for one of our own little children, we knew that God was hearing our prayers. The next day, the boy kissed his momma as he was dropped off and bounded into class. He was ready to play and to pray with the children who had prayed with him the night before.

— 👥 FROM MY CHILDREN'S PERSPECTIVE —

HELL IS REAL!

By Joshua Dunagan, at age eight

One night when I was eight years old, I was sitting in our living room, thinking about my dad. He was away on a missionary trip to Africa, and I started praying for him. As I prayed, the Lord showed me something. I began thinking about all the people in the world who don't know Jesus and how my dad was sharing the gospel at that very moment. Suddenly, it hit me how people who don't know Jesus can't go to heaven . . . they go to hell.

I kept praying and began to realize how terrible hell really is and how people in hell are stuck there—forever!

It's hard to explain what happened, but God did something inside me. I began to cry, for a long time, and it changed the way I thought about the lost. I realized that I had never led anyone to the Lord, and I prayed specifically that God would give me a chance to share with someone that week.

Afterward, I wrote this letter:

> Dear God, I love you so much. Please let me have a chance to share the gospel with someone this week. Lord, you are precious to me.
>
> From Joshua

Dear God
I love you so Much
please let me have
a canc to cher theGospe
With somyon
this week.
Lord you ar
presis to me
From Joshua

(Note: Later that week, Joshua went to a park and shared the gospel with a young boy named Randy, and then Joshua prayed with him to receive Jesus. Within two years, at the young age of ten, Joshua himself was boldly preaching in Africa—about Jesus and about the fire of Elijah—to intent crowds of over ten thousand people!)

— ⚭ FROM MY CHILDREN'S PERSPECTIVE —

WE LOVE TO PRAY!

Mark (age eleven): "I think it's really important to pray! I like to go on prayer-walks outside, and I even made a special 'prayer place' out in the woods. One time I made a prayer closet in my room, and other times I simply put pictures on my bedroom wall. I like to pray for my African prayer partner (his name is Moses) and special friends and missionaries who live in other countries."

Caela Rose (age nine): "When I pray, I know that I'm really talking to God, not to myself. Sometimes God has even helped me to pray and fast (where I didn't eat anything, other than juice and water, for a whole day). No one made me do this, but after our pastor taught about the importance of prayer and fasting, I really felt that God wanted me to do it. Even though I was very hungry, fasting encouraged me to pray harder, and it really drew me closer to God."

Philip (age six): "I'm just six years old, but I like to pray too! I like to worship at church, and sometimes I go to church prayer (even if it's mostly just grownups). I even like to make up songs (good songs) to Jesus. I also like to pray for my special friend, Ivan, in Africa. And I love Jesus!"

Ten Prayer Projects

1. Take a prayer-walk around your neighborhood, quietly praying for each neighbor as you walk by.

2. Have each child pick a neighbor and take that person a small gift—such as flowers, cookies, or a homemade card that says something like "I'm glad you're my neighbor." Pray beforehand for God to prepare the way and soften your neighbor's heart. Encourage your child to mention that he or she has been praying for them and to ask if they have any special prayer needs.

3. Create a map of your country. As each state, province, or region is added, have your child pray specifically for that area.

4. Purchase a simple world map to display on a wall, and add a bundle of dried wheat above it (or display a bundle of wheat in your kitchen as a decoration) to remind you to pray for a great harvest of souls around the world.

5. Add a "10/40 Window" to your world map. Use colored yarn and pushpins or colored tape to highlight this important area of the world where there are so many unreached people who need Jesus. Make horizontal lines along the latitude lines 10 degrees and 40 degrees north of the equator. Make vertical lines to include all of Africa to the west and all of Asia to the east. Pray for this area.

6. Toss an inflatable globe around the room while playing music, as in musical chairs. When the music stops, the person holding the globe prays for the specific place where his or her fingers are touching.

7. Have your child make a "Ten Most Wanted" list or poster. Have them think of ten people who need Jesus. These can be relatives, friends, neighbors, famous people, or the man

who works at the convenience store. Use this list or poster to remind you to pray for these people to come to know the Lord.

8. Use the acronym THUMB to remember the five major segments of people who need Jesus: T for Tribal, H for Hindu, U for Unreligious, M for Muslim, and B for Buddhist.

9. Using your church directory, talk about all the ministries and jobs in your church. Relate each person to a part of a body and how every part is important. Pray for these various individuals, including your pastor, and for the people in your congregation as a whole.

10. Simply pray!!

CHAPTER 7

Missions and
Family Finances

"For where your treasure is, there your heart will be also."

JESUS CHRIST (MATTHEW 6:21)

How your family views money and possessions is intrinsically connected with how you view God's priorities in life. As Christians, we should have the perspective that everything belongs to God: all of our time, all of our talents, all of our life decisions, and, yes, all of our money. I believe it is important to teach our children about God's principle of tithing (giving 10 percent of our income to Him), but even more importantly we need to instill in our family that 100 percent of absolutely everything in our lives belongs to God. This principle is much easier *caught*—by our example—than *taught* by our words.

Every Christian family should live by faith. It doesn't matter if you are called to a conventional occupation or called to be a pastor or a missionary; in actuality, every believer is called to "full-time ministry." Every believer is called to serve the Lord as His ambassador, in whatever area that might be. There is a special grace, a high accountability before God, and many unique challenges for believers who commit to earning their entire livelihood by the gospel; but every mission-minded follower of God should live by faith. Often the most difficult challenge to accepting God's calling to ministry or missionary work is the question of money and trusting in God's provision, especially provision for an entire family.

Nobody wants to be a missionary mooch or a religious bum. The very fact that we have these fears reveals a struggle in our core attitudes about work, faith, and God's provision.

This chapter is written for two purposes. First, I want to encourage each family that is called to forgo a traditional salary or occupation (or that may be called to do so in the future) to obey God's call into ministry or missionary work. Even a traditional pastoral position or an appointment on a church staff seems more stable than a mission-oriented occupation or a ministry with an evangelistic or outreach focus. Lost people don't buy tickets (or pay their tithes) to hear the gospel. But they need to hear, and someone has to be willing to reach out to them. Second, this chapter is written to encourage every mission-minded family to understand the tremendous needs concerning world missions and international evangelism. Every one of us (including pastors, laypeople, and even missionaries) needs to support God's work generously.

The Little Blue Lamp

My husband and I were both twenty-one years old and had just completed Bible school and university education when the Lord began training us to rely totally on Him. We were living in Oklahoma and preparing to move over two thousand miles away, to Oregon, to step into full-time ministry.

Because of prayer, we felt God calling us to mission evangelism and specifically (in our situation) that Jon was not to work any job for pay, outside of the ministry. We had accumulated a modest savings and were beginning to sell our belongings. But no matter how many times we tried to calculate our future budget, there was no way, financially speaking, that it would work. Even if all of our things sold for top dollar, we realized there would be nothing to live on beyond the first few months.

We didn't have a support base. We didn't know anyone in the city where we were headed. And the more we thought about it and tried to crunch the numbers, the more concerned and frustrated we became.

As graduation day drew near, Jon earnestly began to seek the Lord for direction and provision. One day, after a time of fervent prayer, Jon came in and told me, "Hon, you'd better sit down." My husband then proceeded to unload what could have been a bomb for a young wife: "Ann, I believe God wants us to forsake everything and totally depend on Him, not on ourselves. Just as the disciples left their full nets to follow Jesus, I believe God wants us to give away everything—our car, our savings, and everything we've had for sale."

For a moment, I let the words sink in. It sounded crazy, but somehow God instantly confirmed Jon's words in my heart.

It wasn't because of something he and I had heard before. We weren't mimicking someone else's testimony. (And we're not suggesting anyone else try this at home!) Yet somehow, deep inside, we both felt this was indeed what God wanted for us. Besides, if Jon's idea *was* from God (which I felt it was), I knew it would work; and if it *wasn't* from God, we shouldn't be in ministry! A faith came that was unexplainable. All worry and anxiety left, and we were instantly filled with excitement.

That night, we called a few friends and told them to come and take anything they wanted. The next day, we gave our car to a fellow student who had wanted to buy it. In the next church service, we gave our entire savings in the offering. We gave a beautiful hand-carved baby crib to a woman I had prayed with (who, by the way, had been barren, but was now expecting!). And most difficult of all, I presented our church's worship director with a treasured silver flute my parents had sacrificed to buy for my sixteenth birthday.

Now there was no possible way we could step out in ministry on our own. If it worked, it would have to be the Lord's provision. And we just knew He would provide!

But two days before we were to move, reality suddenly hit. We had nothing. The lease was up on our apartment. Our church had already prayed for us and sent us out. We had no vehicle and no money. How would we live? How were we going to get across the country? Could we really expect someone to give us a car within the next few days? It seemed impossible.

Jon looked over at me, sitting on the floor with our newborn, as he suddenly felt a wave of despair, responsibility, and condemnation.

He desperately cried out to the Lord, "God, did I hear You right?"

As he prayed, Jon felt a reassuring peace and a still, small voice: *Yes, and as soon as you do everything I have told you to do, you will see My provision.*

Jon kept asking me all morning if there was something we had not yet done, but we couldn't think of anything. Finally, we got out our "for sale" list and went down the items one by one—until we came to . . .

Blue Lamp—$5

Looking across the room, we saw the little blue lamp sitting on a cardboard box in the corner. We had found it (then an ugly orange) at a garage sale, brought it home, and painted it country blue.

"The lamp! The lamp!" we both shouted. "We forgot to give away the lamp!"

Immediately, Jon grabbed that little blue lamp (along with a handful of pots and pans) and headed to our neighbor's apartment. Our young bachelor friend didn't know what to think when Jon loaded his arms with the strange combination, saying, "Here—God wants you to have these!"

Jon hurried back to our apartment, and within three minutes (that is no exaggeration!) we received a phone call from a man we barely knew.

"Is this Jon Dunagan?"

"Yes."

"Do you need a car?"

Jon attempted to conceal his growing excitement. "Well . . . uh, why do you ask?"

"Well, my wife and I have been feeling that God wants us to give you our car. We've never done anything like this before, so we prayed about it all last night. It wasn't until just a few minutes ago that we finally felt a peace about calling you."

That last step of obedience—giving away that insignificant blue lamp—released God's provision! Before, we trusted in ourselves and our stuff, but now we depended on God.

Within two days, we left for Oregon—arriving in town with our little car, a few dishes (which weren't on our "for sale" list), some clothes, one baby, and only twenty-seven dollars!

We preached in parks and witnessed on the streets; and a roller-skating rink allowed us to use their building—*free of charge*—for weekly services. We even found a nice fourplex with an amazing move-in special: "Move in today . . . and don't pay for three months"!

Our First Mission Trip

After we had been in Oregon a short time, God led us to a pastor who helped arrange our first overseas mission trip: to Hong Kong, Macao, China, and the Philippines. The Lord supernaturally provided money for our airline tickets, but when it came time to leave, we had no money for traveling expenses—not even one dollar to buy gas to get to the airport!

Here we were, a young couple with an eighteen-month-old baby, and I was seven months pregnant. Our only overseas contacts were complete strangers, and we didn't know if we needed to pay our expenses once we were there.

How could we leave with no money? Would we be a blessing or a burden? Was this really God's will?

As we prayed together, God again gave us peace that comes only from Him. He gave us a tremendous burden for the lost in those countries and reassured us that He could provide there just as easily as He could provide in America. For Him, there was no difference; but for us, it was a lesson in trust.

We decided to pack our car and drive toward the airport until our near-empty gas tank ran dry. Right before we left, we made a last-minute check through our apartment and noticed a new message on our answering machine: "Hey, Jon and Ann, if you haven't left yet, I've got something for you down at the church . . ."

That "something" was a twenty-dollar bill—just enough to get us to the airport! On our way overseas, the Lord opened up an opportunity for us to share with a small college group at a church in Maui, Hawaii. We were completely surprised when they offered to take a special missions offering for our trip! These people blessed us and sent us on our way.

Throughout the several-month outreach, no one knew of our meager financial situation. Every step along the way we had enough money to pay for every expense. We were able to bless our ministry contacts monetarily. And we even came home with souvenirs! We saw firsthand the "ripe harvest" overseas, and our lives and ministry have never been the same.

Continuing to Trust God

For over twenty years, my husband and I have not worked a job—for pay—outside of the ministry; and we have never "itinerated" to raise ministry funds (although we realize that many, in fact most, missionaries are led by the Lord to do this). We have simply trusted God. And He has faithfully provided for hundreds of international outreaches and for every need for our growing family.

When we have a financial need, we seek God's direction. Sometimes we share a ministry need in our monthly newsletter (which we only send to those who have requested it). Sometimes we tell no one and simply pray. Other times the Lord directs us to mention something to a particular person. Sometimes He directs us to give generously to someone else. We often practice "tithing in advance" (just as people gave of their "firstfruits" in the Bible): we give 10 percent of what we need for an outreach before any money comes in.

No matter how the details work out, God consistently comes through! Over the years, He has provided for missionary motorcycles and village church buildings, as well as for college tuition and orthodontic braces for our children.

God's provision doesn't always look the same, but it's always there. One time we trusted God for over fifteen thousand dollars for an African outreach; then, soon afterward, we trusted God for us to go back to Africa without even one penny—using a free airline ticket! God's provision was met in a supernatural way for each trip, but the provision came quite differently.

When another "impossible" situation comes, the Lord simply reminds us how we began; and He continually reassures us that He will keep meeting our needs today . . . and tomorrow.

How Does a Missionary Raise Support?

When beginning full-time missionary work, one of the first steps a person will take—while praying and seeking the Lord's will—is to build a support base for prayer, mutual encouragement, and financial partnership. As Betty Barnett of YWAM has written in her excellent book, *Friend Raising: Building a Missionary Support Team That Lasts*, this is a process of raising friends, not funds.

It is important for mission-minded families to do their best to understand the challenging steps new missionaries must take to reach the ministry goal God is calling them to make. As we take time to consider a missionary's initial (and ongoing) challenge to trust God for financial provision, it can help us to be more empathetic and encouraging. Missionaries need constant encouragement—in prayer, friendship, and finances—to see God's visions fulfilled. Even simple comments, such as "I just got your newsletter in the mail, and I'm so proud of you!" or "Hey, I want you to know that I'm praying for people to give toward your ministry!" can make a huge impact.

🎤 TEACHING OPPORTUNITY

Learn How a Missionary Builds a Support Team

Even if your family is not called to full-time missionary service, look at each step a new missionary has to face and consider how your mission-minded family could be a support, help, and encouragement to new missionaries.

- A new missionary usually begins by seeking counsel from a pastor or a mission organization. (Your family could pray with them for God's wisdom.)

- As God leads, the new missionary usually hopes to share the new vision at his or her home church or at a church of close friends or family members. (You could mention this opportunity to your pastor or church leaders.)

- Sometimes a table display needs to be assembled with photos of the people or a map of the projected area. (Your family could stand by their display or, if you're computer savvy, help to make an video or computer presentation.

- It is usually helpful to have a ministry brochure available. This brochure often includes photos, a brief introduction of the missionary and his or her family, a description of previous ministry experiences, and the missionary's vision for the future. (Your family can give encouraging comments or help with mailing.)

- A new ministry brochure usually includes a brief recommendation from a pastor and perhaps others and a simple response card. (Your family could collect recommendations and positive comments about the missionary.)

- When sharing a new vision, missionaries try to remember that God is their ultimate source of provision—not any particular people. "Where God guides, He provides!" Without portraying a begging attitude, new missionaries attempt to convey their burning heart for the lost and to share their vision for the future. Many missionaries see tremendous needs that they are unable to meet by themselves; part of their calling is to help convey this need to others. (Your family can help by requesting prayer support for specific missionary needs.)

- Oftentimes, the thought of facing friends and family to raise necessary missionary support is far more terrifying than the thought of facing a tribe of cannibalistic headhunters! It's a great blessing when a new missionary meets someone with an encouraging and compassionate heart. (Your family can be this encouragement!)

- At the conclusion of a new missionary's presentation, it is very helpful if a pastor (or someone other than the missionary) invites people to join with this new missionary in prayer and/ or financial support. (Perhaps you can fill that role.)

TEACHING OPPORTUNITY

Make an Introductory Missionary Brochure

As a family, you could help a new missionary with an introductory brochure, design a brochure for a missionary who needs an updated design, or even write your own family letter to communicate your heart for world missions or to encourage prayer for a specific need.

Imagine you're a new missionary. Follow the steps below to begin communicating with your supporters. (And when you are in the midst of that tedious job of signing and mailing your annual Christmas letter or cards, remember to pray for God's blessing and anointing on your missionaries—who need to communicate with their partners regularly, nearly every month!)

- Begin with an up-to-date family photo, and design an attractive prayer card.

- Ask the Lord who to include in your first mailing. (Missionaries often begin by making a list of relatives, church friends, coworkers, high school and college friends, those on their Christmas list, or people they meet as they share their new ministry vision.)

- What to include in your mailing to supporters: a simple letter, a quality ministry brochure, a return envelope, and a response card (if desired).

- Make your communication personal. If possible, a new missionary should precede the first mailing with a personal contact. A friendly call or a short note simply to touch base with a longtime friend could make a big difference. And when the initial newsletter is sent, it is always good to include a personal, handwritten note.

It is important to realize that stepping into full-time ministry or mission work usually requires dying to self-righteous pride and reevaluating self-sufficient attitudes. Sometimes a person may listen to a missionary and inwardly mutter: *Ugh! There is no way on earth I would take money from people I know. If God ever provided supernaturally, that would be one thing. But if He ever wanted me to be a missionary, I would never be like some tramp—just mooching off friends and family!*

Do we consider "living by faith" equivalent to begging like a homeless vagabond or perpetually surviving on food stamps and welfare? Thoughts like these degrade God's calling and the obedience of His frontline warriors. As mission-minded parents and teachers, it is vital to esteem God's missionaries and the tremendous sacrifices they make. Remember that our children will grasp our attitudes even more than the things we say.

DARING TO LIVE ON THE EDGE

An excerpt from *Daring to Live on the Edge*, by Loren Cunningham

In his excellent book *Daring to Live on the Edge: The Adventure of Faith and Finances*, Loren Cunningham addresses many challenges of stepping into full-time ministry. As the founder and director of YWAM (Youth With A Mission), Cunningham shares from his vast experience and from his heart as he encourages others to walk in obedience to God's calling—whatever that may be.

For many of us, pride blocks us from being the receivers of generous giving. We would rather be self-sufficient. I have often talked with people who wanted to be missionaries some day—when they could pay their own way to go. But the sad fact is that even if you could manage to remain unentangled with debt and find a way to bankroll your own work, you would miss the terrible-but-wonderful humbling heart link that occurs when people put money in your hand, saying the Lord told them to give it to you.

There is a special bond forever between you and the giver. You will care about and pray for the giver in a different way than you pray for those who have never given to you personally. You will also quite naturally want to share news with your giver about your ministry, reporting what the gift has done in the work of the Lord. And prayer will go up on all sides—the spiritual warfare that is necessary for anything to be accomplished. It might not seem possible to struggling missionaries or pastors, but if a giant foundation were to fund their work or some billionaire were to write out a huge check, it could be a death knell for their ministry. Missionaries need much more help than money. We need people backing us up, praying for the extension of God's kingdom, engaging with us in spiritual warfare through their giving and intercession.

The giver is blessed in the process, too. Jesus told us, "Where your treasure is, there your heart will be also" (Matthew 6:21 NIV). When we give our "treasure" to specific people and their ministries, our hearts are there with them. They may be halfway around the world in an area we may never visit—but we are closer to these people and what God is doing in that country because of our giving. This kind of heart link giving allows any Christian from any part of the world to "go out" and help fulfill the Great Commission. And it is God's way of forging and strengthening relationships.

> "Though your riches increase,
> do not set your heart on them."
>
> PSALM 62:10 (NIV)

A Few (More) Thoughts about Faith and Finances

The next sections are for mission-minded families that are *not* called to be missionaries

Advice from a Mission-Minded Single Mom

Every month I put money aside and work extra jobs to have the means to go when and where the Lord shall direct. I encourage everyone to do what he or she can to save little by little as well. The Lord makes ways when you are working for Him! But it's also important to remember not to be so caught up in saving that we forget to give. (This is a daily reminder that I need to keep giving myself!)

Challenged by Cluttered Closets

With twisted hangers, bulging drawers, and too many clothes, the kids and I began our major closet-cleaning attack. It took days; but as we conquered our last pile, we felt victorious—with sacks for the Dumpster and sacks to give away. Best of all, we finished just in time for me to leave for a short-term mission trip.

I was headed to Uganda and soon was surrounded by orphans with bare bottoms and wearing nothing but rags and ripped-up shirts. I couldn't think of anything but these precious children and my cluttered closets. Then I felt the Lord whisper, *I'm the One naked on these streets!* I immediately went to buy armloads of children's clothing. But the situation turned pathetic: mothers came running from everywhere, holding up naked babies, and begging for help. The need was beyond me; and I tell you, it did something to my heart.

Back home, our family raised funds to clothe that whole village. And this year, we even started an orphanage. The world's needs are huge, but they're not beyond God!

Ten Ways to Raise Money for Missions

There are many ways to raise money for international mission projects. Here is a list of activities commonly used by children's churches, youth groups, and short-term mission teams. The time will come, however, when these efforts won't be enough. A true mission-minded family just needs to earn and save money, managing that money according to what's important.

1. Organize a car wash; rather than charging a set amount, receive donations.

2. Collect newspapers for recycling.

3. Recycle aluminum (and go around neighborhoods to get even more).

4. Use creative offering baskets. The last few weeks at our church, someone held up a big rubber boot to collect money for a mission trip to the Philippines. A missionary wants to buy rubber barn boots and other gifts for pastors in remote villages; the boot was simply a fun way for the church to catch the vision. Another idea is to use African-looking baskets.

5. Track a missions goal on a "thermometer" poster or in the church bulletin.

6. Have a family garage sale.

7. Make and sell something, like crafts or after-church lattes and espressos.

8. Donate a service in exchange for a donation for a mission trip.

9. Collect spare change in special containers, such as a coffee can with pictures related to the mission project and a hole for coins in the lid. I know of a small church in which the kids raised thousands of dollars for missions by doing this.

10. Have a bake sale after church.

A Coast Guard Cutter . . . or a Luxury Liner?

What kind of lifestyle is appropriate for a mission-minded family? Does God want all Christians to subsist just above the poverty line? Is it OK to live in extreme wealth and extravagance? Or does God have a divine balance economically for each family? An interesting perspective is to remember that we are in a spiritual battle, with eternal souls at stake. As mission-minded believers, we should go through life as if we are on a rescue ship, not a luxury craft.

During World War II, the *Queen Mary*, a huge ocean liner, was converted into a troopship. In *Serving as Senders*, Neal Pirolo writes:

> Today the museum aboard the *Queen Mary* affords a stunning contrast between the lifestyles appropriate in peace and war. On one side of a partition, the tables prepared for high society hold a dazzling array of dishes, crystal and silver. On the other side, one metal tray with indentations replaces 15 dishes and saucers. Bunks, eight tiers high, accommodate 15,000 troops in contrast to the 3,000 wealthy patrons in

peacetime transport. To so drastically reconstruct the vessel took a national emergency. The survival of a nation depended upon it. Should you replace your china with metal trays? No! But allow the Holy Spirit to challenge every aspect of your lifestyle.

> "You may say to yourself, 'My power and the strength of my hands have produced this wealth for me.' But remember the LORD your God, for it is he who gives you the ability to produce wealth."
>
> DEUTERONOMY 8:17–18 (NIV)

A Few Startling Financial Facts

- More money is spent each year on chewing gum than on world missions.

- Every fifty-two days more money is spent on pet food than is spent annually on missions.

- The US poverty level is in the top 4 percent of world family income.

— 👫 FROM MY CHILDREN'S PERSPECTIVE —

GRANDPA'S REWARD

By Patrick Dunagan, age fifteen

Recently, my grandpa Dunagan died. At the time, Dad was overseas on a mission trip in Africa and was unable to get home in time for the memorial service. I had the sad honor of taking Dad's place (along with my five uncles) as one of Grandpa's pallbearers.

My dad wrote this letter before he left. As it was read at Grandpa's memorial service, it really showed me how a father's life can impact his children for God and for missions and, in turn, impact his grandchildren too!

Dear Dad,

Well, I am off to Africa again! Lord willing, my team will hold two crusades on this outreach. Months of preparation and planning have gone into this endeavor. I pray that God will honor the labor with multitudes of precious souls coming to know Jesus Christ as their Lord and Savior.

Dad, you and Mom were the first people to plant in me a desire for missions evangelism. For many years you had been faithfully in charge of the missions department at East Olympia Community Church—always making sure that these laborers received their material support and plenty of love and encouragement.

I remember one time in particular, when I was about twelve years old, that a certain missionary from South America had come to visit you at the farm. I knew that at the time your own personal finances were tight. However, I observed how you and Mom wanted to bless this man. You saved a little here and a little there and even sold a cow. When you gave your gift, you gave joyfully and humbly. Little did this man know of the sacrifice behind what you gave . . . and seeing your act of giving stirred something inside of me. I immediately ran to my room and gave the missionary all of my money to help him in his work. I figured that if "missions" was that important to you, it had better be important to me.

Dad, in the event that your body passes away while I am in Africa, I know that your soul and spirit are with Jesus. To be sure, there is nothing I can do to bring life back into your body now. However, through my labors I trust for salvation to be granted to many. More than likely, I would not be able to make it back in time for your funeral; but in that event, I would like to dedicate the souls that come to Christ on this outreach to you. I trust that the Lord will add them to your reward.

I love you, Dad! Thanks for being such a godly example to follow.

Your son,

Jon

> "The question is not how much of my money I give to God, but rather how much of God's money I keep for myself."
>
> R. G. LETOURNEAU

> "He had everything, but he possessed nothing. There is the spiritual secret."
>
> A. W. TOZER (SPEAKING OF ABRAHAM OFFERING ISAAC)

Great families and the Great Commission GO together.

JON & ANN DUNAGAN
MISSION-MINDED FAMILIES

CHAPTER 8

Mission-Minded
Ministry Ideas

When a family ministers together, the spiritual impact is powerful. I strongly believe that even a child, if properly trained and mature in Christ, can effectively share the gospel of Jesus Christ. The purpose for including your children in ministry or on a mission outreach is not merely for your kids to be cute or for your family to look good.

The purpose is to train each member of your family to participate— even now—in Christ's Great Commission, to share with people who desperately need Him.

You can prepare for particular ministries and mission outreaches as a family, but it's important to guard against pushing a child into a particular ministry calling. Allow God to lead each child; and learn, together as a family, how to follow God.

Focus on the Heart of Ministry
(Four Family Ministry "Rules")

- *God deserves all the glory.* Don't take any glory. If someone gives you a compliment, simply say, "Thank you"; then give the praise to God.

- *God deserves all the attention.* Don't distract others. This principle is reinforced by having an attitude that requires attentiveness in church or anytime anyone is sharing or ministering.

- *We're here to build others up, not to tear others down.* Don't criticize others (including your siblings!).

- *We want to make God look good.* Do your best—for the glory of God!

Q. How can I prepare each family member to share a "testimony"?

If your children have grown up loving the Lord, they may think they don't have a powerful testimony. But in actuality this kind of testimony is best, because it doesn't include wasted years of sin and regret and the negative consequences of being separated from God's purposes (although God can use even those "wasted" years for His glory if a person repents).

A Mission-Minded Testimony

When I was about eleven years old, I was asked to share my Christian testimony in a meeting. Right before my turn, a rough-looking motorcycle biker presented the powerful story of God's grace in his life. This man had done many terrible things and had even served time in prison. But he had radically come to know Jesus Christ and was now zealous for Him.

As I compared my simple story with his, I thought my "testimony" was so boring and uneventful. Yet when I stepped off the platform, that biker came and encouraged me to never downplay the power of God in my life. Then he added, "You know, I'd give anything to have a testimony like yours."

 **TEACHING OPPORTUNITY**

Learn How to Prepare a Powerful Testimony

Encourage each member of your family to consider his or her personal relationship with the Lord and to prepare to share this faith with others effectively.

Questions to answer:

- What was your life like without Jesus?

- Encourage a child who accepted the Lord at a young age to share how it wasn't enough to be born into a Christian family. Every person has to receive Jesus for himself or herself.

- When did you accept Jesus Christ as Lord and Savior?

- How did you come to know Jesus?

- Did someone share or pray with you?

- What does it mean to be "saved"?

- What is it like for you to follow Jesus?

- How has God been real and alive in your life? Has God answered a specific prayer, provided for you, or given you peace during a challenging time?

If you share your testimony in a church:

- How can your life and testimony encourage other believers?

- What ages will be in the audience? How can you encourage them?

If you share your testimony with non-Christians:

- How can your experience with God encourage others to follow Jesus?

> - What is the primary belief system or religious background of the people with whom you are sharing? How can you effectively share your faith?

— 👫 FROM MY CHILDREN'S PERSPECTIVE —

COULD YOU IMAGINE WORSHIPING A "GOD" THAT HAS TO BE DUSTED?

By Joshua Dunagan, age fifteen

The smell of incense was strong as my dad and I entered a Buddhist temple in Singapore a few weeks ago. It shocked me to see so many normal-looking people bowing down to such weird-looking idols!

As we stood and quietly watched from the back of the temple, I was so thankful that I didn't have to worship some silent statue. After a couple of minutes, a temple worker walked into the glass case and started dusting off the idols—right in front of everybody! I thought, *How could these people worship a "god" that has to be dusted?*

This mission trip came as a real surprise to me, since I found out only a week ahead of time that I was going. The United States had just declared war on Iraq, so airline tickets were cheap; and we saw it as an opportunity to "go"! Jesus said that in the last days "you will hear of wars and rumors of wars. See that you are not troubled. . . . And this gospel of the kingdom will be preached in all the world as a witness to all the nations, and then the end will come" (Matthew 24:6, 14).

The entire outreach was a great eye opener for me. From witnessing to taxi drivers next to massive Asian skyscrapers to passing out Bibles in a small Malaysian fishing village, I saw for myself that people everywhere need Jesus!

☻ TEACHING OPPORTUNITY

Learn How to Work Effectively with an Interpreter

If your family takes part in a short-term outreach, you will need to learn how to work effectively with an interpreter. A good interpreter will work with you, not against you, and will translate your message smoothly and accurately. It is a great blessing to have a Christian interpreter, especially one with experience sharing and interpreting the plan of salvation. Often, words we take for granted, such as *sin*, *heaven*, *salvation*, and *forgiveness*, are not familiar to an unbeliever and will be difficult to convey. Even so, over the years our family has had the blessing of leading many of our unsaved interpreters to Jesus Christ!

Q. What are some helpful tips for speaking through an interpreter?

- Speak slowly, clearly, and distinctly.

- Say one complete thought (but *only* one complete thought) at a time. Half of a phrase often cannot be translated because the grammatical structure or verb conjugation in the foreign language may be different. The interpreter will usually need to hear your complete thought before he or she can interpret it.

- Use simple, everyday words. Avoid technical and difficult words.

- Avoid slang and figures of speech. Expressions such as "It's cool to be here!" "I'm so fired up about Jesus!" or "Keep an eye out . . ." usually cannot be translated in a way that makes sense to your audience.

- Avoid words with double meanings or jokes involving a play on words (such as "If you've seen one shopping center, you've seen a mall," or "When the actress saw her first strands of gray hair, she thought she'd dye"). Most often your words won't be funny when interpreted, and the people will just stare at you with a confused look.

- If you will be speaking directly from the Bible, share the specific Scripture verses ahead of time with your interpreter so that he or she can look them up and be prepared to translate them correctly.

- To ensure that people understand what you are saying, pay attention to the response from your audience as you speak. Watch for confused expressions or for responses that are not expected. For example, if the entire crowd laughs when you're trying to be serious, your interpreter likely added something.

- Avoid theological terms. If a non-Christian interprets for you, try to substitute simple words for theological ones. For example, in place of the word *sin* you can substitute "the wrong things we do," and instead of *redemption* you can say, "God helps us to come back to Him." Some words, such as *generation*, *legacy*, *information*, and *technology*, may be difficult to translate. If you will be repeating a theme, discuss this with your interpreter ahead of time in order to avoid problems.

- Encourage your interpreter to have the same enthusiasm you have, perhaps even using the same hand motions. This is especially important when ministering to children.

- Practice! When teaching your child how to work with an interpreter, have him or her say a complete phrase and then repeat the phrase again. To flow smoothly and clearly while speaking through an interpreter is not hard; it just takes practice.

TEACHING OPPORTUNITY

Help Your Family Gain a Passion for Kids' Ministry

Over 35 percent of the world's population is under the age of fifteen, and in developing countries this percentage sometimes reaches 50 percent. Over 85 percent of all Christians receive Christ before the age of eighteen; yet this vital reality of evangelism is often overlooked.

Q. How can we have a successful children's outreach?

- *Encourage your kids to reach kids.* A child or young person is a "perfect-sized missionary" to reach other children for the Lord. It is usually nonthreatening for a child to share with another child.

- *Go to a place where kids gather.* Instead of trying to get a group of children to come to you, have a children's outreach in a place where they already are: crowded neighborhoods, parks, beaches, street corners, schools, recreation centers, or by invitation to a home. (In many countries, schools are open for Christian assemblies for the entire student body.) We shouldn't expect unbelievers to come to church; we must go to them.

- *Let people know you're there.* Play fun children's music or circus-style music. Set up a "party" area with balloons and a simple puppet stage (even a brightly colored sheet held between two people). Enthusiastically invite children—and parents—to come and join you. Use a puppet, balloons, or a clown to catch their attention. (I have been amazed at how easy it is to draw a crowd of children overseas; in a foreign country, a few energetic teenagers could draw a hundred children with merely a handful of balloons.) Begin with a few exciting children's contests (such as balloon blowing or pop drinking), accompanied with prizes, to create an exciting atmosphere.

- *When you've gathered a crowd, share the gospel—with ENERGY!* You may want to begin by holding up a newspaper and asking, "Hey! Have you heard the news?" Then share how you have Good News for them. Use simple object lessons to share the plan of salvation with enthusiasm, energy, boldness, and plain language that enables everyone—children, teens, and adults—to understand God's message of salvation. Pray for God's anointing on His Word and realize that the gospel has power to change people's lives.

- *Give an opportunity for people to respond.* Conclude by bringing people to a point of decision, giving them an opportunity to accept Jesus Christ as their Lord and Savior. You may want to ask everyone to bow their heads in prayer, to raise their hands, and/or to come forward—depending on the situation and the receptivity. Make sure everyone understands what it means to receive God's salvation, and then lead people in a prayer to receive and follow Jesus Christ.

- *Help new believers to grow.* Review the gospel message, and share with new believers what it means to grow as a Christian. If possible, distribute follow-up material, and invite them to a nearby church or home Bible study to be introduced to a local pastor or group of believers.

🌐 TEACHING OPPORTUNITY

Learn Easy and Effective Object Lessons

Jesus often taught by referring to a simple object as He shared an important truth about God's kingdom. He used familiar objects that were readily available (such as coins, lilies, and seeds) or easily imagined (such as a woman mixing yeast into bread dough). The teachings of Jesus were always profound, yet simple enough for even children to understand. The following ideas are some of my favorite objects lessons to use on mission trips in developing countries.

- *The Gospel Colors*
  Explain the gospel message through the color *gold* (God wants everyone to go to heaven); *black* (all have sinned); *red* (only the blood of Jesus can take away our sins); *white* (we need God to purify our hearts through salvation in Jesus); *green* (God wants us to grow as a Christian); and *blue* (as believers, we need to be baptized into God's family). You can use large pieces of material or felt (which are easily folded and packed in a suitcase), colored balloons, or even selected children from the audience wearing clothes with these colors.

- *Dirty and Clean Hands*
  Wet your hands and then rub them in dirt (representing sin). Hold up your dirty hands while you share how all have sinned. Wipe your hands on your clothes (representing trying to get rid of our sin by ourselves), noting how the problem only gets worse. Finally, use water (or white shaving cream) and a red washcloth, and clean your hands. Explain how it is only through the blood sacrifice of Jesus Christ and His forgiveness of our sins that our lives can be made clean.

- *Bible Cover Filled with Garbage*
  Use a zippered Bible cover that has a cross or an obvious Christian symbol on it. Note how this looks very good outwardly; but as you slowly open the cover, the audience will see that it is filled with garbage. State that the garbage represents sin. Using a red washcloth, clean out the Bible cover and insert a Bible. Explain how God does not look merely at outward appearances or "religious" motions, but He looks at the heart. Share about the importance of receiving Jesus Christ.

- *Soap and Wash Bucket*
  Show a dirty cloth, representing our sinful lives. The soap and wash bucket represent our salvation through Jesus Christ. (These objects are easy to find anywhere.) Jesus can take our sinful lives and make them clean and pure.

- *Black Balloon*
  As you blow up a black balloon, share how sin usually starts very small but soon grows and becomes worse. Hold up a small pin and explain how the power of Jesus Christ can destroy the sin in our lives—no matter how large or small that sin is. It may seem like a "little thing" to pray and surrender your life to Jesus Christ, but it can make all the difference in the world and for all of eternity. Then pop the balloon with the pin.

- *Large Green Balloon*
  Point to nearby trees and green plants, and talk about how the color green reminds us of things that grow. Blow up the biggest green balloon you can find as you teach about how to grow as a Christian: through loving God and others, praying to God, reading the Bible, going to church, worshiping, sharing the gospel, etc. When the balloon is at its maximum size, point out how we need to continue to grow in the Lord until the day—although we don't know when—our lives on earth are over and we go to heaven. When you (or your interpreter) say the word *heaven*, let go of the balloon and watch it "fly away" as it deflates!

Teaching Your Family to Use Object Lessons

- What you need: The objects mentioned above.

- What to do: Pray for God to help you use these object lessons to share about Jesus effectively. Demonstrate the object lessons, and then have each family member take a turn to share a short section. (For example, one child could share how "*gold* reminds us that God wants us to go to heaven, where even the streets are like gold!")

- Have your family work together to present one or two of these object lessons. Make sure each person speaks clearly and with enthusiasm.

🎤 TEACHING OPPORTUNITY

Learn How to Minister with the *EvangeCube*

One of the most outstanding tools for personal evangelism is called the *EvangeCube*. This simple cube is sometimes referred to as "the *JESUS* film of one-to-one evangelism." If you haven't yet seen this wonderful tool, please look at the online demonstration at www.e3resources.org. The *EvangeCube* is easy to use and to teach to children, and it is amazingly effective in countries around the world.

The *EvangeCube* displays various gospel pictures, including sinful humanity separated from a holy God, Jesus dying on the cross, Jesus buried in the tomb, Jesus risen from the dead, the cross as the only way to God, the choice between heaven and hell, and five ways to grow as a Christian. This ministry has prepared excellent teacher-training guides, including a short DVD and workbooks that explain how to use this tool effectively and how to train others to use it (including other adults, youth, children, and national believers). The *EvangeCube* comes in various sizes, from a tiny plastic cube that can hook to a child's backpack, to medium-sized cubes, to a "BIG CUBE" for classroom demonstration.

In just a short time, news of the *EvangeCube*—and through this tool the powerful message of the gospel of Jesus Christ—is spreading around the world. Teachers, missionaries, churches, and children are using this little cube to share God's plan of salvation effectively. Your mission-minded child will be excited about it!

Teaching Your Family to Use the *EvangeCube*

- What you need: One "BIG CUBE," *EvangeCube* teacher's workbook, the *EvangeCube* demonstration video, and a small *EvangeCube* for each person.

- What to do: Demonstrate the *EvangeCube*, watch the video and have family members practice presenting different sections.

- Have one person use the "BIG CUBE" to share the gospel. Have your children follow along at the same time with their small cubes.

— 👫 FROM MY CHILDREN'S PERSPECTIVE —

IT'S COOL TO USE THE CUBE!
By Daniel Dunagan, age fifteen

What's neat about the *EvangeCube* is that it really grabs people's attention! Its pictures show how we all need God, how Jesus died on the cross for us, and how Jesus is the only "bridge" between people and God. I've used the *EvangeCube* on mission trips to Uganda, while helping in kids' church here at home, and with people in international airports.

The cube is really cool and interesting, and people are usually curious to talk about it. As I turn the cube to show different pictures, it also helps me to remember all the major points of sharing the gospel. It's quick and easy to use, and it really helps people to see how great God is!

 TEACHING OPPORTUNITY

Learn to Use Drama in Ministry

A simple dramatic presentation can be an effective way to share the gospel.

- *Mime:* Dress in black clothes, wear white gloves, and cover your face with white makeup. Without using words, act out simple messages.

- *Skits:* Use costumes, or props to teach basic stories, such as getting rid of sin.

- *Clowns:* Dress in clown costumes and give out candy or balloons to draw a crowd.

- *Human Video:* Act out or create motions for a song with a powerful message.

Leading Your Family in Doing a Live "Human Video"

- What you need: Locate an audio with a powerful message (such as "Asleep in the Light" by Keith Green or "The Champion" by Carman), appropriate costumes and props.

- What to do: Pray together for the Holy Spirit to anoint your family as you prepare and present your drama. Talk about using drama to explain a message. Have family members practice dramatizing different emotions, such as happiness, fear, excitement, confusion, etc. Listen to a song, and create motions to explain the meaning. Practice repeatedly.

- Share the song with the dramatic motions.

A Teen Mania Drama Testimony

Just yesterday I spoke with a fifteen-year-old from our church youth group, Caleb, who just returned from a Teen Mania mission outreach to New Zealand. When I asked him what stood out as a favorite highlight, Caleb shared about a time his team presented a drama about suicide. During their performance, a teenage girl ran out of the room, crying. When the girl returned, she shared how she was seriously contemplating suicide, but she realized God loved her and had a purpose for her life; and she prayed with the group to become a Christian!

 **TEACHING OPPORTUNITY**

Learn How to Use Puppets

Puppets can be a great tool to help reach the lost. Learning puppetry skills can be fun, and knowing them provides a way for a child to participate actively in ministry outreaches.

Puppet Ministry for Beginners

- *Step 1—Master mouth movements*
  Learn to synchronize the puppet's mouth with your voice
  (or the puppet's "voice" on a song or puppet recording). The
  puppet's mouth should open with every syllable, instead of
  merely opening and closing in a random snapping motion. The
  mouth should open wider on accented syllables, while opening
  only slightly on unaccented syllables. When moving the
  puppet's mouth, move only the puppet's bottom jaw (operated
  by your thumb). The top of the puppet's head (operated by
  your other four fingers) should remain still.

- *Step 2—Keep puppet's eye contact*
  Keep your puppet's head down so the audience can see its eyes. Don't have your puppet speak up to the ceiling or down to the floor. Keep the puppet's head looking around naturally without continually bobbing up and down.

- *Step 3—Show the entire puppet, but not the puppeteer!*
  Make sure the puppet's entire body can be seen, not just its head. If the puppet has arms, keep them in the front of the stage. If you are a puppeteer, don't let the audience see you, particularly your arm. And don't let anyone see an empty puppet not in use.

Training Your Family in Basic Puppet Ministry

- What you need: Puppets, a puppet stage, audio recording, video player, a microphone, puppetry video (*Basic Techniques Puppetry Training* video by Puppet Productions is excellent for teaching beginning puppet skills), and a music recording (easy puppet songs are "The Laughing Song" from Puppet Productions and "He's Got the Whole World in His Hands" from *Wee Sing Bible Songs*).

- What to do: Pray for God to help your family use puppets to share about Jesus effectively and to convey God's love for children. Distribute the puppets to your family and review the three steps above. Watch the *Basic Techniques Puppetry Training* video and follow the directions. Practice simple puppet songs: first *without* the puppet stage, then *with* the puppet stage.

- Present your puppet shows.

Let Your Light Shine!
A Mission-Minded Puppet Skit

Two puppets needed: "Ralph" (with a small flashlight) and "Bernie"

RALPH: (Enters with the flashlight, singing "This Little Light of Mine." As he gets to the verse "Hide it under a bushel—No!" Ralph is singing very loudly and waving the flashlight around. This can be done by attaching a small flashlight to a puppet's hand with wire or tape, and the puppet's arm can be moved by using a metal hanger attached to the puppet's arm or an official puppetry rod. Another option is to use a human-arm puppet that takes two arms to operate, one for the puppet's head and the other for the puppet's arm. This second method is my favorite because the puppet can hold a full-size flashlight for the skit.)

BERNIE: Excuuuse me . . . Uh . . . Yoo-hoo! What do you think you're doing?

RALPH: Who, me?

BERNIE: Yes, *you*, Ralph. What are you doing?

RALPH: Can't you see, Bernie? I'm letting my little light shine! I learned this cool song at church, and now I'm shining my light all over. See my neat flashlight? It really works goooood.

BERNIE: Ralph! That's not what the song is talking about.

RALPH: What do you mean? It's not?

BERNIE: Of course not! "Letting your light shine" means that we're not afraid to tell other people about Jesus.

RALPH: Are you serious?

BERNIE: Yes, I'm serious. Jesus said that He is the Light of the World, but He also told us to be "lights" for Him by telling other people about His love.

RALPH: Wow! You mean I don't even need this flashlight?

BERNIE: No, silly! You just need boldness to share about Jesus.
          You could use your Bible or a story, but the important
          thing is that you do what God says and be a witness for
          Him.

RALPH: That sounds easy enough!

BERNIE: With Jesus, it *is* easy. And one more thing, Ralph . . .

RALPH: Yeah?

BERNIE: Do you see how bright it is up here? You hardly need
          a flashlight here because there's already so much light.
          But if you look down there (Have both puppets look
          behind the puppet stage) . . . it's dark!

RALPH: (Shining his flashlight down below the puppet stage)
          Wow! Look how good this flashlight shows up down
          there!

BERNIE: You see, Ralph, we need to spread the gospel of Jesus
          here at home, but did you know there are many places
          where people have never heard about Jesus? There are
          millions and *millions* of unreached people around the
          world, and someone's gotta *go* to them!

RALPH: Isn't that called being a "missionary"?

BERNIE: That's right, and we can *all* be missionaries. When we
          help fulfill the mission of Jesus, we're really letting our
          light shine!

RALPH: That sounds exciting, Bernie!

BERNIE: It really is; and every one of us needs to find God's
          purpose and plan for our lives and do our part in sharing
          His light around the world. Do you get it?

RALPH: You bet! I'm going to let my light shine for Jesus—
          especially to those who haven't heard about Him.

BERNIE: Good job, Ralph!

RALPH: (Singing as he begins to walk "downstairs" behind
          the puppet stage) "Ohhh, this little light of mine, I'm
          a'gonna let it shine. . . . Ohhhh NOOOOO!" (Make
          sound effects of Ralph falling down the stairs)

BERNIE: Ralph! Ralph! Are you all right?

RALPH: (Responding weakly) Yeah, but I really should have
          used the flashlight.

Q. How can we use puppets when we can't speak the language?

- Learn a few key words and phrases, translated into the foreign language, that the puppet can say (such as *hello*, *goodbye*, *yes*, *no*, *Hallelujah*, *Praise the Lord*, and *Jesus loves you*).

- Have the puppet simply make animal sounds. You can "interpret" what the puppet is saying; then an interpreter can translate for the people.

- Have the interpreter interpret what the puppet is saying.

- Teach your interpreter to use a puppet so you can have an interpreter puppet. Children (and adults) usually think this is funny.

- Teach a local worker to use puppets, and let him or her speak for the puppet in the local language. (When you leave the area, you could even give this worker a puppet or two to continue reaching children for Jesus.)

- Purchase an upbeat, contemporary Christian album in the foreign language, and have the puppet mouth the words. Make sure that the words are appropriate, and practice synchronizing the movements.

- Purchase a prerecorded puppet skit in the foreign language, and practice having the puppets mouth the words. (Puppet

Productions has many prerecorded puppet skits available in Spanish.)

- Use a ventriloquist-style puppet, making animal sounds or saying "Hello" while walking up and down a street, as a drawing card. Have a local person walk with you as you invite children to come to a nearby meeting.

- Just have fun; have the puppets sing in English . . . and draw a curious crowd!

🎙 TEACHING OPPORTUNITY

Focus on Music and Worship Ministry

If your family is musical, take time to prepare songs for ministry. You may want to purchase some musical accompaniment audios or practice with your own instruments. If possible, learn a song or a simple chorus in the language of the people you desire to reach, or be prepared to learn a song from a long-term missionary or national. Perhaps you could add some basic choreography or motions to help make your presentation more effective.

Even if you sing in English, or present an instrumental piece with no lyrics, music can be a powerful tool to draw people to hear the gospel. As you practice, prepare your heart to "minister"—not merely to "perform." Pray for God's Holy Spirit to soften hearts and to impact the people to whom you will minister.

Training Your Family in Music and Worship Ministry

- What you need: any type of sound system, and one or two accompaniment audios/songs with a mission theme. Possible ideas: "Carry the Light" by Twila Paris or "Heart to Change the World" from Psalty's *Kids' Praise! 6: Heart to Change the World* . Have the words of the songs written out and available for practice.

- What to do: Pray together and discuss the importance of ministry, as opposed to mere musical "performance." Sing scales. Listen to and then practice the songs. You will also want to practice with microphones and decide where everyone will stand. If desired, add hand motions or choreography.

- Sing the songs with a heart of worship.

Mission-Minded Music Lessons

If a member of your family enjoys music or has natural musical ability, it is good to encourage the development of this talent. Quality music lessons, faithful practice, and active participation in church worship are important. Even though it takes years of time, energy, and expense to establish musical excellence, this is an investment in future ministry. Developing musical talent in a godly child is like preparing a powerful spiritual weapon to win battles for the kingdom of God.

Realize Fitness Affects Your Family's Mission-Minded Purpose

A mission-minded family is healthy, active, and adventurous.

- *We are stewards of our bodies!* It's true that our focus needs to be on God's kingdom and His eternal purposes. Yet we also need to remember that our bodies are temples of God's Holy Spirit (1 Corinthians 6:19). We have been entrusted as stewards of these temples (our bodies); and, as parents, we must train our children to be good stewards of their bodies.

- *We exercise!* "Bodily exercise profits a little, but godliness is profitable for all things, having promise of the life that now is and of that which is to come" (1 Timothy 4:8). To put this into perspective, however, remember that Jesus and His disciples often walked several miles a day. I encourage mission-minded families to participate in athletics and physical activities, since God's mission-minded representatives need to be strong, healthy, and disciplined.

Reaching Out through Sports

Being involved in sports and athletic activities can help individual family members learn about teamwork, cooperation, friendship, evangelism, and community involvement—along with developing athletic skills and staying in shape, of course. If a child is athletic or enjoys participating in sports, encourage him or her to be a mission-minded child and develop these gifts for God's purposes. (At the same time, guard against sports commitments taking control of your family. Spiritual training and church participation should always be a higher priority.)

- If your child is on a sports team, encourage him or her to be a good example of godly sportsmanship and a Christian witness to fellow teammates and their families.

- Realize that athletic activities and games can be excellent drawing cards for Christian outreach and evangelism—both at home and overseas.

- A mission-minded athlete could travel to another country, arrange spontaneous athletic events, draw a crowd, and then share the Good News of Jesus!

— 👫 FROM MY CHILDREN'S PERSPECTIVE —

A BUDDHIST COMES TO JESUS . . .
DURING CROSS-COUNTRY SEASON
About Patrick, at age fourteen

During high school, our oldest son, Patrick, had the opportunity to compete on a local cross-country team. During the season he became friends with a foreign exchange student from Thailand, Tip, who had been raised in a Buddhist family. After several lengthy conversations, Tip prayed to receive Jesus as his Lord and Savior. Though he later moved to another state and enrolled in college, Tip has continued to grow as a Christian. He celebrated his first "Christian" Christmas with our family, and he was baptized on Easter weekend in our family's pond. Tip is active in leadership at a strong Christian church: he works in the media department, leads a weekly "Royal Rangers" discipleship group for boys, and often shares his faith on his university campus.

I'm a Mission-Minded Soccer Mom

I've been a soccer mom, track mom, cross-country mom, and tennis mom. I've definitely "put in my time" going back and forth to games, meets, and matches. I've sat in the rain and stood in the snow, and I've encouraged my husband as he's coached. But most importantly, our family has had many opportunities to share about Jesus on the sidelines.

As a Christian mother, I love to keep focused on God's plans for my kids; but I don't regret the time we've invested in athletics. His purposes may require a healthy body, a daring mindset, and an adventurous attitude. Participating in sports is not just for competition and family entertainment; it can help our kids become disciplined, goal oriented, and even a witness for Jesus. On the sidelines, our family has met new friends and shared our faith—and we've had fun in the process. We keep balanced, and spiritual activities and church involvement are our priorities.

Even as a soccer mom, I cheer on my kids . . . toward God's goals!

Use Your Family's Skills . . . for Missions!

Instead of dwelling on what you lack or what you are unable to do, seek God for ways to use your abilities for His glory. Sometimes we consider only traditional missionary occupations, such as church work, medicine, Bible translation, or aviation; but the many needs overseas are as diverse as the talents you have been given.

- *Do you have construction experience?*
  You can help build a church or an orphanage. If you know how to paint, you could paint a Bible school or teach efficient painting techniques.

- *Do you have educational experience?*
  You can teach in an elementary school, hold a workshop to encourage local teachers, or introduce a curriculum to missionary families.

- *Do you have computer skills?*
  You can teach a missionary how to use a new software program, or you can conduct a training seminar overseas.

- *Do you know how to operate a film projector?*

  You can show the *JESUS* film, currently available in nearly one thousand languages, or another gospel film.

- *Do you speak English and have a college degree?*
  You can teach English as a second language. Many countries that are "closed" to missionaries are "open" to qualified teachers.

- *Do you have a happy family?*
  You can teach a marriage or parenting class or organize a seminar on being a godly father or mother.

- *Do you know how to wash your hands?*
  You can share information about cleanliness and sanitation in a remote village.

- *Do you know how to pray?*
  You can visit a country to pray and intercede or to teach a seminar on prayer.

Ideas for Helping the Poor

- Give clothes to needy children!

- Distribute toys or school supplies to an orphanage!

- Deliver gift boxes . . . or soap . . . or sheets . . . or food!

- Assist in a free health, dental, or midwifery clinic!

- Help distribute free Bibles or gospel tracts!

WHEN YOU DON'T FEEL "STIRRED" FOR SOULS

A Family VBS Story

One time when I wasn't feeling "in the mood" for missions, God renewed my passion for souls and challenged me afresh about the urgency of reaching the lost.

Jon and I were watching our little ones swim in our pond (which is more like a giant mud hole) and were talking with our fourteen-year-old son, Joshua, about an upcoming vacation Bible school closing service. Josh had been asked to preach alongside me, so he was trying to decide whether or not to say yes. And if he agreed to do it, he was trying to figure out what he could share.

Right at that moment our four-year-old daughter, Caela, stepped out too deep—and, without making a sound, she began to sink. Jon yelled, "Josh, get Caela!" Immediately—clothes, shoes, and all—Joshua leaped into the water, swam over to little Caela, and quickly pulled her out. Once we saw she was fine, Jon turned to Josh and said, "There is your sermon!"

All day long, I too had been thinking and praying about my message. Specifically, I was trying to decide how to minister to both the children and the adults who would be present, including some visiting parents who had likely never been in church before. It was going to be the final night of a weeklong VBS, and I was scheduled to share a "stirring" message about the importance of "getting out there and winning the lost." At the moment, however, I wasn't feeling very "stirred" myself.

Of course, I have a heart for missions and evangelism. It's what we do. It's our life. But quite honestly, at the moment I was more concerned with how to delicately preach a "strong" missions message—without offending those unchurched parents.

The next day, when Joshua and I arrived at the church early for preservice prayer, we were surprised to see many of the VBS workers crying. Their news was sobering and shocking. Just the night before, four children who attended VBS tragically lost their dad. The young father had been suddenly killed in a work accident.

This was one of those unchurched families I'd been thinking about. Only two days earlier, one of these boys received Jesus. Only one day earlier, after learning how children can be mighty in prayer, this same little boy filled out a prayer card that read, "Please pray for my Mommy and Daddy to know Jesus."

Who could have known how serious that little prayer would be?

Who could have known that in less than twenty-four hours that daddy's life would be over and that he would be face to face with eternity . . . either in heaven or in hell?

Who could have known?

As we prayed for the family, tears streamed down my cheeks. I was challenged afresh about the urgency of the gospel. How could I not be stirred about reaching the lost? How could I have been more concerned about offending unsaved parents than caring for their souls?

That night, Joshua and I both preached to a church full of children and adults about the importance of reaching the lost—even when we don't feel like it. Just like Joshua simply jumped in to rescue Caela, we need to rescue the lost. When our heavenly Father says, "Go!" we need to instantly obey! Joshua told the audience, "When Dad shouted at me to get my little sister, I didn't have to pray about it to see if it was God's will or not. I just had to jump in and get her!"

Over the years, specific life-and-death situations (at home and overseas) have challenged us to renew our passion for missions and the lost. Right at this moment, whether or not we realize it or can see them, multitudes of precious people are dying without Jesus Christ. Our Father sees them. If God calls us to reach out and help with a rescue, may we be ones who instantly leap to obey!

CHAPTER 9

You *Can* Go!

Taking a Mission Trip with Your Family

For many families, taking an overseas mission trip with a child (or perhaps several children) sounds utterly impossible. "How could our family afford it?" "How could we ever take that much time off work?" "How is it possible to travel with kids?" "But what about school?"

These are all legitimate questions, but more importantly, why not ask, *Dear Lord, would You ever want our family (or me, or one of my children, or a group from our school, or a team from our church) to go on a mission outreach?*

If God answers, "Yes," then the only legitimate questions to ask are *When?* and *Where?* and, in faith, *Well, Lord, then how do You want us to obey?*

Instead of responding with fear and doubt like Zacharias (Luke 1:18), have a willing heart like Mary (Luke 1:38), when she said, "Let it be to me according to your word." If God calls you or your child to missionary work, He will open the way for you, and He will provide more than enough of His grace and provision.

Q. But what if I'm at the peak of my career?

On the day Jesus called Peter to be a "fisher of men," Peter's nets were bursting with fish (Luke 5:6–7). Most likely it was the best day of Peter's fishing career, but Jesus called him to drop everything and follow Him (Matthew 4:18–20)! Jesus also called a rich young ruler, but this man was unwilling to surrender his money and his security (Matthew 19:16–22). If Jesus asks *you* to follow Him to the mission field, which of these two responses will *your* answer most closely resemble?

Q. But what if I just got married?

Congratulations! As you begin your life together, this is a great time to readjust your priorities and seek God's will for you as a married couple. Many newlyweds have gone straight from their wedding to the mission field. Read about young missionaries such as Adoniram and Nancy Judson or Jim and Elisabeth Elliot. Another perspective, from the Old Testament, presents a principle of newly married men being exempt from war and encouraged to stay home for a year to establish their marriage foundation (Deuteronomy 24:5). Early married life is a perfect time to find a godly mission-minded balance, with a fervent commitment to marriage and a lifelong commitment to God's purposes.

Q. But what if I still have children at home?

My husband always laughs when he hears this excuse. "Oh, that's right," he says. "You could *never* travel with kids!" But then he grins and raises his eyebrows, because we never traveled *before* we had children! For us, raising and training our children are a primary calling; yet through *every* season of our parenthood (pregnancy, chasing toddlers and little ones, homeschooling, raising teenagers and keeping up with their activities, and sending young adults to college), God is continually calling us to be an active part of world evangelization.

Sometimes our entire family goes on mission outreaches together. Other times Jon goes by himself or takes one of our older children. We've gone together as a couple or as a couple with a nursing baby and a few other children. (We've been blessed to have the option of godly parents, relatives, and friends who have taken turns caring for our children while we minister overseas on short-term trips.) Each time God calls us to a specific outreach, we pray and seek His will for that particular mission trip . . . and then we obey!

Q. But what if I'm in the prime of my life?

Does God deserve less? Midlife is a great time to readjust your priorities in order to reach the world! Try a short-term outreach (either you, or your spouse, or together as a couple, or together with your children) to minister and to seek God's will. Another option is to attend a short-term mission training school as a family, such as YWAM's six-month Crossroads Discipleship Training School.

There's No Excuse!

Our good friends Nels and Lorrie had every reason to stay home when God called their family to full-time missionary work. They had seven children still living at home, including little children and a son just graduating from high school, along with an elderly mother who lived with them. Lorrie was having health problems due to several miscarriages. And they had no financial support!

Even so, both Nels and Lorrie felt in their hearts God calling their family to start a Bible school on a remote island in the Philippines. So what did they do? They went—with all seven children and Nels' eighty-seven-year-old mother! And to top it off, they invited a paraplegic friend to join them! They must have been quite a sight as they arrived on that remote Filipino island of Catanduanes: seven exhausted children, luggage everywhere, Grandma with her walker, and Jeff in his wheelchair!

But God was so faithful. The family adjusted better than expected, God provided for every need, the Filipino people loved and appreciated their family's example, and the tropical sunshine helped improve Lorrie's health. Today their Bible school is established and growing strong, with graduates pioneering many Christian churches in unreached areas and on other remote islands.

Even with every excuse to stay home, Nels and Lorrie went!

Who, who will go,
salvation's story telling,
Looking to Jesus,
minding not the cost?

GO YE INTO ALL THE WORLD

A missions hymn, by James McGranahan (1840–1907)

Far, far away, in heathen darkness dwelling,
Millions of souls forever may be lost;
Who, who will go, salvation's story telling,
Looking to Jesus, minding not the cost?

"All pow'r is given unto Me,
All pow'r is given unto Me,
Go ye into all the world and preach the gospel,
And lo, I am with you always."

See o'er the world wide open doors inviting,
Soldiers of Christ, arise and enter in!
Christians, awake! your forces all uniting,
Send forth the gospel, break the chains of sin.

"Why will ye die?" the voice of God is calling,
"Why will ye die?" re-echo in His name;
Jesus hath died to save from death appalling,
Life and salvation, therefore go proclaim.

God speed the day, when those of ev'ry nation
"Glory to God!" triumphantly shall sing;
Ransomed, redeemed, rejoicing in salvation,
Shout Hallelujah, for the Lord is King.

Q. But what if my child wants to go on a mission trip and I'm afraid he or she is too young?

You may want to consider accompanying your child on a short-term children's mission outreach, such as YWAM's King's Kids or a Teen Mania outreach for preteens. Take seriously God's calling for you as a parent or teacher to nurture your child's desire and to adequately train and equip your child for this possibility. Let's encourage our children to pray regularly for world needs and to learn all they can about world missions.

Q. But what if my child needs to focus on school right now?

If you have a high school or college student interested in missions, encourage him or her to check out short-term opportunities with mission organizations such as Teen Mania, YWAM, Teen Missions, Master's Commission or through your own church or denomination.

Along with encouraging youth in what they do *for* God, especially encourage their personal walk *with* God. Challenge them to develop their relationship with God and to guard their relationships with others, keeping their lives pure and set apart for God's calling and purpose. One of the biggest hindrances to a young person fulfilling his or her calling to missions is marrying someone—even someone who is nice and loves the Lord—who is not also called to world missions. Communicate to your child that if God has given a desire and a calling for missions *at* a young age, He wants him or her to prepare for this calling *from* a young age! There is a time to focus on educational preparation, but encourage your child to "seek first the kingdom of God" (Matthew 6:33).

Q. But what if we have a large family?

What a blessing! So did many missionary heroes, including the founders of the Salvation Army, William and Catherine Booth, who had eight children, and African missionary John G. Lake, who had a dozen children (seven with his first wife and then, after she died, five with his second wife). Some missionary organizations may limit the number of children they allow, or "prefer," their missionaries to have, but there are always other options available. Your big family can be a great benefit to many missionary ministries.

Large families are common in many developing countries. If you have substantial parenting experience, others will highly regard your opinions. Your children and teenagers can be involved in your ministry, especially if you have trained them to be mission-minded. Buying airline tickets for many family members obviously will cost more; but to God, that makes no difference! Your monthly living expenses in a foreign country may be even less than they were previously.

Schooling is a major challenge and expense for many missionary families. For large homeschooling families, however, the children's education can continue nearly the same as before. If God is calling your family to missions, He will direct you and provide all your needs.

Here are a few other ideas. Perhaps Mom and Dad can go together on a mission trip (and perhaps enjoy a second honeymoon before or after the mission outreach) while the kids enjoy a few weeks at Grandma's. Or you can all work together (praying, seeking God, and raising support) to send one parent or teenager on a short-term outreach. You can even establish a new family tradition: when each child reaches a certain age (e.g., sixteen or eighteen), you will present that teenager with an airline ticket for a summer mission trip.

If your quiver is full of arrows (see Psalm 127:3–5), don't limit God's ability to send them wherever He wants them to go!

Q. But what if I'm getting too old? Isn't it too late for my family to make a change?

Consider Moses, Abraham, Sarah, and other mighty men and women of God who began their ministries later in life. It's never too late to obey God's call!

I once read about a woman in her mid-eighties who travels throughout the world, sharing the gospel. As I stared at her photograph, I marveled at her adventurous attitude. She reminded me of eighty-five-year-old Caleb, ready at last to take his inheritance in the Promised Land, shouting, "Give me this mountain!" (see Joshua 14:6–12). In the photo, this elderly woman—with a huge smile on her face—was sitting on the back of a mule in a remote mountainous area. Her white hair wasn't a hindrance but an asset to her ministry. Because of her age, nationals honored and respected her; and because of her willingness, many have come to Christ.

Young in Faith

Bob and Carol were nearing retirement, but they longed for something more in their lives. One day, during a time of discouragement and seeking direction, they came to our home for dinner. Jon and I shared some exciting mission testimonies and challenged Bob and Carol to do something different. We invited them to teach at a village pastors' conference overseas. Despite major challenges, this elderly couple decided to *go*—and their lives have never been the same.

Overseas, they were challenged by the need for godly discipleship and pastoral training. But instead of just complaining about the need, these two were led by God to do something about it. After much prayer, they made the big decision to move overseas as full-time missionaries.

This last year (at Thanksgiving), we met again for dinner; but this time we were near their home in Kampala, Uganda. As we shared our strange holiday food (including zebra and ostrich), this couple shared highlights from the past few years. Over ten Bible schools are training ministers all over East Africa. Over 1,500 pastors have graduated from their yearlong program. Mobile health clinics and volunteer doctors are ministering to the physical needs of the people. Carol teaches women cooking and sewing skills, enabling them to earn extra income. As Bob and Carol shared their vision for an orphanage they were about to open, my mind went back to that day in our living room only a few years earlier. This incredible couple wondered if God's ministry for them was over . . . but it had barely begun!

Q. But what if I don't have anything to offer?

So you don't think you have special talents. You can't speak a foreign language. You don't even like to go camping. Well, you are in good company!

- **Gladys Aylward** initially was turned away in her attempt to become a missionary. Yet eventually, in 1932, she went to China and became a beloved Christian servant. In her own words, Aylward thanked God that "one so insignificant, uneducated, and ordinary in every way could be used to His glory for the blessing of His people in poor, persecuted China" (from the back cover of *Gladys Aylward: Missionary to China*, Heroes of the Faith Series, by Sam Wellman, Barbour Publishing, 1998). (For more about Aylward's exciting missionary life, watch the classic movie *The Inn of the Sixth Happiness*, starring Ingrid Bergman. Although not completely accurate, this wholesome film is mission-minded and inspirational.)

- **Bruce Olson** was shy and weak as a child, hating outdoor activities and Scouting. Yet God chose him to reach the remote and primitive Motilone people of Colombia. Much of this tribe has now turned to Christianity, and the Motilones are reaching surrounding areas with the gospel of Jesus Christ! (Read Bruce's book, *Bruchko*, for the exciting details.)

- **Elisabeth Elliot** wondered why God had chosen her. She couldn't sing, and she wasn't a nurse or a gifted linguist; but God has used this woman mightily through her missionary work and inspirational writing! (Read her story in *Through Gates of Splendor* and *The Savage, My Kinsman*.)

There is no perfect time to step into missionary work. At every stage in life there will always be challenges to overcome and barriers to cross. No matter what your current situation, God can make a way for you. He does not expect you to use what you *don't* have; He simply expects you to love and serve Him with what you *do* have. As you obey the Lord, step by step, He will multiply your gifts and talents for His purposes. It is not all about doing things *for* God, but being *with* God: living in His presence, hearing His voice and direction, and being available to serve Him—through His strength and gifts, not your own.

🎙 TEACHING OPPORTUNITY

Practical Steps for "Stepping Out"

If God has given you or your child a specific direction for the future, realize that He spoke this now because He wants you to *do something now*. If He didn't want you to do anything right away, why would He bother to tell you at this early time? If God has given you His direction, it's likely He wants you to begin—by preparing your heart, learning, or praying—to pave the way for future outreach.

Gather Information

- Begin preparing by praying and interceding for the specific people you desire to reach. At the same time, learn everything you can about them. If you have a burden for a particular country, do some research at the library or on the Internet, or write to the country's international embassy for information.

- Find out what you would need for travel: passport, visa, inoculations?

- If you are interested in a particular missionary organization, write or call for information. Compare and evaluate the opportunities they have available; and explore their focus, policies, and particular mission. How long are their mission outreaches? Are there educational requirements? Do they train team members? How extensive is their training? What are their views on children and families? Can children be involved in the ministry outreach? What are their opinions on schooling? What are their basic theological beliefs? What is the living environment like? What is their leadership or authority structure? Is there potential for career missionary opportunities? And, of course, how much will it cost (and is there training for raising support)?

Seek Godly Counsel

- As you gather information, pray for direction and seek godly counsel from other mature believers, from missionaries you know, from your pastor or youth leader (if you're a young person) . . . and listen to their advice!

Research Airline and Travel Prices

- If you are considering traveling on your own or taking care of your own travel arrangements, check with a local travel agency for approximate travel costs.

- You can usually get a better price if you check with several travel agencies or directly with international airline companies.

- Some travel organizations have missionary discounts. We have found over the years, however, that missionary travel restrictions and date limitations are usually too difficult to work with. We can generally beat the price by shopping around or looking into different international connections.

- Compare various travel award programs. For years, we traveled on whatever airline had the lowest fare, regardless of routes or services. After years of accumulating a hodgepodge of expiring mileage on various airlines, we decided on one airline to use on a regular basis. By using its mileage award program, we now earn at least one free international trip each year.

Get Your Passport

- If you or your child are considering going on a mission trip someday and haven't yet applied for a passport, what are you waiting for? This is one thing you can do right away. If you are serious about being available for God, get ready! You can pick up a passport application at your local post office, get a passport photo, show identification, and then submit the application and required fee.

- When traveling, it is vital to keep your passport either with you at all times or in a secure location. This is your most important travel document. Without your passport, you cannot legally remain in a foreign country, travel to another foreign country, or return home. Your passport guarantees your citizenship and is your best form of identification.

Find Out If You Need Travel Visas

- Certain countries require a visa, in addition to a passport, for entrance. A visa is a stamp or sticker inside your passport granting permission to enter a particular country for a designated time. Contact a travel agency or check the Internet for international embassy addresses to inquire about specific requirements for the country you wish to enter. Travel agencies often pay for necessary visa or passport photos if you purchase your tickets through them.

Find Out If You Need Inoculations

- Pick up international travel inoculation certificates from a doctor. In many developing countries, certain health requirements are necessary for entrance.

- Some inoculations require a series of shots taken over time. Other recommended inoculations may be unnecessary. Opinions differ on the potential risks of certain inoculations, so seek advice and seek the Lord.

Short-Term Mission Travel Tips

Q. Do you have any packing tips?

- *Pack light.* When selecting clothes for a short-term mission trip, be sure to pack lightly. Clothing is often washed daily in other countries, so only a few changes are usually necessary. In warmer climates, lightweight, quick-drying clothing is best. Select clothes that coordinate with a few basic colors and that will be appropriate for the work planned. As you leave home, check for the three most important items: passport, tickets, and money. (All the rest is luxury!)

- *Pack modest clothes.* Be sensitive to the culture of the people to whom you will minister. Clothing that is perfectly modest at home may be perceived as immoral in another culture. In many places, women cannot wear pants, and neither women nor men can wear shorts. In some areas, women's necks and ankles must be covered. In other locales, certain colors (such as red) are considered taboo.

  Modesty is a heart issue; but at times it can be "relative," depending on cultural practices. Many times as I've traveled through African or Asian jungles in my khaki safari skirt, I've secretly wished for pants. Pants would be more practical and modest when I'm standing in the back of a truck with my skirt blowing in the wind or as I climb over things. It's funny to see women in these same places remove their shirts to nurse their babies while sitting in the front row of a church or use a pit toilet or shower with no door. In their culture, these very "immodest" actions—by our standards—are perfectly acceptable.

- *Pack with sensitivity.* As Christians, we must be culturally sensitive and as inoffensive as possible when selecting items to bring. (For example, check the wallet photos you take with you for culturally inappropriate dress. A family photo at the beach could be devastating to your ministry!)

  You may want to bring small gifts and thank you cards for people who show you kindness or for people with whom you stay.

A Few Extra Hints

- When packing, try to bring no more than one suitcase per person, in addition to your carryon luggage. On short-term mission trips, the second allotted suitcase is usually used for ministry supplies or gifts for missionaries and national ministers. When our family travels, I often limit my personal luggage to my carryon bag.

- As my husband constantly tells me, don't cram your suitcases too full. If you have to force your luggage to close, remove a few items (which is much easier said than done!) to prevent broken hinges or zippers.

- Fill your shoes with underwear and socks, and then stuff them inside a pair of socks to protect other clothing.

- Instead of folding your clothes, try rolling them. You will fit more clothes in your suitcase, you will see everything at once, and your clothes will get less wrinkled.

- I have found that a small spray bottle is excellent to have along for straightening messy hair, cleaning children's dirty hands and faces, and spraying wrinkled clothes when an iron is unavailable.

- Take along a small empty duffle bag to use for day-long outreaches or to accommodate for a lack of space later.

- Because of varying electrical systems around the world, you may want to research on the Internet to find out if you need to bring a converter or adapter. Some countries (such as North American countries and parts of South and Central America, the Pacific, and the Caribbean) have an across-the-board standard of 110 volts, while others (such as European and African countries) have a standard voltage of 220. Without a proper converter, your electrical appliances (hairdryer, curling iron, cell phone, and camera battery charger, etc.) will be unusable.

A Few Notes about Travel Money

- When traveling to a Third World country, you usually need to bring cash. Many developing countries will not accept traveler's checks, while others will accept them, but at a low exchange rate. If you are departing from the United States, bring crisp one-hundred-dollar bills in order to get the best exchange rate for your money.

- When traveling as a foreigner in technologically advanced countries, credit cards are often required to secure a rental car or a hotel room. In developing countries, however, a credit card is of no use.

- A calculator is helpful for calculating confusing exchange rates and prices. Chances are your cell phone includes a calculator.

- Worldwide communication has dramatically improved in recent years, with expanding Internet and cell phone coverage, especially in international cities. A cell phone is still of no use in many areas, although we are often pleasantly surprised. Many developing countries skipped the step of establishing telephone landlines and went directly to building cell phone towers; and sometimes we receive better cell phone coverage in remote villages than we do at home! At other times a cell phone may not be able to make calls, but text messages will get through.

- To avoid being a victim of thieves, wear a money belt instead of using a purse or wallet. Also, to get better deals (and to avoid being cheated), try to have a faithful national friend assist you with shopping.

Q. What are some health tips for international travel?

- In addition to travel inoculations, be sure to secure any necessary medications you may need (such as an antimalarial drug).

- Carry at least a thirty-day supply of any necessary medication, along with a copy of your prescriptions.

- If you wear eyeglasses or contact lenses, take extra pairs and a copy of your eye prescription. (Because of dust and heavy pollution in some developing countries, many people find it difficult to wear contact lenses.)

- Be careful to drink clean water (professionally bottled or thoroughly boiled and purified). Some people travel with a small water purifier.

- When packing, always keep your medications, passport, tickets, and other important papers and valuables in your carryon luggage. Because there is always the possibility of luggage being misplaced, don't pack in your luggage any items you would desperately miss. Put all liquids and lotions in plastic bags, leaving room for expansion due to air pressure while flying and—because of security regulations—pack these items in your checked suitcase rather than your carryon luggage.

- Include in your carryon luggage a small first-aid kit and over-the-counter medications for upset stomach, diarrhea, motion sickness, and constipation.

- You may also want to bring sunscreen and a mosquito net in your checked luggage. You may opt to purchase these items overseas, but only if you will have time for shopping and access to them.

Q. Do you have any other practical advice?

- *Learn a few foreign phrases.* Introduce yourself and your children to basic phrases and simple worship songs in the language of the people you desire to reach. Buy a small dictionary or teaching audio with commonly used words. Commit yourself to learn at least a friendly greeting and a word of thankfulness.

- *Take care of things at home.* There are many details to take care of before leaving home. Decide whether you are comfortable with just locking your home or if you need to arrange for a friend or relative to house-sit. Cancel or hold newspaper subscriptions, and have your mail held at the post office. Schedule someone to mow your lawn, shovel snow, care for animals or plants, etc.

- *Do your best to resolve relationship problems.* Before leaving on a mission trip, make sure you are on good terms with friends and extended family members. If there has been unforgiveness or hard feelings in the past, repent and ask forgiveness for any wrongs you have done, and do your best to make things right. Even though you will likely be busy with travel details, now is the time to get things worked out. Being separated by distance will probably only hamper your communication and any hope of future reconciliation. Unforgiveness could hinder your prayers and your ministry.

Some Things We Don't Want to Think About

- Secure any necessary details concerning your family's health insurance, life insurance, and wills.

- If traveling overseas, prayerfully determine ahead of time what you want to happen to your body in the event of your unlikely death. On my husband's first trip to Africa, an elderly pastor traveling with him came down with cerebral malaria and died within one day. This man would have preferred to be buried in Africa—a *much* less expensive option than transporting his body back to the United States—but he hadn't clearly conveyed that to his family before the trip. The result was confusion, added stress, and tremendous hassles with the foreign government.

- Whatever you do, don't be afraid! As Christians, we should already be "crucified with Christ" (Galatians 2:20). Your mission goal, of course, is not to go and be martyred for Christ! The goal is to go and come back . . . so you can share an inspiring mission report . . . and then go again!

We Died before We Came

When James Calvert went out as a missionary to the cannibals of the Fiji Islands, the ship captain tried to turn him back, saying, "*You will lose your life and the lives of those with you if you go among such savages.*"

To that, Calvert replied, "*We died before we came here.*"

An "Opportunity of a Lifetime"

A few days ago I received a sobering e-mail from a mission-minded college student. A friend of hers, a sixteen-year-old girl, had gone on a short-term mission outreach; and on the last day of the trip, while the team was having a fun free day, this girl accidentally drowned in the ocean.

I've had such a burden for this whole situation. The girl, one of ten children, was very sweet and had already been on several other mission trips. I've been praying for her parents, siblings, church, friends, and mission team. It's very hard and very sad.

In hindsight, I found the promotional ad for this mission trip a bit unsettling:

> Don't miss the opportunity of a lifetime! Pack your bags and hop on a plane . . . where you will set foot on one of the most beautiful tropical landscapes in the world! During your ministry days, you will reach out in schools, parks, villages and churches. . . . You will have the opportunity to minister through practical drama, testimonies, and service projects. On your free day, be ready make the most of the sandy beaches, catch some sun, hit the waves, and cool off in the ocean. The summer can't get any better than this!

Who would have known a precious teenage missionary would "hit the waves" . . . and never come back? I know the church that sponsored this outreach, and it's a fabulous mission-minded church with a great world vision. But what do they do now? They grieve. They support the girl's family and friends. They seek God's wisdom for future precautions so this won't happen again.

I heard about this situation as I was completing this chapter, and I felt I couldn't ignore it. As mission-minded families, we do need to realize that international travel can be dangerous. A mission trip is not just about fun times and exotic destinations. Travel today is easier (and safer) than ever; but we still need to seek God's direction. Yes, there is risk involved; but we still need to *go*.

As a final note, at this precious girl's funeral service, several people surrendered their lives to Jesus Christ. Her father addressed the congregation and encouraged other mission-minded families not to be moved by fear because of this situation. This man urged everyone in the audience to continue to support youth missions, and he even shared how he and his wife had prayerfully decided to send another daughter on the church's next mission outreach.

Taking Photographs

- Taking photographs during your mission trip will enhance your experience and help you remember this time for years to come.

- Before you go, know how to use your camera (especially if it is new), and make certain that everything is in good working order. Make sure you have everything you need (batteries, memory cards, or film, etc.).

- Thinking you may be "taking their soul," people in remote areas may be hesitant for you to take their photo. Or a local police officer may see you taking a photograph of an interesting bridge and accuse you of spying for the CIA. (Avoid wearing army camouflage for this same reason!) In other places, both adults and children may beg you to take their picture. Be sensitive to cultural differences.

- It is great to capture your special memories on film or video, for your own sake as well as to help share your mission vision when you return home. But may your first impression be a loving smile and a courteous greeting, not that of an impersonal tourist flashing pictures.

Traveling with Young Children

- When traveling with children, put together a small backpack for each child with activity books, art supplies, reading materials, small toys, and a few snacks.

- If you are traveling with a ministry team or with a large family, assign each person a partner to help keep track of everyone.

- When spending an extended time in an international airport, look for a nursery or a children's play area. Many major airports even provide cribs for little ones to sleep.

- In order to alleviate the effects of increased air pressure, attempt to nurse or bottle-feed your baby during takeoff and landing. Don't feed your baby for a while beforehand, so that he or she will be a little hungry when the plane is taking off. For young children, sucking on a piece of candy or chewing a piece of gum will help.

- While traveling, watch for people with whom you can share Jesus Christ. You and your child can meet people from all over the world in an international airport, many with nothing to do as they wait for their flight. Be prepared to witness by packing small New Testaments or gospel tracts in your carry-on luggage.

Food and Mission Trips

- Bring along snack foods, such as crackers, beef jerky, or a bag of trail mix.

- Expose your children to different kinds of food, and train them to eat whatever is set before them. This may be challenging at times. Our family has eaten nearly raw dog meat and fried intestines, sea slugs with oyster sauce, chicken feet, snake, eel, and monkey. Encourage your children to think of it as a great adventure.

- If your family has a usual eating preference (such as vegetarian, vegan, or particular food allergies), ask God for extra grace, and clearly explain any necessary requirements with those who need to know. Be willing—with a positive attitude—to be flexible. Adapt as much as possible to cultural norms.

- Realize that the most challenging things to eat will make the best stories back home!

Discipline of Children

- Be very cautious about the physical discipline of your children, especially if you are staying with people from another culture. In some countries, spanking is not practiced and is seen as abuse.

- Pray for extra grace and patience, and prepare your kids to be well behaved. Cultural misunderstandings are especially common on short-term outreaches.

Homeschooling and Missions

Homeschooling Overseas

Years ago, many mission organizations had negative attitudes toward homeschooling, believing it could hinder missionaries from their "primary" responsibility of ministry. (As parents, raising our children should be our primary ministry.) However, as homeschooling has become more mainstream, this option has become more encouraged.

Yes, teaching your children is very time consuming and demanding; but all homeschooling parents have to deal with that. What parent isn't busy, with time demanded on every front—home, ministry, church, and work? Homeschooling families know this route takes work and is often hard, but we make the sacrifice. Why? For some, it's simply the best of several (perhaps all of them challenging) options. For many, it's what the Lord has shown us to do. But regardless of your family's educational decision, it's important to remember that God has called parents to train their children; and the ultimate responsibility should not be relinquished to anyone else.

Missions work may, at times, involve periods of family separation. God may call you to travel short term into a volatile area, where it would be extremely dangerous to take your children. Sometimes one spouse may travel alone to a remote village, or perhaps a husband and wife may go together. But for the most part, God has called you to be a family. Homeschooling and missions fit together perfectly. You have the flexibility to travel, and your children can be involved in ministry. You *can* do it!

Homeschooling on a Short-term Mission Trip

- If taking a short-term mission trip, immerse yourself and your children in the culture you are reaching to make the most of your outreach.

- When our children travel overseas on short-term outreaches (for two or three weeks), they usually leave behind all of their regular schoolwork, other than their Bible and journal, in order to have time for all there is to learn and enjoy.

- Have your children compare their experiences to typical life back home. Taste the local food. Attempt to communicate in the local language. Watch unique characteristics of the people. Learn about the local geography, arts, and technology (or lack of it). Note different animals, birds, and plant life. Soak in the sights, smells, and sounds; and enjoy your time of ministry. Think of it as an extended field trip and an exciting cross-cultural experience.

Homeschooling on a Long-term Outreach

- When living among another people group for an extended time, you and your children will need to develop a routine for regular school subjects.

- Instead of isolating your children, encourage them to play with nationals and to learn their language. A child can often learn a foreign language by exposure alone.

- Most likely you will not have access to resources found in a quality library. A solution to this challenge is to acquire a good supply of online or off-line educational resources. Get a laptop that can connect to a car battery, enabling your child to access important reference information anywhere in the world—even when Internet access is unavailable.

- Begin to build your own library or work with other missionary families to build an educational library. Perhaps your church, mission partners, or a local school group from home could specifically support you in the area of your schooling. They can help you with challenges, send interesting Internet links or encouraging care packages, or simply be available (through e-mail or traditional mail) to assist your educational endeavors.

The Culture Shock of Coming Home

Individuals and families are often unprepared for the culture shock and emotional letdown following a mission outreach. It may be frustrating to find friends and church members unconcerned about your experience or uncaring about the world's needs. The blessings of home may suddenly appear wasteful and extravagant, and you may feel critical toward others or confused about what to do next.

In their article on Crosswalk.com, "Mission Trip Anyone?" David and Laurie Callihan share about the positive (yet challenging) impact of a mission trip: "For our daughter, returning home was heartbreaking. Rebekah cried off and on for a week straight. Her heart was changed as a result of this experience. She has wanted to be a nurse since she was a child. Now she is dreaming of possibly returning as a missionary nurse to this remote village, to share the gospel message of the love of Jesus with these underprivileged children. This experience was a supernatural intervention by the Holy Spirit in the life of a young Christian girl."

🌐 TEACHING OPPORTUNITY

Prepare to Share
(It's not over when it's over)

At the conclusion of an outreach, prepare to share with others about your experience. Ask yourself questions that will help you evaluate your time of ministry, including both positive aspects and negative challenges. Lead those in your family who went on the trip in discussing how you adjusted to change and in summarizing highlights of your journey.

Be prepared to share an encouraging testimony of your experiences. Have a one-minute version (for the casual inquirer), a three- to five-minute version with a few pictures (for an information update for a class, youth group, home group, or school), and a more detailed summary of about ten to fifteen minutes (for your church or more intent audiences). Include in this summary the overall picture of where you went, why you went, what you saw, and what you did, as well as a few specific examples and personal testimonies. Keep your reports brief, positive, and full of enthusiasm.

When you come back, your vision for missions should be contagious. Even a brief contact could spread God's heart for the world to others.

Post-Outreach Debriefing with Your Family

Our Expectations

- How did this trip compare with what I (we) expected?

- How has my (our) view of world missions changed?

- Is my (our) view of a "missionary" different from before?

- What did I (we) think of the people? The culture? The food? The transportation?

Our Positive Experiences

- What aspects of the culture did I (we) enjoy most?

- What person stands out most—in a positive way?

- Share a specific positive ministry experience.

- Think of one person in particular who was helped by my (our) ministry.

Our Greatest Frustrations

- Describe any frustrations you may have had with the culture.

- What was your greatest frustration in ministry? With the team?

- Was it challenging to adjust to the local people? The food? The transportation system? The living conditions? Time considerations?

- What could I (we) have done to make the trip more positive?

Our Personal/Family/Class Evaluation

- How well did I (we) portray Christ? Through my attitudes? Through our unity?

- Did I (we) cooperate well? with missionaries? With nationals?

- How did I (we) do during travel times?

- Did I (we) adequately prepare for this outreach?

- Do I (we) appreciate things that I (we) previously took for granted, such as hot water, toilets, sanitation, home?

Our Ideas for Future Improvement

- How could this trip have been more beneficial to me (us)?

- How could I (we) have prepared better to help those I was (we were) ministering to?

- What area and attitudes do I (we) need to work on most?

Our plan to share a positive report with others

- How can I (we) effectively and briefly share about this experience?

- If I (we) had only one minute to share, what would I (we) say?

- If I (we) had only three to five minutes to share, what would I (we) say?

- If I (we) had ten to fifteen minutes to share, what would I (we) say?

- How can this experience help encourage world missions?

Our new view for the future

Taking your first mission trip is only the beginning. Upon returning home, it's important to look to the future and seek God for your next step. Here are a few questions to consider during your debriefing time:

- What does God want me (us) to do when I (we) get home?

- How can I (we) continue to reach out to the people I (we) just visited?

- Does God want me (us) to pray more? Give more? Recruit others?

- How can I (we) reach out more to my (our) neighbors and community?

- What would I (we) think about the possibility of another outreach?

- Would I (we) be open to long-term missions?

- How can I (we) prepare for the future?

IN PURSUIT OF THE PERFECT FAMILY VACATION

By Laurel Diacogiannis

What is your dream of the Perfect Family Holiday? Relaxing on a Caribbean cruise? Tanning on the beaches of Hawaii? Or, perhaps, shopping in New York City?

What are your children's ideas of the Perfect Family Holiday? A week at Disney World? A houseboat trip on Lake Shasta? Or, maybe, snow skiing in Colorado?

Although all of the above sound like quite a treat to me, my children have humbled me, this year, by asking for a very different type of family holiday. I shouldn't be surprised, however, because I have encouraged them for many years to look more toward the needs of others than toward their own pursuit of pleasure.

For many years, I have had a heart and passion for missions. I used to dream of going to Africa to share the love of Christ. As our family grew, however, I began to wonder if maybe I was just supposed to be raising my children for mission trips, rather than pursuing them myself. So I passed my dream along to them. Gregg has been to Mexico. Cassie has been to Haiti, Africa, and India. Carissa and Lindsey have been to Costa Rica and Mexico. They have enjoyed their travels and have dreams of more exotic places that the Lord may lead them to.

While some of the children have traveled abroad, our family vacations and holidays have been limited to road trips. And we've had some great ones over the years. This past summer, however, we began talking about going on a family mission trip to Costa Rica. I was excited! Although we would spend time doing missions work, I was really looking forward to the beautiful condominium we were going to rent, the sunshine in the middle of winter, and the beautiful beaches to play on with the children and walk along with my husband. It was going to be the Perfect Family Holiday.

Before making our plane reservations and renting the condo, however, I discovered that my children, and the Lord, had other ideas. Rather than being excited about the beaches of Costa Rica, I discovered that the Lord had called my children's hearts to the people of New Orleans.

I do admit, though, that it probably is my fault. When we were planning our cross-country road trip for this past summer, I thought it would be nice to work in New Orleans for three days. We toured the city and were in shock at the devastation that remained a year after Katrina. We did some painting at a church. And we worked at the St. Bernard Parish distribution center. Our time there was good. We all had compassion for the people living there. We all enjoyed working at Pastor Jon's church. And, we all talked about coming back "some day." But, I didn't know that "some day" would replace the beaches of Costa Rica.

Please don't think I am complaining. I am just truly humbled that my children would ask to spend their entire two-week vacation ministering in New Orleans. We won't be walking on the beach or swimming in the surf in Costa Rica. We won't be snow skiing in Colorado or shopping in New York. We won't be enjoying a luxurious condominium.

We will be walking the streets of the city, going door-to-door, giving presents to children, praying with parents, and inviting everyone to a few events. We will be hosting a tea for ladies and The Best Party Ever (a two-day event) for children. We will be doing construction projects and working at the distribution center. We will be sharing the love of Christ with the people of New Orleans. I know that, for our family, this will be the Perfect Family Holiday.

As you begin planning your summer vacation, I encourage you to think outside the box. Rather than asking, "Where do I want to go? Where does my husband want to go? What do my kids want to do?" maybe, as a family, you should all be asking, "Where does Jesus want us to go?" When you allow Him to plan the itinerary, you can be assured that it will be the Perfect Holiday for your family.

Long-Term Missions

Living long term in a foreign country is much different from visiting during a short-term trip. Cultural differences, which previously were amusing and fascinating, may become extremely frustrating.

Short-term outreaches often focus on high-impact evangelism or projects that can be thrilling and encouraging. Long-term missionary work often focuses on the nitty-gritty—much needed but often not as exciting—work of discipleship training, tedious translation work, or church planting. Even the task of raising your family in another country is a time-consuming (and vitally important) ministry in itself.

As you prepare to make a move overseas, be sensitive about your standard of living. Material possessions often can be the biggest hindrance to your witness. It is easier said than done—and sometimes not feasible—but usually the best way to reach a people is to live among them with a similar, yet sanitary, standard of living.

In our travels, my husband and I have seen Western missionaries supposedly "suffering for the Lord" in conditions far beyond what they could afford back home. One time we were driving with a local pastor in a large Asian city. As we passed a neighborhood of huge, extravagant houses—each with a walled gate and several personal guards—we asked if these were homes of important government officials.

"No," he answered, "this is where most of the American missionaries live."

We were shocked; but over the years we have seen this situation repeatedly. Sometimes new missionaries may not have a choice in the matter, since many agencies and denominations have overseas housing already provided.

Fourteen Barrels and Two Large Crates

A young family went to live overseas. Their baggage did not arrive, so they had to make do with what they could find. They began developing relationships with the local people and started their missionary work.

After four months of successful ministry, their bags finally arrived. Consisting of fourteen barrels and two large crates, it was like Christmas in the summer. However, the arrival of their things brought isolation from the people they were trying to reach. Their "shipment of blessings" brought a tremendous barrier that actually hindered their work.

It's a challenge, but the fact remains: to reach a group of people effectively, a missionary must learn to live among them.

When our family travels overseas, we usually stay with nationals—eating, bathing, washing clothes, sleeping, etc., like they do. We have also stayed with many long-term missionary families that generously open their homes and their hearts to us. At times, missionary families need to facilitate large groups of foreign visitors, which usually requires more-spacious-than-normal living quarters and a higher living standard than the local people. Sometimes a missionary's home may be large, but continually shared with others. Continual hospitality is a challenge in itself.

Poverty is not a virtue, but we must be led by the Lord and by His law of love. Throughout history, the missionaries who have had the greatest impact on societies generally were those who learned to identify with the local people and not isolate themselves in a much higher social class. If God calls you and your family overseas, may He pour His blessings upon you—especially in the areas of spiritual favor and extra grace. May you and your children be blessed with God's faith, hope, and love . . . and may you fulfill all the plans He has for you.

FROM GREENLAND'S ICY MOUNTAINS

A missions hymn, by Reginald Heber (1783–1826)

From Greenland's icy mountains,
From India's coral strand;
Where Afric's sunny fountains
Roll down their golden sand:
From many an ancient river,
From many a palmy plain,
They call us to deliver
Their land from error's chain.

Shall we, whose souls are lighted
With wisdom from on high
Shall we to men benighted
The lamp of life deny?
Salvation! O Salvation!
The joyful sound proclaim,
Till earth's remotest nation
Has learned Messiah's name.

WHO WILL GO?

A missions poem, by James A. Barney

Hark! I hear a voice from o'er the waters
'Tis the cry of anguish and despair,
'Tis the cry of precious souls in darkness,
While waiting for the light of Jesus there:

Hear the idle laborers near us saying,
"Master, what wilt Thou have us to do?"
The harvest now is great!
Oh haste, my brother!
The reapers—few!

Will you go and tell them of a Savior;
Tell them how He suffered on the tree?
Will you give your very life to save them?
And tell them Jesus died to set them free?
Will you take the way, endure the suffering;
Finding in the Cross your only rest?
For suffering here with Jesus brings the glory.
His ways are best.

Who will go? Who will go?
To the ends of the earth
Hast thou a passion for the lost?
Dost thou realize what a soul is worth?
Who will go? Who will go?
Tell of Jesus' death upon the tree;
Oh, who will answer quickly,
"Here am I, Oh Lord, send me!"

We will follow, we will follow Jesus.
Willingly and gladly we'll obey.
He will never leave us nor forsake us;
He is our Friend, our Comforter and stay!
Though He lead us
O'er the briny ocean;
Though He lead us
O'er the sandy plains;
We will trust in Jesus Christ our Savior.
Oh, praise His Name!
After we've received the Spirit's fullness,

> Filling all our hearts with love divine;
> We're to witness to this blessed Gospel,
> In every nation, country, land and clime.
> When we give the Gospel as a witness
> Unto every people far and near;
> With lightning flash,
> We'll see in clouds of glory
> The King appear!

# ARE YOU CALLED?

A final word, by Keith Green

It's not God's fault that the world isn't being won. It's not His will that any should perish. There's a little command in the Bible that says, "Go ye into all the world and preach the gospel to every creature."

We like to think that was for the disciples, for the missionaries, for old ladies that can't find husbands that need to bury their troubles on the mission field, or for humanitarians, for real Christians that are so spiritual they can't stay in society so they go overseas. . . . The world isn't being won because we're not doing it. It's our fault. Nowhere on earth is the gospel as plentiful as it is here in the United States. You don't need a call—you've already had one. If you stay here, you better be able to say to God, "You called me to stay home." If you don't have a definite call to stay here, you are called to go.

WHO WAS KEITH GREEN?

Keith Green was a popular Christian musician whose ministry had an impact for world missions. During his concerts, he consistently emphasized "No compromise" and "Get right with God." At the end of his life this focus went one step further to the importance of reaching the lost, especially overseas.

Only weeks before the fateful plane crash in which Keith and two of his children died, Keith and his wife, Melody, together with Loren and Darlene Cunningham of YWAM, interceded for world missions. Keith fervently cried to God for the lost and prayed that God would use him to raise up thousands of young missionaries. The words above, filled with passion and urgency, were spoken at one of his last concerts and later repeated by video at Keith Green Memorial Concerts across the United States, and multitudes responded to the call.

Today, the former property of Green's Last Days Ministries is an international missionary training headquarters where thousands of young people from around the world are trained in missions and sent throughout the world. Keith Green's songs continue to inspire many, especially "Asleep in the Light" (based on William Booth's classic vision, "Who Cares?" about drowning lost souls).

— 👫 FROM MY CHILDREN'S PERSPECTIVE —

SHARING GOOD NEWS
By Joshua Dunagan, at age ten

I was interviewed after my first mission trip to Africa, and our local newspaper, the *Dalles Chronicle*, printed this feature article. I saw it as a chance to share the gospel at home and was excited when the editor included my comments about Jesus!

First sermon exciting for 10-year-old

■ By DAVID CLEAR
for the Chronicle

The music from the African choir and drums has scarcely died down as Joshua Dunagan steps onto a makeshift platform made of wooden planks.

Before him stretches a sea of dark-skinned faces, clad in a rainbow of colors. The people - 10,000 of them at least - wait quietly and intently Beyond the mass of people is the desert-like prairie of northern Uganda.

Joshua, 10, is about to preach his first sermon. On a mission trip with his parents, Jon and Ann Dunagan of The Dalles, Joshua is about to experience a moment that, until now, he's only been able to dream about. He grips the microphone and lays his Bible and notebook on a small, wooden pulpit.

"I want to tell you about the most important person in the world," Joshua begins, and for the next several minutes this 10-year-old with short-cropped brown hair and a big arm tells his audience about the life of Jesus Christ and the Christian beliefs of salvation and eternity in heaven. His message is interpreted by a native Ugandan woman, and as the words are conveyed in their language, the attentive listeners break into smiles and applause.

It was a moment Joshua doesn't think he'll ever forget.

"I was excited and happy," he says, though he admits he was "a little nervous the first time. They listened so attentively, and I had all the time I wanted."

His first speech was on the life of Jesus. On another night he spoke on the life of fiery prophet Elijah, an Old Testament figure known for performing miracles.

All his life Joshua has dreamed of going on a mission trip with his parents. As a small child he traveled with his family to several countries in Asia and Latin America, but the trip to Uganda in November of last year was his official mission trip. "It's something I've dreamed about for years," he says.

He's been influenced by his missionary parents, Jon and Ann Dunagan, founders of Harvest Ministry. Since 1987 the Dunagans have led more than 100 city-wide evangelistic crusades in remote areas overseas. The couple moved their headquarters from Bend to The Dalles last year where they're raising and homeschooling their six children. About four times a year Jon travels to Africa, India, the Philippines or some other part of the world to hold a crusade. When he can, he takes Ann and another member of the family. When they're home the family attends Covenant Christian Community Church.

For Joshua, the mission has been a long time in the making. For years he's viewed pictures and videos of his parents' mission trips, and even met guests from Africa, India and Russia that the Dunagans have hosted in their home. All of this has kindled a flame of desire in Joshua to travel to a foreign country.

When he got the OK from his father to go on the Uganda trip, Joshua immediately began preparing. He outlined several sermons and Bible lessons, ordered his passport, and visited a doctor to get shots to protect himself from malaria, yellow fever and a host of other diseases prevalent in Uganda.

The three-week adventure began Nov. 12 at SeaTac International Airport in Seattle. The Dunagans flew to London and spent three days in Europe to adjust to the change in time zones. While there they visited popular tourist sites such as Big Ben and Buckingham Palace.

From there they then flew to the metropolitan city of Kampala, Uganda, then squeezed into a single engine Missionary Aviation Fellowship (M.A.F.) bush plane for a two-hour flight to Arua. Then came the final leg, a planned two-hour van ride to Koboko, a remote village near the border of Sudan and Congo that took four hours because of muddy roads.

For five days the Dunagans held crusade meetings in the evenings and adult and children's seminars in the mornings. While more than a thousand adults gathered to hear the morning teachings, Joshua and Ann taught Bible lessons to 300 children under a group of mango trees. Joshua schooled his Ugandan peers on the 10 Commandments and the story of Jesus.

While the work in Uganda was serious and consuming, Joshua found time for fun. He played with Uganda children, and learned the trick of putting chickens to sleep. The team also spent a day on a wildlife safari to the Queen Elizabeth National Park. "I saw tons of animals," Joshua said, including more than 60 elephants, hundreds of hippos, an alligator, water bucks and African kobs (a type of deer). He also took a 45-minute canoe ride to Bussi Island on Lake Victoria.

But the business of meeting people's spiritual and physical needs was foremost in the mind of this delegation from The Dalles. Like Jesus, Joshua's heart swelled with compassion as he saw multitudes of needy people. Poverty is extreme in northern Uganda. Large families are crammed into 12-foot by 12-foot huts with mud floors. Disease is rampant, and scores of Sudanese refugees who have crossed the border to escape war are ravaged by years of fighting. Hundreds are blind and lame or have distortions and growths on their bodies. The children are dressed in rags.

"I've never seen so many poor and sick people," Joshua said. "Seeing people living in little huts with practically nothing made me a lot more thankful for what I have here in America."

The trip may have imprinted Joshua for life. He wants to return to Africa some day to communicate God's love to the people in any way he can. "I care about the people of the world now. They need God as much as we do. I'm more willing to do whatever God wants me to do with my life."

HERE HE IS seen in action, preaching his first sermon in the city of Koboko, Uganda.

10-YEAR-OLD Joshua Dunagan is seen at the equator in Uganda in Africa.

Conclusion

God has a destiny for your family.

He has an individual plan for each member, as well as a corporate purpose for you as a family unit. Psalm 127:4 says, "Like arrows in the hand of a warrior, so are the children of one's youth." God wants you to "aim" each of your children, and your family, toward the "bull's-eye" of His purpose. But a powerful bow must be strong and fastened tightly on two ends. As a mission-minded family, your family's "bowstring" must be aligned to biblical priorities, with two passions in balance: God has a passion for your home (including your personal relationships with Him), and God has a passion for your world.

As your family focuses on these two priorities, your home will begin to function as God intended. As a mission-minded family, you'll sense a growing, God-infused energy. You'll have worldwide purpose, and you'll have passion for the lost. Even among your children and teenagers, there will be a spiritual depth and hunger that will reach beyond the maintenance mode of cultural Christianity. You'll emphasize leadership, calling, and destiny. You'll have a prevailing attitude of self-sacrifice and a desire for total submission to God's will. And in your home (and wherever God sends you) there will be an unmistakable and contagious joy.

Psalm 112:1–2 says, "Praise the LORD! Blessed is the man who fears the LORD, who delights greatly in His commandments. His descendants will be mighty on earth; the generation of the upright will be blessed." As you follow God's mission-minded priorities, may this promise be true for you.

May you release your family to God's destiny!

Recommended
Resources

Mission-Minded Prayer

- *Kids' Prayer Cards* (Caleb Project, 2006). More than just cards, this pack is a window into the lives of kids around the world! Discover what they think is fun, exciting, and cool with these twenty-five colorful cards. People Group Cards give you a look at the lives of kids in different cultures, and Activity Cards give you everything you need to paint tribal art, eat their food, and even meet and make friends with internationals in your own neighborhood. This prayer card set is built on the THUMB acrostic, and the cards are shaped like the letters: T is for Tribal, H is for Hindu, U is for Unreligious, M is for Muslim, and B is for Buddhist. Available from Caleb Resources: www.calebproject.org.

- *Operation World: 21ˢᵗ Century Edition*, by Patrick Johnstone and Jason Mandryk (Authentic Publishing, 2001). With over two million copies in print, this handbook for global prayer is highly recommended as a resource for mission-minded families. Packed with information about every country in the world, this book is inspiring fuel for prayer.

- *Window on the World*, by Daphne Spraggett and Jill Johnstone (Lion Hudson, Ltd., 2002 by Authentic Publishing). This children's accompaniment to *Operation World* is an outstanding tool for parents and teachers and my number one recommendation for your family. Filled with stunning full-color glossy photographs, this A-to-Z guide to one hundred countries and people groups will provide an exciting learning experience and tool for prayer.

- *Personal Prayer Diary and Daily Planner* (YWAM Publishing, 2005). Every year YWAM produces a new daily planner, which includes illustrations of unreached people, highlights for prayer, maps, monthly calendars, and Scriptures. This is an excellent organizational tool for older children, teens, and adults.

- *Walking with God: The Young Person's Prayer Diary*, by Michelle Drake (YWAM Publishing, 2005). This energetic diary will encourage your child to establish the mission-minded discipline of daily prayer. With cartoon illustrations, practical Bible-reading charts, world maps, prayer teaching highlights, and plenty of encouraging spaces for a young person to write, this tool is child friendly and highly recommended.

- *From Akebu to Zapotec,* by June Hathersmith and Alice Roder (Wycliffe Bible Translators, 2002). This second alphabet book introduces children to twenty-six of the world's Bible-less people groups. Today most of the twenty-six people groups from Wycliffe's first alphabet book, *From Arapesh to Zuni*, published in 1986, have some part of the Bible in their language—demonstrating that prayer is powerful!

- *God's Got Stuff to Do! And He Wants Your Help* (Caleb Project, 2003). This thirteen-week curriculum was created to expose kids to what can be done to help share Jesus with the nations. It includes a teacher's resource kit and a student booklet (a journal-style Bible study that leads kids to discover opportunities to go, send others, pray, give, welcome internationals in this country, and connect with others for service). Also available are *Kids Around the World* curriculum sets and the *THUMB Teacher's Resource Kit*. Available from Caleb Resources: www.calebproject.org.

- World Prayer Team, current information for international prayer: www.worldprayerteam.org

- Dare to Be a Daniel (D2BD): www.daretobeadaniel.com

- The Voice of the Martyrs: www.persecution.com

International Ministry and Ideas

- Mission-Minded International Decorations:

    Oriental Trading Company: www.orientaltrading.com

- Mission-Minded Music:

    Wee Sing Around the World (especially the song "Hello to All the Children of the World"), by Pamela Conn Beall and Susan Hagen Nipp (Price Stern Sloan, 2006)

    "Heart to Change the World" (*Kids' Praise!* 6): www.psalty.com

- Mission-Minded Drama Ministry:

    "Asleep in the Light," by Keith Green: www.lastdaysministries.org

    "The Champion," by Carman: www.carman.org

- Puppet Ministry:

    Puppet Productions (Puppetry-training, and recommended songs "Laughing Song" and "Let's Go to the Church," and Spanish puppet skits): www.puppetproductions.com

- International Information:

    Country profiles and world maps: National Geographic: www.nationalgeographic.com

    Geography and history: Geography Matters: www.geomatters.com

    International embassies: www.embassy.org

    International time zones: www.timeanddate.com/worldclock

    The World Factbook: www.cia.gov/cia/publications/factbook

Mission-Minded Evangelism Tools

- *Good News Comic Book*, an excellent children's evangelism tract: www.ccci.org/good-news

- *Steps to Peace with God* (small tract), by Billy Graham Evangelistic Association (1998): www.billygraham.org/Grason.asp

- The *EvangeCube*: big cubes, small cubes, training tools and DVD, and outstanding gospel tracts in many languages. One of the most powerful evangelism tools available: www.evangecube.org

- *The Four Spiritual Laws*, by Bill Bright (Campus Crusade for Christ). Available online in almost every language. An excellent resource for international one-to-one witnessing: www.4laws.com/laws/languages.html

- The *JESUS* film, the powerful film of Jesus based on the Gospel of Luke. Over six billion exposures globally and available in nearly a thousand languages: www.jesusfilm.org

- Wycliffe Bible Translators; this premier Bible translation ministry also has many outstanding mission training books and tools for children: www.wycliffe.org

- *Planet Word Bible* (Thomas Nelson, 2005). This is my all-time favorite mission-minded Bible! It's for kids and families that want to put their faith into action. Using the NKJV translation, this Bible is filled with energetic encouragement for reaching the world. The theme is based on the GPS (Global Positioning System) of pinpointing any location in the world using four coordinates. *Planet Word* highlights four "P" Coordinates: Purpose, Power, People, and Partnership. It features 140 "Planet Messengers" (from the Bible and history), 50 "Planet Impacts" (short first-person stories of real mission-minded kids), 50 "Planet Verses" (which show Mark 1:1–4 in different languages), plus "God's Plan" introductions to every book, colorful world maps, and much more. I give this outstanding tool my highest recommendation!

- Family mission opportunities:

Adventures In Missions: www.adventures.org

Operation Christmas Child: www.samaritanspurse.org

Teen Missions: www.teenmissions.org

YWAM (Youth With A Mission): www.ywam.org and

YWAM King's Kids International: www.kkint.net

ShortTermMissions.com: www.shorttermmissions.com

(Note: These are just a sampling of the many mission opportunities available. Look on the Internet for more possibilities, and talk with your pastor or church organization for specific short- or long-term mission outreaches that could be of specific interest to your family.)

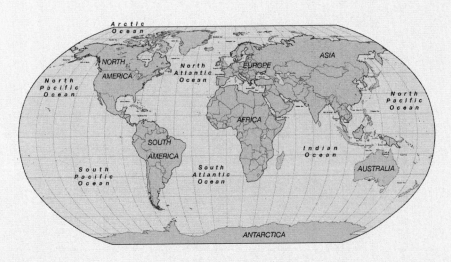

THE WORLD
ROBINSON PROJECTION
©2005 Geography Matters
www.geomatters.com

THE "10/40 WINDOW"
ROBINSON PROJECTION
©2005 Geography Matters
www.geomatters.com

Notes

Chapter 1

Calcutta, India, analogy: special thanks to a favorite Bible teacher and friend, Bo Stern, who allowed me to adapt her analogy.

"Pursuing God's Purposes": excerpted (with minor variations) from *The Missions Addiction: Capturing God's Passion for the World*, by David Shibley (Lake Mary, FL: Charisma House, 2001), 29–30. Used with permission.

"We've a Story to Tell to the Nations": H. Ernest Nichol, 1862–1928. Words of this hymn are in public domain.

Chapter 2

Funeral example: from *The Seven Habits of Highly Effective People: Restoring the Character Ethic*, by Stephen R. Covey (New York: Simon and Schuster, 1989), 96–97.

Recommended Resource: *God's Smuggler—35th Anniversary Edition*, by Brother Andrew, John Sherrill, and Elizabeth Sherrill (Grand Rapids: Baker, 1991).

"The Call for Reapers": John O. Thompson, 1782–1818. Words of this hymn are in public domain.

Chapter 3

"The Difficult Dilemma of Jonathan Goforth": from *Goforth of China*, by Rosalind Goforth (Grand Rapids: Zondervan, 1937), 189.

"Divine Order for Each Day": from *Extravagant Worship*, by Darlene Zschech (Grand Rapids: Baker, 2004). Used with permission.

"Farewell to the Balanced Life": from *The Missions Addiction: Capturing God's Passion for the World*, by David Shibley (Lake Mary, FL: Charisma House, 2001), 78–79. Used with permission.

Chapter 4

1. Sources for Perpetua monologue: *From Jerusalem to Irian Jaya: A*

Biographical History of Christian Missions, by Ruth A. Tucker (Grand Rapids: Zondervan, 1983), 32–34; Edith Deen, *Great Women of the Christian Faith* (New York: Harper & Row, 1959), 6; Mark Galli, *131 Christians Everyone Should Know* (Nashville: B & H Publishing Group, 2000), available at http://www.christianitytoday.com/history/special/131christians/perpetua.html; Elliott Wright, *Holy Company: Christian Heroes and Heroines* (New York: Macmillan, 1980), 236.

2. Sources for John Eliot monologue: Tucker, *From Jerusalem to Irian Jaya*, 74–79; Galli, *131 Christians Everyone Should Know*, available at http://www.christianitytoday.com/history/special/131christians/johneliot.html.

3. John R. Weinlick, *Count Zinzendorf* (Nashville: Abingdon, 1956), 225.

4. Tucker, *From Jerusalem to Irian Jaya*, 116.

5. Quoted in Tucker, *From Jerusalem to Irian Jaya*, 119.

6. Tucker, *From Jerusalem to Irian Jaya*, 119.

7. Quoted in Tucker, *From Jerusalem to Irian Jaya*, 119.

8. Quoted in Deen, *Great Women of the Christian Faith*, 193–94.

9. Cecil Northcott, *Robert Moffat: Pioneer in Africa, 1817–1870* (London: Lutterworth, 1961), 189.

10. Quoted in Deen, *Great Women of the Christian Faith*, 187.

11. Tucker, *From Jerusalem to Irian Jaya*, 150.

12. Tucker, *From Jerusalem to Irian Jaya*, 153.

13. Deen, *Great Women of the Christian Faith*, 193–94; Oliver Ransford, *David Livingstone: The Dark Interior* (New York: St. Martin's, 1978), 118.

14. The story about God's provision of food for breakfast is in George Müller's own words; from *The Life and Ministry of George Müller*, a booklet by Ed Reese (Christian Hall of Fame Series, Reese Publications, Lansing, IL), available at http://www.uvm.edu/~sbross/biography/muller.txt.

15. George Müller, *A Narrative of Some of the Lord's Dealing with George Müller, Written by Himself,* 2 vols. (Muskegon, MI: Dust and Ashes, 2003), 2:392–93.

16. Denny Kenaston, "William and Catherine Booth's Home Life," an article published in *The Heartbeat of the Remnant* magazine; available online at http://libertytothecaptives.net/booth_home_life.html.

17. "Rescue the Perishing": Fanny Crosby, 1820–1915. Words of this hymn are in public domain.

18. "God's Hidden Inheritance": from *Frontier Evangelism*, by T. L. Osborn (Tulsa: Osborn Foundation, 1964). Used with permission.

Current missionary biographies were checked with each minister's official ministry website, updated 2006–2007.

Chapter 5

Holiday celebrations, music, and international ideas compiled and adapted from various sources, including the following:

Bev Gunderson, *Window to India, Window to Japan*, and *Window to Mexico* (Milaca, MN: Monarch Publishing, 1988).

Mary Branson, *Fun Around the World* (Birmingham: New Hope, 1992).

Phyllis Vos Wezeman and Jude Dennis Fournier, *Joy to the World* (Notre Dame, IN: Ave Maria Press, 1992).

Ruth Finley, *The Secret Search* (Mt. Hermon, CA: Crossroads Communications, 1990).

"I Gave Myself": Author unknown. Story excerpted from *The Harvest Call*, by T. L. Osborn (Tulsa: The Voice of Faith, Inc., 1953), 61. Used with permission of Osborn International.

Quote by Bernie May excerpted from the second edition of *From Jerusalem to Irian Jaya*, by Ruth A. Tucker (Grand Rapids: Zondervan, 2004), 391.

Chapter 6

Sources and ideas for this chapter from the author's personal experience in prayer, along with the following sources:

Danny Lehman, *Before You Hit the Wall* (Seattle: YWAM Publishing, 1991).

James P. Shaw, senior editor, *Personal Prayer Diary and Daily Planner* (Seattle: YWAM Publishing, 1995), 12–15, 192.

Chapter 7

Special acknowledgment goes to Betty Barnett and the excellent information presented in her book, *Friend Raising: Building a Missionary Support Team That Lasts* (Seattle: YWAM Publishing, revised edition, 2002).

"Daring to Live on the Edge": from *Daring to Live on the Edge: The Adventure of Faith and Finances*, by Loren Cunningham (Seattle: YWAM Publishing, 1991), excerpted from Chapter 8, "Missions Support the Jesus Way," 87–100. Used with permission of YWAM Publishing and Loren Cunningham.

Biblical examples of giving the "firstfruits" and "tithing in advance": Exodus 34:26; Leviticus 23:9–14; Deuteronomy 26:1–15; Proverbs 3:9; Ezekiel 44:30.

"A Few Startling Financial Facts" and quote about the *Queen Mary*: from *Serving as Senders: How to Care for Your Missionaries While They Are Preparing to Go, While They Are on the Field, When They Return Home*, by Neal Pirolo (San Diego: Emmaus Road International, 1991), 77, 78, 80.

In this area of missions and family finances, I highly recommend *Money, Possessions, and Eternity*, by Randy Alcorn (Tyndale, 2003).

Chapter 8

Special thanks to my precious prayer partner, Nanci Miller, for sharing her "Four Rules of Ministry" for children and for inspiring my children to be mighty lions for God, not only in ministry but also in their personal relationship with Him.

Chapter 9

"Go Ye into All the World": James McGranahan, 1840–1907. Words of this hymn are in public domain.

"From Greenland's Icy Mountains": Reginald Heber, 1783–1826. Words of this hymn are in public domain.

"Who Will Go?": James A. Barney. Original source unknown. Poem found in *The Harvest Call*, by T. L. Osborn (Tulsa: The Voice of Faith, Inc., 1953), 6. Used with permission of Osborn International.

"Are You Called?": excerpted from *Winning God's Way*, by Loren Cunningham (Seattle: YWAM Publishing, 1988), 52–53. I also recommend reading *Why You Should Go to the Mission Field*, a tract Keith Green wrote shortly before his death; available online at http://www.lastdaysministries.org/nations/whyyoushouldgo.html. For a tract catalog or to order this article in tract form, contact Last Days Ministries at 825 College Blvd. Suite 102 #333, Oceanside, CA 92057-6258 (toll-free fax 1-877-228-9536) (Ref. #043).

ABOUT THE AUTHORS:

Jon & Ann Dunagan founded Harvest Ministry in 1987. They are international mission leaders, convention speakers, and veteran homeschooling parents of seven grown children (born in 1986 to 2000, with an ever-increasing number of graduates, married-in-spouses and grandchildren). Collectively, the Dunagans and their family have shared the love of Jesus in over 100 nations on every continent, including Antarctica — winning souls, loving orphans, equipping nationals (National Evangelism Team Support — NETS), serving churches, and mobilizing Christian families for God's Great Commission.

You can find the Dunagans on:
Instagram, Twitter, LinkedIn, Pinterest, and Facebook
Podcast on iTunes: Mission-Minded Families

Video Series on YouTube — for churches, families, and small groups
7 Simple Keys for Mission-Minded Families - with Jon & Ann Dunagan

HarvestMinistry.org
MissionMindedWomen.org
MissionMindedFamilies.org

PODCAST

On iTunes: **Mission-Minded Families** ("Kids & Family" category)

27 minute episodes (listen while you drive, organize, or exercise)
Subscribe, Rate, Review, and Share with others!

or 4-minute Mission-Minutes — Q & A's with Ann Dunagan

7 P's in a Pod:

Prayer.
Passion.
Perspective.
Parenting.
Priorities.
Progress.
Purpose.

On iTunes:
http://tinyurl.com/iTunes-MMF

On the Web:
http://missionminded.libsyn.com

SCAN ME

KIDS MISSION BOOKS

3-D KIDS COURSE

KIDS MISSIONS TRAINING

Passion & Clarity Course
7 Keys for Families

FREE ONLINE COURSES

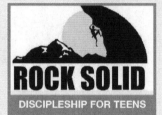
ROCK SOLID

DISCIPLESHIP FOR TEENS

Communication Skills &
Mission Support Raising

MISSIONS & MONEY

Ideas for Teaching Kids
at Home & Church

FAMILY MISSION IDEAS

LOVING ORPHANS

MISSION-MINDED WOMEN

MISSIONMINDEDFAMILIES.ORG/INFO

FREE Video Series on YouTube:
7 Simple Keys for Mission-Minded Families

FREE Video Series for Christian families
with Jon & Ann Dunagan

Designed for churches, families or small groups
Gather a few friends for a 7-week study!

7 videos (20-24 minutes each)
Motivational. Encouraging. Biblical.
FREE workbook pages — for group handouts.

Made in the USA
Columbia, SC
25 September 2024

43044371R00265